HELLO HUMAN

HELLO

A History of Visual Communication

HUMAN

Michael Horsham

First published in the United Kingdom in 2022 by
Thames & Hudson Ltd, 181A High Holborn, London WCIV 7QX

First published in the United States of America in 2022 by
Thames & Hudson Inc., 500 Fifth Avenue, New York, New York 10110

Hello Human: A History of Visual Communication
© 2022 Thames & Hudson Ltd, London

Text © 2022 Michael Horsham
Pictures as credited on page 227
Design concept by Fraser Muggeridge studio

British Library Cataloguing-in-Publication Data

A catalogue record for this book is available from the British Library

Library of Congress Control Number 2022931215

ISBN 978-0-500-02388-4

Printed and bound in India by Replika Press Pvt. Ltd

Be the first to know about our new releases,
exclusive content and author events by visiting
thamesandhudson.com
thamesandhudsonusa.com
thamesandhudson.com.au

Contents

The DUMB LANGUAGE or the Art of talking with the FINGERS.

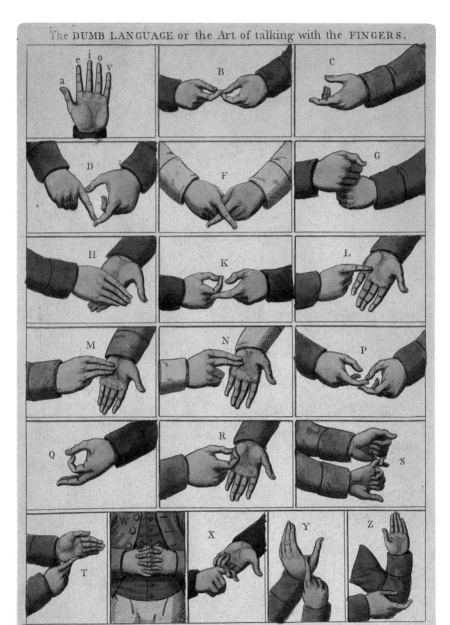

Printed for BOWLES & CARVER, N°. 69, S.¹ Pauls Church Yard, LONDON.

Extinction Rebellion's cut-through owes much to their brilliant use of imagery and old-style guerrilla *affichage*. Here, in an empty shop doorway in Clapham, London, in 2021, the beneficent gaze of the Green Man is overlaid with digital symbology and the XR logo.

Introduction

The idea for *Hello Human* came to me via a realization that, amongst our many other achievements, we have, all through time, continued to invent a variety of channels that we then fill with communication. (As an analogy we make the buckets, fill them with swill and then bash our sticks on the side. The swine come running, eat their fill and are temporarily satisfied.) It seems we are compelled to communicate with one another. The quality of the communication of course varies. It's by no means all 'swill'.

We do this to reach one another, to move one another, to persuade, inform and entertain. To accomplish these things successfully, we have to learn how to use the available technology, but that technology is always moving on. This is as true of the cave-dweller painting a buffalo on a wall at the dawn of 'civilized' time as it is of the influencers populating Instagram or Weibo today. The truism linking both is that by learning the tools and techniques of communication, you have a greater chance of creating the emotional hit that will connect you effectively to the human(s) on the receiving end. I have been working in this field, first as a researcher and commentator and then as a practitioner and educator, for more than three decades, so I'm hoping that the conclusions I have reached are useful – and that they will chime in some way with fellow practitioners, students and anyone else interested in how we make, and have made, the tools we use to communicate with one another.

There are huge differences, of course, between the cave-dweller and today's influencer, at least in terms of the work they produce. I would suggest that the principal difference lies in the nature of human relationships to tools and technology. Using your hands to make something is a markedly different experience to creating a piece of work digitally. The haptic feedback experienced in the process of painting, creating letterpress, making a plasticine model, even developing a photograph in trays of developer, fixer and stop (or making a cyanotype) is a world away from swiping across an iPad or a Wacom tablet. So, if the act of making by hand is imbued with humanity as a matter of course, how do we create works of beauty, resonance and humanity where the hand is not directly involved?

The answer is: it's not easy. The proliferation of ways to create and share visual communication has changed the landscape of what it means to be, and to be seen to be, a creative person. The world of 'viscomm' used to be entirely top-down, governed by the mastery of skill, technique and craft, save for some home-made postering and graffiti. The gatekeepers used to be publishers and art galleries, presses and editors, design studios, governments and laws. Now it's more or less a free-for-all. An extremely successful campaign or a piece of music, art, propaganda, pornography or misinformation can come to the attention of the world without the need for an authoritative voice giving permission or authenticating its value. Sanctions, editorial control, demonetization and deplatforming tend to come after the fact.

Joseph Beuys's assertion that 'Every man is an artist' ('Jeder Mensch ein Künstler') reflected his interest in building 'a social organism as a work of art'. By way of the participatory impulse Beuys was talking about back in 1973, anyone could 'become a creator, sculptor, or architect of the social organism'.[1] That was prescient, but I have to ask: how's it going now, Joseph? How's the old social organism coming along?

From my perspective, it's very much a mixed bag. Partly because there's just so *much* material being created, all the time, that it's increasingly difficult to sort the wheat from the chaff. Because of this, we tend to connect to the things we know. Recommendations for our access to the digital multiplex come from our friends, for sure, but they come more regularly from the algorithms that continuously track and trace our likes and dislikes, computing what we might like to see next. We are encouraged to form our own echo chambers, a natural consequence of the 'if you liked "x" you will like "y"' system and the impossibility of working your way through everything that is available in order to form your own critical opinion of it.

The individuated nature of much digital experience is masked by the 'netiquette' of likes and follows, views and subscriptions. Notwithstanding the activism and political action facilitated by networks, or the joy of shared music, the numbers attached to our participation in the digital world can make it feel and look like a community experience, but it's often not.

So humanity has travelled from small-scale visual communication – the written word and incunabula – through to the revolution in the printing press, taking place first in Korea with Choe Yun-ui and then in Europe with Johannes Gutenberg, through to the mastery of dimensionality in terms of perspective, abandoning the rigour of the page and embracing surrealism on the way, to arrive at a place where the mastery of the pixel and computational power means it's now possible to create deepfake imagery that is indistinguishable from real footage.

Underpinning this amazing journey is a curious constant that exists in the form of the non-cursive numerical characters of one and zero. One and zero join East and West: mathematically and culturally, they bridge two states.

Something and nothing. There, not there. On and off. Two states. Binary. Once they were written by hand; now they appear at a keystroke. They were there at the beginning when proportion, value and position had to be calculated, and they are here now wherever machine code delivers instructions to the handheld devices, editing software and server farms that support the current orgy of visual exchange and communication.

I'm not suggesting that this is a groundbreaking insight, but it's the thought that set me off on this journey – and a journey it has been. I've tried to imagine the history of visual communication as a landscape through which we can find a way, with our route shaped by waypoints on what we know of the map. It might be useful to think of the journey as a *dérive*, an undirected wander that creates a form; this idea originated with Guy Debord, the activist, artist and articulator of situationist thought and action. Of course, while the map is busy and densely populated, we cannot know or see everything; omissions are inevitable and, I hope, forgivable.

This journey is in part a search for insight into the experience of making (or seeing something made) by hand or by machine. It's about understanding how the evolution of techniques and technologies has helped to change what is possible in terms of visual communication. It embraces the shift away from the handmade to the chemical, to the machine, the electronic and the digital. In the wake of that shift it's about veracity, too. Truth matters, both in terms of how we come to believe in what we see through the power of our own emotional responses, and how those responses are provoked, shaped, mapped and understood. It's also about learning that it's OK to be outraged when we feel we are being lied to, scammed, manipulated or controlled.

As we reach the end of the journey we get back to where we once belonged, discovering that the most important element of everything we do and create, however we do it, is our love for it. If we communicate with love, we cannot help but be successful in connecting with our fellow humans in a good and positive way. Hello Human, you may say, in any number of ways – but make sure you mean it.

ABOVE *Right hand of Artemisia Gentileschi holding a brush*, 1625, Pierre Dumonstier II. Dumonstier II's drawing is a useful illustration of the precision grip, which is unique to human beings, allowing for precise manipulation of objects and tools.

OPPOSITE An early arteriogram by Alfred G. Fryatt, published in *The Archives of the Roentgen Ray* (1904). The image is of the hand of a cadaver and reveals the complexity of joints and musculature.

Part One

Gesture

A big hand for gesture

In 1625, in Rome, the artist Pierre Dumonstier II made a chalk drawing on paper of a woman's right hand. The hand holds a paintbrush. On the reverse of the paper is an inscription praising the hand for 'knowing how to make marvels that send the most judicious eyes into rapture'. The hand depicted by Dumonstier in red and black chalk belonged to Artemisia Gentileschi,[1] the now renowned Renaissance artist. Dumonstier was drawn to divorce the hand from its owner in order to make the point that manual dexterity, when deployed in image-making, is the means by which emotion can be triggered in the heart of the viewer.

Some three hundred years later, the philosopher and soon-to-be Nazi Party member Martin Heidegger wrote: 'Through the hand occur both prayer and murder, greeting and thanks, oath and signal, and also the "work" of the hand, the "hand-work", and the tool. The handshake seals the covenant....No animal has a hand, and a hand never originates from a paw or a claw or a talon.'[2] Leaving aside his appalling political views, Heidegger's general position on the indivisibility of the subject and object is useful. The hand performs many subjective and objective functions. It is tool, manipulator and transmitter: twenty-seven bones, connective tissue and muscle, providing a

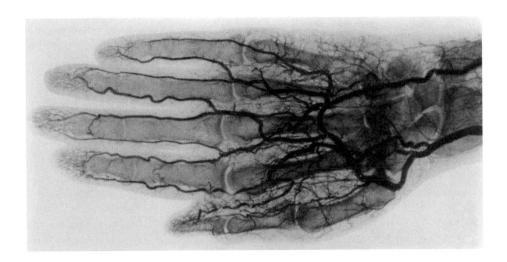

rotatable, positionable, gripping versatility that other mammals on the planet do not have. Sure, other primates have opposable thumbs, as do some frogs, possums and koalas. But it's not the fact of opposable thumbs that defines us, it's what we do with them in the context of our work. It's about what we make. For us, on our journey through some of the historical and cultural weave of visual communication, the hand is fundamental.

That's part of the reason we find ourselves, to begin with, in the cool of a European cave. The El Castillo cave, part of the Monte Castillo cave complex in Puente Viesgo, Cantabria, northern Spain, contains some of the earliest known attempts at visual communication. There in the darkness, waiting for the light and the eyes of a visitor, is the silhouette of a hand on the cave wall created some 40,000 years ago, possibly by a Neanderthal. Of course, the purpose of this mark-making, the intention, cannot be known; but still the form communicates.[3]

In December 2020, the BBC and other news outlets reported that vandals who daubed red handprints onto a Neolithic monument, the 5,000-year-old Stoney Littleton Long Barrow in Wellow near Bath, might have damaged it permanently. This mark-making exercise had no obvious point or meaning other than to make the human presence felt in the environment; and of course the rocks in Puente Viesgo were already ancient when they were defiled by Neanderthal attempts at what we now call art. The point is in the compulsion to make marks, and in the significance of the hand as a sign. Later, in January 2021, the BBC announced the discovery of a similarly ancient cave painting of a 'warty pig' in Indonesia. Significantly, the warty pig image was accompanied by two handprints above its back.

So powerfully embedded and encoded in our psyche is the raised hand that we cannot escape our programming. In this case, the shape of the right hand – palm towards us, fingers slightly splayed, gentle and relaxed, the thumb in its natural place, the whole raised to the level of the eye – says to us now, for some reason, 'Hail'. Hello. Hello, human. During the early part of the COVID-19 outbreak in 2020 the artist Mark Wallinger proposed that every child all over the UK should draw an outline of their hand on an A4 piece of paper and display it in their front windows as a nationwide 'wave'. Wallinger, inspired by the Neanderthal impulse, tried to get us all to raise our hands in greeting.[4]

That gesture, with its atavistic power, is everywhere: TV presenters, YouTubers, TikTokers, Zoomers and Facetimers greet their audiences and colleagues with the same gesture. But for all its simplicity, the raised hand has the capacity to communicate in a wide variety of ways depending on the cultural context. In the USA, at crosswalks, a stylized raised hand symbol illuminated in orange means 'Don't Walk'. In places as far apart as Greece

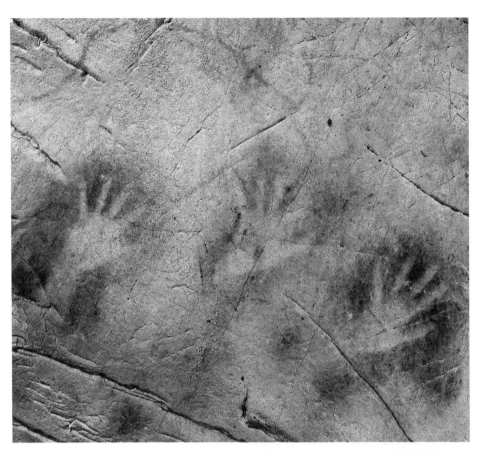

ABOVE 40,000-year-old paintings in the El Castillo cave. Haematite blown over the hand gave these images their reddish colour. There is something about these traces of ancient existence that I find emotionally compelling; our ancestors' marks speak to our modern compulsion to create images.

RIGHT The meaning of the raised hand is contingent on cultural and semiotic context.

and Mexico, the action of raising an open hand, palm out, with spread fingers in front of someone's face is a sign of displeasure – the *moutza*, as it's called in Greece, can cause serious offence.

So the human hand delivers many permutations of greeting and salutation, movement and meaning. Another case in point is the furore around the use of the *quenelle*, a gesture described as a cross between the *bras d'honneur* (essentially 'up yours') and the straight-armed Nazi salute. The *quenelle* originated with French comedian Dieudonné M'bala M'bala and was then taken up by the footballer Nicolas Anelka as a goal celebration. An arcane arrangement of downward-pointing arm and shoulder-clutching, it has the power to shock and stir the emotions. The outcry when the gesture was deployed in public is a testament to the interpretive impulse of humans when faced with visual stimuli with encoded meaning. In a further illustration of the power of symbolic gesture, NFL teammates Colin Kaepernick and Eric Reid of the San Francisco 49ers chose to 'take the knee' during the playing of the US national anthem in 2016 as a protest against continuing racism and police brutality. To move things back toward the hand, there's also the athletes Tommie Smith and John Carlos, who raised their gloved fists in the Black Power salute on the podium at the 1968 Olympic Games in Mexico City. It was Peter Norman, the third man on the podium, white and

Nicolas Anelka's *quenelle* as a goal celebration for West Bromwich Albion in 2013 was claimed to be simply 'anti-establishment', yet it attracted an £80,000 fine and the withdrawal of the club sponsor. Gesture can be powerful and should be used with care.

The England team were pressured by the Football Association to give the Nazi salute before a match against Germany on 14 May 1938. The only player to refuse, Wolverhampton Wanderers' Stan Cullis, was subsequently dropped. England won 6–3.

Australian, whose hands remained by his sides as he suggested Smith and Carlos share the gloves. Gestures all, and powerful with it. Smith and Carlos were pallbearers at Norman's funeral.

Clearly, the hand is both tool and transmitter. It's this dual function that underpins the first part of this foray into how we have developed visual languages in order to communicate with one another. Before industrialization and mechanization, before machines, it was the hand that used the tools that made the materials with which we communicated.

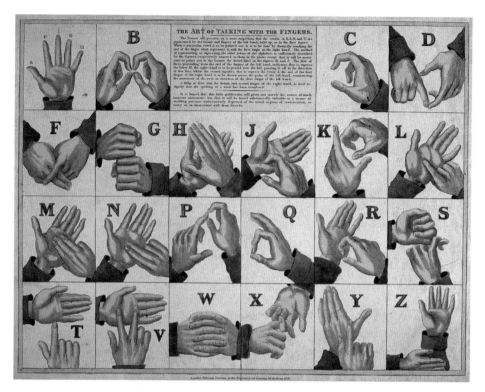

The Art of Talking with the Fingers, artist unknown, is an early depiction of the sign language alphabet. British Sign Language was partially recognized as an official language by the UK government in 2003.

The mark-making in the El Castillo cave is a rudimentary example of the meeting point of technology and technique. Technology-wise, the Neanderthal artist/communicator/bored cave-dweller needed tools and materials with which to work. Things were pretty advanced 40,000 years ago, and we would recognize many of the things our Neanderthal or Denisovan forebears carried around with them. The toolkit used by Middle Palaeolithic people has been found to include hand axes, plaited cords and antler hammers as well as hafted spears and sticks for dragging or digging.[5] There is evidence, too, of the cultural and communicative life of Neanderthals and *Homo sapiens* – not only in cave art but in small, sculptural figures, tools that carry decoration, and ornamental items fashioned from found materials such as ivory, bone, shell or stone. Just like us, these people liked to decorate things to transmit meaning. They liked to communicate visually.

Colours were and are important. The pigment used in cave art like that found in Spain would have been derived from limonite and haematite. Later in the history of painting, these would be the earth pigments from which red ochre, yellow ochre and umber would be made. In the cave, the method of application would have varied, with everything from feathers to lichen performing the work of a brush. At Puente Viesgo, it was the pneumatic power of a mouthful of pigment forced through pursed lips by a lungful of air that left the negative space of a hand on the wall, its form ornamented and outlined by spit spots, droplets and blobs.

However rudimentary (albeit powerful) these early examples of mark-making may appear to us today, they are linked to how we communicate now. Intriguingly, we can infer what they might mean without much difficulty; our understanding of some signs, symbols and gestures appears to be innate. The roots of gestural communication have been studied by anthropologists, behaviouralists and linguists, and the consensus seems to be that the innate use of hand movements was a feature of proto-hominid ability to develop a means of communication independent of speech. Once established, gesticulation could underpin the development of language or, in the lingo of the scientists, glottogenesis.

A gesture is a form in space and time: a repeatable design, a performance-form imbued with meaning that, according to scholars, helped to bridge the gap between the communication of meaning and spoken language. No wonder, then, that the results, the record, the form occurs and recurs throughout the history of visual communication. After all, the human hand and its capabilities are behind the making of visual communication up to and beyond the industrialization of media that started with Gutenberg.

Look around. Evidence of the power of gesture can be found in all sorts of places. You've the flailing, tubular inflatable man at car dealerships, the big foam finger at American football games, the fellow with the table tennis paddles guiding planes at the airport. Other examples are more culturally loaded. Take the *maneki-neko*, a beckoning, waving cat figure that is an integral part of Japanese streetscapes (see page 20). Its raised right paw is clearly a greeting as well as a symbol of strength and calm. Shop windows in the streets of Japanese cities from Sapporo to Hiroshima are populated by hordes of these little creatures, many of them animated and automated. They wave at

The hand axe is a rudimentary tool that evolved over some 500,000 years. It is formed to nestle in the palm of the hand, to cut, flense and shape skins, carcasses, wood and reeds.

Maneki-neko, the beckoning cat, engaged in trans-species communication. The raised paw is perhaps as powerful as the raised hand.

passing humans in a trans-species gestural greeting designed to make us feel a connection – to make us feel, once we see it, the thing that we call empathy.

Examples of empathy-inducing hand use abound in what is known as inter-species communication and particularly in popular culture. Sci-fi offers a rich seam. I have a favourite film of the genre from the era of cold war paranoia: it's Robert Wise's 1951 *The Day the Earth Stood Still* (see page 22). When Klaatu, the interstellar traveller played by Michael Rennie, emerges from his seamless silver ship, his greeting to the assembled army, press and public is the simplest and most empathetic human gesture: the raised hand (though he speaks in good English only moments later). As he emerges from the ship, Klaatu's gait, movement and communication, his adoption of the human impulse, all turn out to be well judged: they stop the assembled, terrified Earthling military from opening fire. After all, even though he's emerging from a silver ship with a big silver robot called Gort, that hand gesture suggests he might just be human, too.

It's not only in science fiction that interplanetary communication is a thing. The potential of the simple gesture to communicate visually, graphically, with whoever may find it has been redeployed in real science, too. The Pioneer 10 space probe was launched by the National Aeronautics and Space Administration (NASA) in early March 1972 at Cape Canaveral, Florida, carrying with it an attempt at inter-species visual communication (see page 23). Significantly, this was the first craft launched by humans to reach a velocity that would allow it to escape the gravitational fields of the solar system we inhabit. The implication was that the craft might get far enough to be discovered by extraterrestrials. With this in mind, the cosmologist and author Carl Sagan, along with astronomer Frank Drake and artist Linda Salzman Sagan, had the idea to include upon the craft a calling card of sorts: a gold-anodized aluminium plaque engraved with symbols of location, consciousness and human existence, just in case an alien civilization should come across the machine somewhere in deep space.

Bolted to the antenna struts of this fragile little bleeping outrider, the plaque bears the graven images of a naked man and woman. Significantly, it is the apparently Caucasian male, with his 70/30 hairstyle, his direct gaze 'to camera' and his foursquare stance, who is raising his right hand in greeting. His 'Eve' has a different and diffident stance, her face turned slightly away. The sexual and gender politics of this aside, the message is clearly intended to be one of empathy to an unknown species, an expectation of a universal recognition of greeting via eye contact and the raised hand. No one seems to have considered whether aliens would actually have hands, or eyes – however, this is a boldly crafted composition designed to communicate visually both with an unknown audience and, of course, with humankind here on Earth.

There's a lot of encoded information on the plaque, which was made by precision engravers in California. The figures are rendered in proportion to the spacecraft carrying the plaque; Earth is depicted as part of our solar system, and there are references to nearby stars and pulsars as a map of our position in the galaxy. The processes of mining, smelting, rolling, anodizing, designing and engraving stand behind this effort at visual communication: handwork and handcraft used to depict a fundamental human gesture made by tender, naked humans. Then let's not forget the rest of the creative, scientific and technological endeavour involved in getting a spacecraft out beyond our solar system. All that effort to raise a hand in potential greeting to a species we will probably never know. Pioneer 10 is heading towards the star Aldebaran in the Taurus constellation and, according to NASA, will take more than two million years to get there.

The Day the Earth Stood Still (1951): Klaatu, with his long-term robot partner Gort, greeting the assembled Earthling military prior to his warning to abandon the path humanity has taken.

This is a big subject!

What exactly do we mean by visual communication? As I've already suggested, the invention, use and mastery of tools – the development of technology – is a theme that runs through and underpins the history of our efforts to communicate with each other using visual media. It could be argued that anything we can see should be included in this journey, but of course that would be too broad a catchment. Setting aside the performative elements of human gesture, posture and gait (we can recognize threat, for example) and the ways the natural world signals to us (the wasp, the thorn, the ripened apple), it is of course human mark-making and composition that is the foundation of human visual communication.

In the pre-industrial phase of societal development, the human hand was the driving force of making. The manipulation of tools and materials – pens, brushes, burins, gouges, chisels and quills, charcoal, sponges, pigment, ink, paint, tempera, paper, canvas, wood, metal – governed the invention and expression of two- and three-dimensional visual commu-

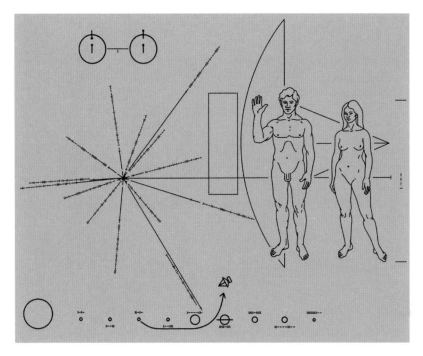

The plaque placed aboard the Pioneer 10 and 11 spacecrafts. The man looks out
of the image with a gimlet eye, a raised brow and a raised hand. The woman looks out
of frame and her stance is contrapposto. The gendered assignment of power is clear.

nication. Now it's the touchpad and capacitive screen that dominate;
and soon it may be possible to design simply by gesturing in space.
Professional designers today will use a touch pen and pad in a mode of work
redolent of the old ways; I can confirm that sketchbooks are still in use, too.
Manufacturers of tablets and phones are nudging customers towards the
use of the stylus or finger. It's as though we have come full circle: gestures
create and manipulate words and images on new technology, linking language to the visual via the hand.

So, our ability to repeat the controlled movement of our hands in space is
key to how we create visual communication. This fact holds whether we are
gesticulating to underline a point we are making as we speak, or creating
cursive characters in the fluid, repetitive act of writing.

Around 2008/9 I spent some time working in Italy, creating a visual identity for an art museum. At one point, gathered with my Italian colleagues
around a table in a trattoria, I was taken through the myriad gestural languages they used. My favourite involved joining the right-hand forefinger
and thumb, palm upward at waist height, and drawing the hand across the

waist from left to right. While doing this, turn the corners of the mouth down. Make the gesture and you may instinctively understand what it conveys: you are drawing a line under whatever argument you are having, or situation you find yourself in. Drawing a line; making a shape in space; recording it; creating and communicating meaning.

Whatever it is we make, be it an argument or an advertisement, visual communication by its very nature straddles modes, boundaries, disciplines, materials and purposes. It takes countless, amazingly diverse forms; within this multistranded and non-linear attempt to explain how we got where we are today, I'll aim to illuminate some of them with examples. A case in point (with no light-based pun intended) is the heliograph.

The heliograph is an ancient form of telegraph.[6] Around 405 BCE, in Xenophon's *Hellenica*, there is a reference to armies communicating with one another by means of a polished shield, and it's probably safe to assume that this method of visual communication remained in use across the ages. Certainly Henry Mance, credited with inventing the modern working version of the heliograph in 1869, was more responsible for the device's

The Mance heliograph is reliant on our ability to repeat gestures in time and space.

technological specification as a standard method of field communication than its pure invention.

What is interesting here is the relationship of heliographic 'sun writing' to the act of writing on a page, and hence gesture. With Mance's mahogany and brass contraption, a mirror is aligned to the sun and to a distant recipient. A switch positioned behind the mirror deflects its angle. By timing the gaps between deflections, long and short bursts of reflected sunlight can be transmitted as code. Writing, calligraphy and the operation of the heliograph are linked, as each relies on the ability of the human hand to create and repeat gestures and motions that will codify communication: the first as flashes of light, the second as letterforms. Mance's heliograph was admirably suited to the hot sun of Afghanistan and India at the peak of Britain's 19th-century colonial expansion; less so to daily usage in, say, fog-bound London or the rainy Pacific Northwest coast of America. Of course, other modes of visual communication designed to telegraph meaning across distances were developed; some of them are discussed later in this book. The heliograph had its moments, but in terms of repetitive, gestural action it was the rendering of letterforms by hand – in other words, writing – that became the means by which knowledge was best marshalled, codified, preserved and transmitted, both locally and over distances.

Where technology and gesture meet

When I started to study design history in Brighton in the mid-1980s, my handwriting was appalling. My first-year essays and notes looked as if they'd been written by multiple people with multiple personalities. Cursive though the notes and outpourings were, some slanted acutely, others obliquely.

The notes on the mark sheets returned by my tutors, however, were instantly recognizable. Their hands had been honed by countless hours of writing out responses to our mostly ill-formed arguments. By the final term of the first year, my own writing too had coalesced into a recognizable hand. This was a testament to the power of repetition, the effect of a favoured pen, and my left-handedness. The old adage that 'practice makes perfect' does not apply here: the formation of my letters was by no means perfect, but it was regular. I could cover page after page, comforted by the rhythmic scratch of the pen on the paper, like Eminem's 'Stan'.[7]

The gift of a Corona typewriter by my parents at the beginning of my second year put paid to the incessant scratching when writing essays, but my note-taking continued in the same vein. In spite of the subject I studied, it didn't occur to me at that point that I was privileged in having access to technology and tools that had been developed and refined over thousands of years.

The green-barrelled Pentel R50 rollerball I used was launched in early 1972: a wonder of injection-moulded design that came out of the mysterious (at least, to most of us in the UK at that time) culture of Japan. It was a highly fashionable thing, that pen. There is a photograph of Queen Elizabeth marking her race card with one, if that's evidence of fashion. The R50, with its cushioned rollerball, was both a writing revolution and a revelation: smooth, ergonomic and able to deliver more than two kilometres' worth of ink. The pen's design was contemporary and groundbreaking, but the water-based ink within it and the paper on which I wrote (close-ruled, spiral-bound notepads, bought from the art school shop) weren't much different from the writing technology that had been around for millennia.

Of course, writing existed prior to the use of ink. The briefest trot through the halls of the British Museum reveals all sorts of scribal evidence: words scratched upon wood, wax and slate, hieroglyphs on sarcophagi, the Rosetta Stone. The early development of the technology of writing was determined by the materials available and the kind of information with which people were working. Socrates famously felt that writing was not the best way of transmitting information, but many in the ancient world seem to have disagreed. The scribal culture around knowledge emerged thousands of years ago, matured and then persisted unchallenged at least from the 5th century to the 15th.

My contention here, though, is that ink, paper/parchment and pen, and formalized scripts and hands represent the starting point of modern visual communication. So the generation of the script, the various hands, the style of writing, the ink stain left on parchment and later paper by a pen wielded by a trained hand, is for our purposes the wellspring of the modern gesture-made mark. It's these marks – written words – that would transform one strand of visual communication and, in the process, transform humanity.

Prior to the invention of the printing press and moveable type, the making of pigmented inks and dye-based inks was in the gift of scribes and their apprentices. The 'ruled' page that guided the scribe's hand, shaping the prototypical wood-plank book page that printers like Gutenberg and Caxton later reproduced, had within it organizational principles to frame the hand-made letterforms. In other words, pages had a grid, an underlying system of proportion and organization.

In Europe, the visual conventions of writing were developed and spread principally by monks. The brethren would travel, taking to other centres of learning their *majuscule* text for religious manuscripts and *minuscule* variations for more workaday applications. Writing styles cross-fertilized as monasteries, cathedrals and abbeys became centres of power and learning across Europe within the Holy See.

Ways of writing, the shapes of letters, developed via a process of experimentation and hard physical work. Is writing hard physical work? Think of the postural discipline involved in maintaining a steady hand; the repetitive, meditative action of the hand and pen on vellum or parchment. The painstaking illumination of capitals; the preparation of materials; the working day divided by prayer, song and sleep. It's not quite the same as my own process, stretched out here on a sofa with a MacBook, notebook, books and a cup of coffee. I would say writing in the medieval period was pretty hard physical labour.

The assiduous work of monks, scribes and scholars characterized a project begun in medieval Europe under Charlemagne and King Alfred of Wessex to improve the state of knowledge and its visual expression. In the late 9th century, the marks (rendered with goose or swan quill nib and oak gall ink) and the bright pigments of the illuminations and marginalia steadily improved in form and execution. This was civilization made manifest, made visual and portable.

As 'book hands' of varying types emerged across Europe, scripts became laterally compressed – perhaps because it was easier and quicker to write this way. The rhythm of writing shapes the hand. The emergence of Caroline minuscule script – which, in the spirit of Charlemagne's unifying influence, combined elements of insular and Anglo-Saxon scripts – arguably made possible Alfred's own project to create the symbolism of coherence, with a pan-European and papal bent. The spread of the new letterforms, with their open and rounded, legible, cursive character, from the scriptoria of Aachen and then Tours as Charlemagne converted Europe to Christianity (often on pain of death) can be seen as episcopal power encoded in the formal language of the Word.

It's hard to imagine the process by which scribes were retrained in their writing skills. Did a manual exist? Or would a single page have been transcribed over and over, until the cursive gestures of the hand were enshrined in the mind and the muscle memory of the copyist? My own experience would suggest the latter. The emphasis on improving the visual quality of the written word, in the late Carolingian and beyond, signified two main principles: firstly, that ownership of the means by which knowledge could be stored and transmitted was the key to power; and secondly, that in developing technologies to create the best possible version of writing, several ambitions could be realized. These would include a uniformity of purpose, the control and spread of education, and the signification of the all-embracing power of the Holy Church of Rome. This was the trinity of civilizing ambitions backed by the military might and political nous of the first emperor of Europe, *Pater Europae*, Charlemagne.

It was, however, the blackletter *textualis quadrata* style that came to dominate both written and printed words. Developed in what is now Germany, the curvatures of the Carolingian were replaced with angles, providing the basis for the moveable type cut by Gutenberg and paid for by his partner, the goldsmith Faust (or Fust). Technological pragmatism and efficiency drove the invention of moveable type: angles are easier to cut than curves.

Letters as symbols of power

The letters formed by monks in their manuscripts were not just for making words to be read. In their growing uniformity, they became a sign system for the presence and power of the Church. Whether or not you could read (and most could not), the sight of the serried lines, the columns of letters – some book hands could fit up to ten lines of dense writing into an inch – glimpsed in the pulpit or on the lectern spoke of industry and inclusion, of unification and uniformity, of education and episcopal power.

There is a system of signification at work here. Medieval letters, with their short, vertical minims, hairline ascenders cut with the edge of the nib on the European medieval page, tend to sit within a grid. The grid and margins ruled on the vellum in turn may take their proportions from the golden section. Fine lead lines would determine the proportion of the letters in the text and that of the dropped, illuminated capital initial. Each stroke, ascender and descender, each counter, bowl, terminal and serif, would be rendered by hand to the glory of God. At times this would be tedious work, repetitive and exhausting. Naturally there are no records of repetitive strain injury in monastic records, but there are marginalia that suggest boredom was an element of life in the scriptoria.

For example, the trope of the knight battling the snail appears in the margins of 13th-century Flemish and English manuscripts. Knight v. Snail can be seen in numerous psalters and books of hours. It's unclear what these little cartoons mean. Scholars have seen them as satirical commentary – the knights are sometimes shown running away from the snails, or confronting their foes while naked. Whatever their intended meaning, they are diversions and probably would have been fun to design, draw and discuss.

OPPOSITE The Knight v. Snail trope appears on this late 13th century or early 14th century page from the Smithfield *Decretals* of Pope Gregory IX. By the 15th century, the manuscript had travelled from Toulouse to the Priory of St Bartholomew in Smithfield, London.

Blanche of Castille and Louis IX: ink, tempera and gold leaf are used here in the depiction of scribal culture, perhaps supporting the hierarchies of state. This extraordinary image brings together so many techniques, trades and materials. The blue would probably have been derived from crushed lapis lazuli.

Craftsmanship drove the production of books; that, and faith in the one true God and the desire to spread the word. Like cleanliness, good work has a relationship to godliness. The minute attention to the angle of attack of the nib on the writing surface; the attitude of the scribe, bent over the high oaken desk with the tools of ink horn, nib, quill, knife and powder at hand; the precision and patience required for preparation and execution; the investment of time in the rendering of each letterform – all of this was testament to the human effort required to produce books before printing was widespread. Books were made in the name of God. But it is in the craft and labour and not in godliness, I feel, that the empathetic kick of a well-turned hand is delivered. For me, it's in the craft, the skill, the time and the work, not in the belief in monotheism.

Around the 9th century in what is now Iraq, other hands were being developed in the ongoing work of the transcription of the Qur'an. The Kufic hand developed to confer authority on the manuscripts of that holy book in the same way as *textualis quadrata* did for the Bible. To my Western eye, untrained in reading Arabic hand, Kufic script has about it an open, abstract, geometric, brush-derived lateral precision that occupies the page in an entirely different way to the output of the monks of northern Europe.

Each system of writing, the Islamic and the Christian, evolved a hand that signified the authority of the pope or the Prophet through the skill of its execution. Scribes came at the page with different materials and levels of ability, but they were all aiming at a similar outcome. This diversity of approach and execution is plain to see today, should one care to look. Some years ago, I was asked to give a short evening talk at Tate Britain. The deal was that I could choose two objects from the collection and then address a small group of visitors on some of the themes that might arise from juxtaposing them. I chose a 16th-century printed Bible and a diplomatic passport to the court of Queen Elizabeth I, granted by Suleiman the Magnificent in roughly the same era.

These two items could not have been more different in execution. One was printed, the other written. The Bible's pages, though beautifully wrought, were modular and orthogonal, the columns creating cruciform gutters and margins, tightly organized as, at that time, a product of a printing press had to be. The passport, on the other hand, was a flowing crescent of handwritten diplomatese; a curvilinear occupation of the page in a wonderfully flowery hand, evoking the contours of a cornucopia and ending in an ornamental flourish and seal. Each object underlined the differences in approach of the two cultures: the crescent met the cross in my little comparative exercise, and each expressed its power through its form.

After the talk, to counter the adrenalin, I had a pint in a local pub in Pimlico and got chatting with a man at the bar. It emerged that he was an importer of cashmere wool whose landlord had just foreclosed on him. It struck me that he was using the same trade routes that Suleiman's ambassador to Elizabeth I, the owner of the passport, would have travelled. As trade routes and the need for passports have persisted, so have the differences in cultural expression via type, type forms and typography. There are few examples of a successful crossover between so-called Arabic and Western forms.

I must have given that talk more than a decade ago, but the memory of the two objects I chose has stayed with me. Of course, there is technology involved in the production of all such meticulous works of wonder, be they printed or written; and the tools and materials that brought these elements of visual communication into being, over hundreds if not thousands of years, were developed through experimentation without precise knowledge of the chemistry and physics involved.

The methods of reproduction were handed down by the written word as well as by word of mouth, apprenticeship and practical demonstration. Some of these practices continue in the guild system still to be found in some European countries, where apprentices become journeymen before becoming master craftsmen or women.[8] It's a positive that the transmission of skill and craft is still in the gift of various closed shops that demand a knowledge of the rudiments of making (whatever it is they are making) before being unleashed on the world. These guilds, apprenticeships, undergraduate courses and training schemes are bastions of quality, maintained to hold back the hordes who have access to tools (often digital) but no real idea how best to use them.

Ink, pen and parchment

Let's backtrack a little, before we dive into discussion of the digital. My hand rests on the writing surface and holds the pen. The pen contains the ink. This triumvirate of ink, pen and writing surface is a tripod upon which the development of Western civilization rests. If I make a mark, I am drawing on history. Each element of the triumvirate is a technologically derived component of a system; each has its own history.

Ink has a particularly curious origin story: one that involves chemistry, the industry of insects, trial and error, and the pressures of necessity. Essentially there are two types of ink: pigmented ink and staining ink. Pigmented ink uses pigment in suspension – in the case of carbon ink, the pigment would be soot – and sits upon the surface of the medium to which it is applied. A staining ink, on the other hand, is made by chemical reaction:

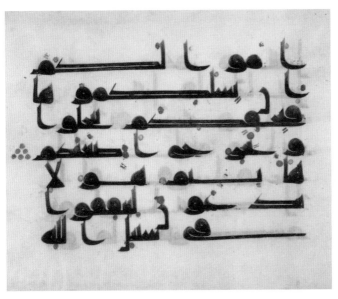

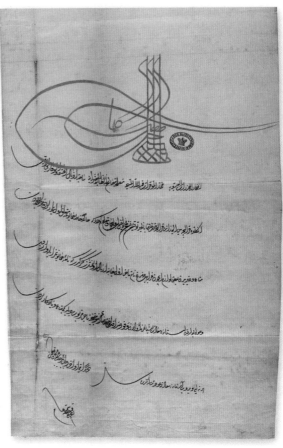

ABOVE The Kufic hand is the oldest form of written script, developed in Kufa on the banks of the Euphrates in what is now Iraq. It features an open, lateral brush-derived precision.

RIGHT The Ottoman passport features a series of flowing crescents of handwritten diplomatese, in direct contrast to the orthogonality of the printed Bible.

it will do what it says on the tin and stain or dye the medium, making a more permanent mark. The distinction is important, the chemistry and history intriguing. Carbon ink is reckoned to be the oldest form of ink and consists in its most rudimentary form of three basic components: soot, tree sap and water. The other kind of ink is iron gall or oak gall ink, whose colour is derived from a chemical reaction between a tannic solution and copperas (ferrous sulphate).

In both types of ink the tree sap in question is gum arabic, taken from the numerous varieties of the acacia tree and other sappy weeds that flourish in sub-Saharan Africa and the tropics. Trade in this water-soluble gum has thrived since well before the Common Era (CE) on routes between Africa and the Mediterranean, and onwards into northern Europe. Its uses have since multiplied, extending into areas such as food production and medicine; but when a quinquereme butting its way through the Adriatic docked in Venice or Piran, its cargo of acacia gum would have been destined for use predominantly in inks and paints.

Ferrous sulphate is produced by roasting iron pyrites, otherwise known as fool's gold. The mining of fool's gold and the trade in pyrites – Italy's geology is particularly rich in pyrites, but the mineral appears in geological seams all over Europe and beyond – accompanied complex networks of buying and selling. Gums, spices, wine, wood and ceramics together with staples such as oils, wheat and barley accompanied the movement of people across continents. Some cargoes also comprised the scrolls and codexes that were the forerunners of books (more of which later).

The process or inspiration by which alchemists discovered ferrous sulphate's ability to react to the gallotannins extracted from oak galls has been lost to time. As with the brewing of beer or the making of leavened bread, little is known about ancient methods of achieving precision in chemistry before it was codified as the science we know today. But the constituents of the inks used in the early civilized world are still around, should we care to look.

Oak galls are a particularly fascinating crop and a key element in the making of 9th-century-style inks. Here's where the industry of insects comes into play. The gall wasp burrows into a healthy young oak and lays its eggs there. The larvae grow within the tissue of the tree, which produces a gall – a kind of benign tumour. This gall is rich in gallotannins, which can be extracted by boiling the galls. They then react with the ferrous sulphate to

OPPOSITE *Spider, Sweet Cherry Flower, and English Oak Leaf with Galls* by Joris Hoefnagel 1561–1562; illumination added 1591–1596. The oak gall is a fascinating crop integral to the development of staining inks.

make a black dye. That dye is thickened with water-soluble gum arabic, which increases the surface tension of the liquid, allowing it to flow via capillary action into the calamus (hollow tube) of a feather and then out through the slit cut in the nib, onto parchment or vellum.

In the distant past, before the Pentel R50 and its rollerball, a pen would be a moulted feather from a goose, swan or other large bird. The quill, dressed with a convex knife to create the writing edge and the slit in the calamus, would be chosen so that it curved over the right forearm of the scribe, ensuring a clear sightline to where quill met parchment. (Left-handed scribes were not encouraged, though the association of the sinister with evil was perhaps a later conceit.)

So the accoutrements of writing in the 9th century, of creating visual communication, stood at the centre of a web of technology and trade. If the production of ink relied on a combination of chemistry, agriculture and transcontinental trade, the making of the writing surface had its own equally arcane gestation involving specific recipes, tools and practices.

The parchment on which many manuscripts were written can be made from any dried and processed animal skin, but vellum is specifically derived from calfskin. Both writing materials are produced by a laborious process of de-fleshing, de-hairing and then washing the skin, first in water and then in lime, followed by further immersion in lime and then repeated soaking and drying in water while stretching on a frame. While on the frame, the skin is scraped (to thin the vellum or parchment) with a curved, sharpened mild steel blade called a lunellum. The steel used in making blades would also rely on the action of lime to remove impurities, increasing the overall quality and improving the honed edge. It appears that lime, limestone, slaked lime and its derivatives were crucial to the birth and growth of all kinds of visual media.

Lime x geometry = the rose window

I am a Londoner, so I am surrounded by limestone. Emerge from Green Park tube station in the West End of London on the south side of Piccadilly, and you will see an artwork by John Maine entitled *Sea Strata*. It is made from Portland stone and granite. The Portland stone has etched into it countless ammonites and other creatures of the kind that would have been sedimented to death when the limestone was laid down, some 167 million years ago, in what is now Portland on the Isle of Purbeck.

Limestone and lime are integral not just to London but to the cultural life of Europe and, it could be argued, the world.[9] Hawksmoor's western towers at Westminster Abbey are built from limestone; Canterbury Cathedral is built in part from Caen stone; parts of the Tower of London and the first London Bridge used the versatile material.

In Europe, the building of the great cathedrals served to concentrate and advance many aspects of the culture. If abbeys and monasteries were factories of learning and study, cathedrals were department stores with glittering shop windows: they needed to communicate with their largely illiterate visiting population through symbols and saints, relics and religiosity, mystery and magic. Somewhat ironically, sedimentary rock, encasing rudimentary life captured at the beginning of evolutionary time, became the material through which the wonders of the six days of creation were promulgated. They could not have done it without limestone and lime.

Standing in the holy light of Lincoln Cathedral, beneath the rose window known as the Dean's Eye, I am struck by just how many different techniques and tools have been involved in the development of visual communication, both in the form of written words and in the built environment around me.

It starts with the use of lime (calcium oxide, CaO) in the making of the vellum or parchment on which a decree was written in 1192 by Henry II, appointing Hugh of Avalon as bishop to raise taxes for the rebuilding of the old cathedral. The process continues with arcane chemistry. The extraction of lime from the ashes of a hardwood fire or from shells is an ancient practice – perhaps, like the roasting of pyrites, initially discovered by accident. Later, through the quarrying of limestone and its heating in kilns, lime came to be used in plaster, washes and early mortars and concrete, in the fertilization of fields, and then in soap-making and food production. It has been a constant in the growth of civilization.

Just as lime, slaked lime and its derivatives became essential to the processes of creating leathery pages, scrolls and codices, the oölite and pisolite rocks laid down in sedimentary prehistoric processes also played a role in the construction of the cathedral, and in communication through liturgical symbolism. Limestone's sedimentary composition means that it lends itself to being quarried, cut and carved with precision. This meant that the palette of medieval media used by craftsmen was expanded and the journey from two dimensions into three, now the bedrock of so much visual communication, was prefigured in the work of medieval craftsmen.

Moving from 2-D to 3-D may sound simple, perhaps because we are so used to the process today. Buildings, products, type, clothes, cars: all may start out as drawings or sketches, and the image of the designer finding a form through the iterative process of drawing is a familiar trope. In medieval times, the making of a piece of visual communication in three dimensions was necessarily predominantly artisanal; machines of all kinds were mostly rudimentary, so the hand and the eye drove the process. The means by which, for example, a rose window such as the Dean's Eye would come into being would involve a combination among other skills of geometry, drawing, stonemasonry, kiln-building, glass-making, lead mining and smelting, iron-making and carpentry. Underlying the whole process was the need to incorporate a range of symbols and codifications that were designed to communicate meaning to worshippers, pilgrims and peasantry.

The Dean's Eye is a pictorial gem. The stained glass features Adam and Eve (he's digging, she's spinning – activities understood by the locals in 1220 or thereabouts),[10] angels of judgment, the apostles, and an angel swinging a censer, together with bishops and clergy presented in the same medium as Christ the Judge.[11] The production of these narrative scenes was necessarily labour-intensive, involving not only illustrators and painters but lead formers, kiln stokers and cement mixers.[12] Underlying all this effort, of course, was the liturgy as it was designed to be communicated by the Church. There are layers to the codification of this communication, some of which relate to the geometric harmony of the whole.

I look into the Dean's Eye. Sixteen roundels encircle the quatrefoil at the centre, with four equidistant trefoils around it. The roundels create other geometric elements, and each is illuminated with coloured glass. Each has a scene, a symbol. My eye can trace the square, the circle, the vesica, the tangent and the chord. The spaces described by these intersections create what seems to be a perfect mandorla. The geometry is complex and multilayered: it's possible to overlay the tetractys, a mystical Pythagorean symbol, upon the Dean's Eye. A tetractys comprises an arrangement of points forming an equilateral triangle and, within it, a hexagon. It symbolizes the four elements – air, fire, water and earth – as well as the idea of dimensionality: a point is zero dimensions; a line drawn between two points is one dimension; lines drawn between three points create the triangle and form a plane in two dimensions; and four points represent three dimensions in the possibility of extrusion. Three-quarters of the tetractys also appears in the diocese's coats of arms as a tasselled ornament.

I could easily lose myself in the geometric puzzle of the rose window, the composition, the meanings. From down here on the transept floor, it looks perfect. But the apparent precision of the window's construction may not have been overseen by master builders or masons. It is possible that it was driven by glaziers or clerics who were in effect experimenting with plate tracery, the thick, carved segments of limestone laid out on the ground before being hoisted into place and cemented.

A companion window to the Dean's Eye – the Bishop's Eye, in the south transept – experienced catastrophic failure within one hundred years of its

The Dean's Eye in Lincoln Cathedral is both a pictorial gem and a geometric puzzle.

construction, reinforcing the theory that the builders were rather making it up as they went along. The collapse of the cathedral's central tower in 1237 would suggest the same. When its rebuilding was completed in 1311 it made Lincoln Cathedral the tallest building in the world, a status it maintained for the next quarter of a millennium; the spire atop the tower collapsed in a gale in 1549. Tall buildings fight both nature and entropy. Over time, close on eight hundred years, the prevailing winds and structural thrusts created a pressure system that effectively began to suck and push the Dean's Eye window out of the facade in which it sits. It started to bow out, creating compression in some joints and opening others, and destabilizing the structure. The window was restored from the year 2000 using Anstrude Roche Claire stone from Auxerre in France, as the bed depth of available Lincoln limestone from which the original window had been built was not adequate.

In spite of the fact that I am looking at a modern reproduction of the tracery with original glass, I find I am moved by the stories it tells. There's the representation of biblical stories, certainly, and the depiction of life as it was lived by the peasantry. But there's also the vision, the craft and the time spent and skill exercised by the people who built it. It's this element that excites and exercises me. The human endeavour involved in the construction of beauty in order to better tell a story delivers an undeniable emotional kick. It's something from which anyone involved in visual communication can learn.

The craft of the medieval master builders and their use of geometry was not necessarily consciously, theoretically Pythagorean or Euclidean; rather, it was the result of judicious use of dividers, compasses, set squares, t-squares, rules and plumbs. The intersections drawn on the ground at 1:1 scale; the window raised piece by piece. Is it possible to imagine the role a window like this might have had some 800 years ago? A lay brother points aloft and describes to a newly arrived pilgrim just what they might be seeing. The geometer's craft encodes a language of popular theology as visual communication. 'Look,' the brother might have said, 'the triangle speaks to the trinity, the square points at the winds and the seasons, the elements and the cardinal points of the compass; the five-pointed pentangle suggests Christ's stigmata and the geometry of man.'[13]

Geometry and beauty

Geometry is an international unifier of human communication: it spans millennia. In Renaissance Italy, the art and science of geometry was called the *ossatura di Dio*, which loosely translates as the 'framework of God'. All the Abrahamic religions use geometry to ornament and decorate their sacred spaces. In eschewing figurative representation, the Islamic traditions of decoration in particular use geometric progression to evoke the relationship of the believer to the works of the godhead, the universe.

In the decoration found in the sacred and secular spaces of the Islamic world, the orthogonal, the square or rectangle, represents the directional human experience of the world in constant motion within the universe, within creation and within the spiritual world which is symbolized by the circle. The intersection and division of these basic shapes creates the basis

The complex geometry of *muqarnas*, with their stalactite-like, honeycomb forms, evokes the dome of stars of the known universe, the Fibonacci sequence of a seed head, or, quite simply, the infinite.

of the decorative forms that ornament buildings, scrolls, books and fabrics. Pattern-making of the kind that ornaments the sacred spaces of Islam tends to be made using interlocking stars and polygons. These are derived from inscribing concentric circles and subdividing them using rays and chords, thereby developing arrays of complex constellations of radial geometric patterns.

Interestingly, where the Christian geometer would usually work 'in the field', as it were, there is evidence that by the late 12th century and certainly the 13th, designers working on mosques, palaces and scrolls in the cities of Iran and further east were working out their geometric designs for *muqarnas* and friezes on the upper parts of the *qibla* wall – that which faces Mecca – on paper.

The arrival of the Mongols from the east brought technologies and techniques for drawing and the transmission of information as visual

Mandana, Rajoli, Alpona or Kolam: there are many names for the making of geometric decorations from chalk, pigments, lime, rock dust or rice flour that adorn the thresholds and architraves of houses and floors all over India.

communication from China. Combining drawing on disposable, easily man-ufactured and transported material (paper) with the Arabic advances in mathematics creates an interesting contrast with the contemporary work at Lincoln. The complex geometry of *muqarnas*, with their stalactite-like, hon-eycomb forms, evokes the dome of stars of the known universe, the Fibonacci sequence of a seed head, or, quite simply, the infinite.

Patterns draw us humans in. We are driven by pattern-spotting and pat-tern-making. Geometric Kolam, drawn with chalk, rock dust or, in other times, rice flour – to feed small insects – on the doorsteps of Hindu dwell-ings in southern India (Kolam have similar expressions and different names all over the subcontinent) are redolent with meaning evoking harmony with nature. This idea recurs wherever humans create communication. Platonists believe that our connection to geometry is innate, having been inculcated in us when our souls were in touch with the infinite state of 'ideal being' before birth. They may have a point, those Platonists, as the visual harmony of geometry underpins designed things to which human eyes are drawn. Whether it is single-point perspective in cinema like that favoured by

Kubrick, the grids underlying the work of Romek Marber for Penguin Books, the Jaguar grille designed by William Lyons, or the harmony of music, the resolution of proportion and form via geometry is a thread that runs through all kinds of successful visual communication.

(An aside: Each human interaction with a piece of visual communication involves a journey from abstraction in the brain of the maker, through to mark-making with the gestural precision of our tools, to the rendering of a creation in two or three dimensions. This journey is at the heart of the mysterious, magical and sometimes sacred relationship between the conception and the making of a piece of visual communication and its consumption. In the pre-industrial world, a work of art, a page of scripture, a sculpture or a window – or, latterly, a scribal book, a painting or a palimpsest of some kind – would make the journey from inside, from the heart and the mind, to outside by way of our human dexterity and developing mastery of gesture and movement in space; in other words, our work, underpinned by skill and craft. The work is made in order to gain access to the interior world of those who see and interpret the results. This is a timeless human occupation with the drive to communicate at its core.)

There is a distinction in the use of geometry by different cultures. The Islamic traditions took arabesques, vegetal forms and geometric interplay and interlacing to create enormously intricate and beautiful patterning with which to adorn palaces and holy places. An aniconic tradition emerged using sacred geometry wherein the representation of people, prophets and creation was forbidden by scripture. In the Christian tradition the same geometric abstractions, interplays and overlays, and snaking vegetal forms are used to frame the pictorial imagery of God, his acolytes, angels and archbishops.

Perhaps the Islamic tradition uses the universality of geometry to force the contemplative mind inward to the self, while the Christian tradition uses that same universality in the service of a powerful, albeit apocryphal story, simply framed and told in images. Whatever the case, numbers, proportion and composition matter and have always mattered in visual communication – whether they govern the making of the work, as in a mosque, or inspire revolution and rejection of order, as in the work of, say, Jamie Reid for the Sex Pistols (see page 45), Malcolm Garrett, or others inspired by the abandonment of old ways in favour of the revolutionary, lawless new frontiers of visual communication.

Robert Lawlor states: 'Ancient geometry starts with *One*, while modern mathematics and geometry start with *Zero*.'[14] He goes on to explain that some monastic orders, including the Cistercians, rejected the idea of zero as the devil's work and that it was their gnostic, mystical view of their relationship to the cosmos and transcendence that underpinned the idea of the great gothic cathedrals as 'cosmic temples to the Piscean age'. Even if this is true, certainly none of the devil-fearing Cistercians or the mercantile classes could have predicted the degree to which one and zero would come to dominate the production of visual communication. For one and zero are the essential 'on and off' states that govern the binary code underpinning all present-day computation. Without Gottfried Leibniz and binary, without one and zero, on/off, true/false, the culture of visual communication we have today would not exist.[15]

Long before we got to machine code, the mercantile classes adopted the Arabic system of numeracy with alacrity, using zero in the swift calculation of prices, profit and loss. The division of faiths and cultures along these numerical lines may be spurious, as it's difficult to imagine any cathedral coming into being without the support of the mercantile classes and the architects, masons and builders whose maths perforce had to include zero. Who would design and manage the build, quarry and price the stone, provide the glass, the pigments, the cords for tapestry, the tallow and beeswax for candles, the gold for the bishop's robes, the silver for the monstrance, the incense for the censer? Who if not the architects, masons, builders and merchants?

In Europe, at least, cathedrals and their constituent parts stand at the crossroads of all early western European medieval human endeavour. They are designed to communicate visually a set of ideas and narratives that are complex, mystical and educational, while at the same time inspiring wonder and faith and underpinning political power – not to mention leveraging the groat from the pilgrim's purse for the sight of the relic, the piece of the true cross or the saint's finger bone in its bejeweled reliquary.

Workmanship, risk and character

Have you ever tried to make an *ensō*? *Ensō* is the Japanese word for circle – or circular form – but an *ensō* is not just any circle. It's a circle with particular properties.

An *ensō* is made in ink using a *fude* (brush) on *washi* (ultra-thin paper). The paper is traditionally made from *kozo* – fibres from mulberry bark, *mitsumata* (*Edgeworthia papyrifera*), or the fibres from the gampi/ganpi tree, or combinations of all three. The fibres and bark are harvested (preferably in winter, when water is frozen and impurities are in suspension and thus easy to spot and remove) and then steamed, separated and pulped, laid into trays, shaken and dried. Traditionally, the *fude* is made from the hair of the tanuki

Jamie Reid used décollage to subvert the symbols of nationhood in 1976/77, the year of Elizabeth II's Silver Jubilee. Here the flag is the grid, the medallion centred and the letters randomly cut and pasted onto the face of Her Maj. Former rules did not apply in so many ways. The shock, then, was palpable.

(a Japanese raccoon dog).[16] The brush is bound to the handle in such a way that ink flows cleanly onto the paper. The density of the brush creates a reservoir for the ink. Japanese ink, once derived solely from soot, lampblack and animal glue, came to include other plant soots, animal and plant oils as well as graphite produced from charcoal, plant dyes and elements of other mineral inks. The ink is formed into a cake or stick and in use is mixed with water on a *suzuri*, or ink stone.

There is a complex web of invention, happenstance and circumstance that led to these tools being available for use. Paper-making, for example, involves a mixture of chemistry and construction in the collection, stripping, mulching and laying of plant fibres to create the basis of ultra-thin *washi*, the construction of wooden forms in which the pulp is laid to dry. Then consider making a brush: the labour of catching a tanuki, killing it, skinning it, blanching the skin to remove the hair, sterilizing the bristles, forming the handle from bamboo – which, by the way, would need a sharpened, forged metal tool – then binding with twine, spun from hemp or other plant material and wound closely around the barrel of the handle to create a ferrule holding the bristles in place. The bristles must then be trimmed and shaped so that, when wet with ink, they fall into a point, allowing the ink to flow smoothly and also creating the familiar 'drag' at the end of a circle where the amount of ink released from the brush, determined by pressure, matches the desired form.

But to draw the *ensō* is to experience mark-making, and its whole point is in the experience. The experience *is* the meaning. This dance between eye, hand and material in time is ancient and mysterious. Gesture drives communication. It says: 'I made a mark. Can you read it?'

As I hope is becoming clear, it's essentially human, this mania for mark-making. The relationship between the scripture and the scribe, the mark-maker and the mark, is necessarily symbiotic. Neither can exist without the other. The drive to communicate language and meaning through the human-made mark is a shared trait across time the world over. That drive has always been supported by invention. Around 1,000 years before the architects at Lincoln were setting out and then installing their first rose window, unknown Chinese experimentalists were creating the first versions of a new writing material: paper. Mulberry bark mixed with water and other materials – rags, strands, plant fibre, silk – were pulped and mixed then stretched across frames to dry, creating a friable but stable enough surface on which the brush and later the pen could make its mark.

The *ensō* is the remnant of a physical act in space and time. Once finished, it should not be altered.

Arguably, the development of brush use over stylus or pen was a corollary of both the fragility of the new writing surface and the compatibility of the geometry of human gesture with mark-making by brush. In the pre-typographic era, what David Pye calls 'the workmanship of risk'[17] was inherent in the work of calligraphers, whose control of their tools and materials in terms of gesture, flow and pressure resulted in the pictographic forms of alphabets and the meditative, expressive qualities of *ensō* and other Zen-inspired brushstrokes.

In the moment of execution of perfect calligraphic strokes, there is no room for error, but uniqueness and imperfection created by the action of writing are embraced. In the world of *ensō*, error contributes to perfection. The making of *ensō* is freighted with symbolic meaning directly derived from the transfer of energy in space and time, through the movement of a body, to create a mark on paper with a brush and ink. The *ensō* should be completed swiftly and, once completed, remain unchanged.

But what does an *ensō* visually communicate? The finished circle is, in essence, evidence of a human action in time, frozen. And this mystical meta-meaning applied to simple mark-making could be applied to any visible product of such gestures – from handwriting to the books of hours and psalters produced by monks; from calligraphy on vellum to the application of complex brushed letterforms onto silk in the Shang and Zhou periods (1045 BCE – 256 BCE); and from artworks and sculptures, through *muqarnas*, through pre-industry and back, to the hand upon the cave wall.

Character-building activities

I wondered why letters were called 'characters'. The Greek word *kharaktēr* means 'a stamping tool', conveniently prefiguring (and helping to name) moveable type. Then the meaning of the word transmutes through French and Middle English to denote something with particular qualities. It works: some characters have, well, *character* conferred on them by the way they are made.

For example, the Chinese character for 'man' (transliterated as 'rén'). The dynamic nature of this mark maintains the stroke weights – a thin point of origin and increasing thickness – of its original brush-derived character, even in its digital form. This is, in its way, an emoticon, a dynamic representation of the human form that suggests soul and emotion. Its profile is akin to that of a person walking, and even in its most simple printed form it carries the 'mark memory' of its origins in brush-made calligraphy. The image of the walking figure connects to the calligraphic execution of letterforms as an expression of energy in motion. The controlled gesture,

The Chinese character 'rén', meaning 'man', retains its brush-derived form and has also an animated, purposeful significance. It is redolent of a walking figure, a human in motion.

practised ad infinitum, results in the thicker stroke at the top of the left-hand element, where the brush first connects with the paper (or previously, perhaps, the silk), thinning as the hand pulls the brush tip downward. The second and final element starts with a delicate thin downstroke, thickening as the brush creates a natural serif. There are deeper Confucian elements to the rendering of characters such as these. In fact, so important was the practice of calligraphy to ancient Chinese culture that it was seen as part of a quad of beaux-arts pastimes including music, painting and the playing of the board game Go.

The primary point to be drawn from the analysis and description of such methods – from the hand on the cave wall to the calligraphers of old – is that the creation of such marks is by definition connected to, evidence of and the product of human movement in space and time. As such, the humanity of the simplest handmade mark connects with our human drive to communicate, to connect with each other. The tag 'handmade' has value still. With the handmade, there is little or no distance between the intention to communicate and our means of accomplishing the task, the primary determinant of success being the development of skill.

It has been successfully argued by many that post-industrial tools of communication necessarily divorced the person from the means of communication. Typography, printing, filming, signalling – all are mechanistic and mechanized systems, designed to replace or reproduce the gestural. The maker divorced from the mark. Machines transfer work. So the gap that has opened up between human mark-making for communication, and communication achieved through industrial systems *after* the invention of typography and printing (and later, other machinery), has had to be filled with something. But what? With what do we fill this gap? Could it be the signification of emotion, and attempts to trigger empathy?

The writing surface and the writing implement are interdependent. Early papers were fragile and friable; the brush was the natural ink carrier for writing the character sets of ancient characters on fragile surfaces.

49

Playing with the page

There are many ways of triggering the emotional understanding of a piece of communication in the viewer or reader. The calligram, an arrangement of text that creates an image, is one such form.

The experimentation with and manipulation of typed and mechanized letterforms into calligrammatic compositions has a long history. The ancient Greek poets – Simmias of Rhodes is one example – would create texts that represented, in their set form, the shape of the subject of the verse. Thus, the poem 'Wings', preserved in later re-editions, has the word forms set into the shape of a pair of wings. This approach also characterized 'The Axe' and 'The Egg'; all three poems date from around 325 BCE. Later, a poem by the 4th-century Latin poet Optatian Porfyry[18] has within it a kind of *carmina cancellata*, wherein certain letters are obscured or overwritten to create what 21st-century puzzlers might recognize as a word search problem, but which uses these pathways drawn across the text to depict the *chi rho* – the combined 'P' and 'X' forms that echo the first two letters of Christ's name when written in the Greek.[19]

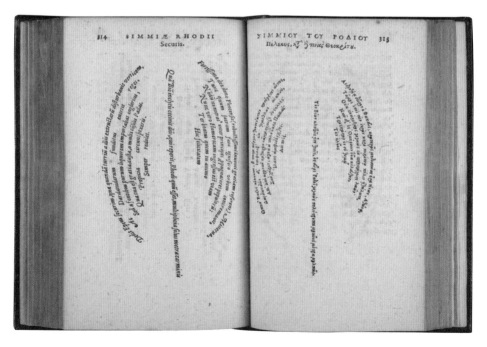

Simmias of Rhodes, 'The Axe' – a calligrammatic treatment of the text assumes the form of the subject matter.

Guillaume Apollinaire's calligrams were in part composed in the trenches during the First World War. The text on the Eiffel Tower shape translates therefore as something like 'Hello world, of which I am the eloquent tongue, O Paris, that will forever shoot out at the Germans'.

The manipulation of page and type to occupy the orthogonal area of a sheet of paper in an unorthodox way has many expressions springing from this tradition. Stéphane Mallarmé's *Un coup de dés jamais n'abolira le hasard*, from 1897, is another case in point. It's a remarkable example of a kind of fin-de-siècle design freedom that inhabits the page as if passing poetic thoughts had formed themselves into typographic interjections on the white ground of the paper.[20] To read it is to experience simultaneity of meaning and form. Mallarmé's requisitioning of the page in the service of poetic form, in the service of modernity, places the reader in what was then the unique position of determining their own rhythmic experience of the word images presented by the poet.

With each turn of the page or roll of the dice, Mallarmé confounds the reader's expectations and throws the weight of interpretation onto the viewer. Across the pages, he prefigures vorticism, the 'liberated pages' of Rodchenko and Bayer, the drifting, colliding juxtapositions of the Dadaists' word-ideas, and the sometimes weighty poetics of animated typography in film titles and advertising of the later 20th century.

Mallarmé was not alone. Prior to *Un coup de dés...*, the apocryphal genesis of 'The Mouse's Tale' had the typesetters of *Alice's Adventures in Wonderland* pleading with Lewis Carroll to rewrite the poem, as the demands of typesetting it in 1865 proved too complex for the snaking form of the original design. Later, Guillaume Apollinaire's calligram 'La colombe poignardée et le jet d'eau' showed the potential of moving type across the bed, holding the typefaces in a forme that did not rely on the orthogonality of a standard galley and, with the jury-rigged printing plate in place, running off multiple copies of *Poems of Peace and War*, a collection delivered after Apollinaire's shrapnel injury and published in 1918, the year of his death from Spanish flu.

The ambivalence of absolute meaning encoded in the rendering of word forms as images asks questions of the reader-as-viewer. Again, as with the columns of text in a Bible or prayer book, the setting of words on the page forms and transmits meaning with or without literacy. Literacy, as in the ability to read, is not essential for visual communication to work.

It was Apollinaire who reputedly coined the idea of the 'sur-real'; and what could be more surreal than finding the nature of the page – so fixed and determined by the mechanization of typography, and for so long so widely distributed via the growth of newspapers and posters and advertising materials – reformed into a fluid wordscape, where meaning and form are elided in the pursuit of poetic power? If Mallarmé and Apollinaire, in the fermenting modernity of the late 19th-century European salons, effectively 'broke' the orthogonal orthodoxy of how letters and lines should sit on a printed page, others found themselves able to manipulate the type and the page when the mechanized wonder of the typewriter became accessible.

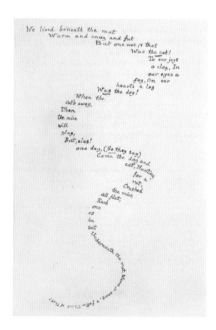

RIGHT AND OPPOSITE Lewis Carroll's original handwritten draft of 'The Mouse's Tail' proved too difficult for the typesetters of the 1865 print edition of *Alice's Adventures in Wonderland* Carroll's original calligram has the tail inverting the type toward its end.

so that her idea of the tale was something like
this :——"Fury said to
a mouse, That
he met
in the
house,
' Let us
both go
to law :
I will
prosecute
you.——
Come, I 'll
take no
denial ;
We must
have a
trial :
For
really
this
morning
I 've
nothing
to do.'
Said the
mouse to
the cur,
'Such a
trial,
dear sir,
With no
jury or
judge,
would be
wasting
our breath.'
' I 'll be
judge,
I 'll be
jury,'
Said
cunning
old Fury ;
' I 'll try
the whole
cause,
and
condemn
you
to
death.

Metal machines and movement

When I received my Corona typewriter from my parents, as a second-year design history student, I was thrilled. This would have been 1985/86. There were no word processors available to students then: although the Amstrad PCW 8256 was launched in September 1985, its *Matrix*-evoking green letters on the cathode ray tube were by no means in widespread use. There were programs in their infancy, sure – WordStar was the first – but they would not run on personal computers, as such things had yet to be invented. The few dedicated machines designed to manipulate manuscripts, in the way we have all come to see as normal, cost thousands.

Having the means to make my submissions to my tutors look 'professional', with double-spaced text on one side of the paper, made a huge difference to my ego and, I think, my grades. I also remember, from even further back, the huge IBM Selectric typewriter on which my mum bashed out letters on behalf of the local residents' association. I would have been twelve or thirteen. Occasionally, as a special treat for me, using the percentage sign and the for-ward/backward slash, alternating between the red and the black ribbon, she would make a row of marching guardsmen with arms at slope, like so:

O O O O O O O O O O O O O O O O O O O O O O O O O O O O O O O O O O O O O O O
%%%%%%%%%%%%%%%%%%%%%%%%%%%%%%%%%%%%%%%
/\

This was my first introduction to typewriter art, though I didn't necessar-ily realize it at the time. But as a student at Brighton I used to play with bits of paper rotated through the platen and lines of type, inspired by my 'discov-ery' of concrete poetry: the likes of Richard Kostelanetz and Eugene Wildman, who with their type experiments seemed to me to be building on the work of Mallarmé.

Like my attempts at this kind of poetry, typewriters had a difficult gesta-tion. The first machines could only write in upper-case letters, prefiguring the 'shouting text' of the current caps-lock Twitter codes. It was not until the Remington was developed, from the original patents of the Sholes/Glidden design of 1874, that the typewriter took a form and function that writers of today would recognize.[21]

As with all forms of technology that have been developed by us for the purposes of human-to-human communication, the typewriter stands at the confluence of many other technologies. The steel for the casing and the gears, levers and keys; the rubber for the platen; the cotton weave for the ribbon;

the inks and the paper. Material science and manufacture are the end results of technological progress. Modernity is inherent in new machines, and it's perhaps inevitable that artists and poets should choose to express their own modernity through their use of the new tools.

That the first commercially successful machine, the Remington, was manufactured by a gun-maker underlines its modernity. The modular nature of gun manufacture is essentially modernist, prefiguring as it does the much-lauded examples fancied by Mies, Gropius and Corbusier: the liners, the cars, the modular houses. In the right hands, though, the typewriter mechanism could produce a form of poetry that rivals Mallarmé and Apollinaire for innovative use of the page.

Dom Sylvester Houédard was a 20th-century Benedictine monk whose output on his Olivetti typewriter provides a useful link between the monks in the scriptoria of old and the meaningfully modern web of concrete poetry practitioners, who developed a way of working involving the physical act of rearranging and overtyping, switching between red and black ink and rotating the page through the platen (see page 56). As he wrote in the 1960s: 'A printed concrete poem is ambiguously both typographic-poetry and poetic-typography – not just a poem in this layout, but a poem that is its own type arrangement.'[22]

Arguably, these 'type arrangements' would not have grown into a recognizable movement – from a solitary poetic pursuit, to sharing as mail art, to underground magazines, to the Lisson Gallery in London – without the democratizing effects of domestic typewriter ownership. You might say that mass access to typewriters as tools for the production of concrete poetry prefigured the opportunities that later arose to manipulate the computerized version of ASCII, generating emoticons, emoji and kaomoji. Give people the means to manipulate type, it seems, and in the fullness of time other meanings and uses will emerge.

Shorthand for emotion

As with concrete poetry made with the typewriter, the grammar of the language of emoticons was at first determined by the available character sets and the imagination of individual communicators. The global *Zeichensalat* (character salad) that the Germans have so succinctly named points to the nature of the world of the emoticon and emoji. The naming of this phenomenon is also worthy of note – Gretchen McCulloch in her book *Because Internet* points out that the naming of the emoji, the form that preceded the emoticons, did not refer to emotion but to the conjunction of the Japanese

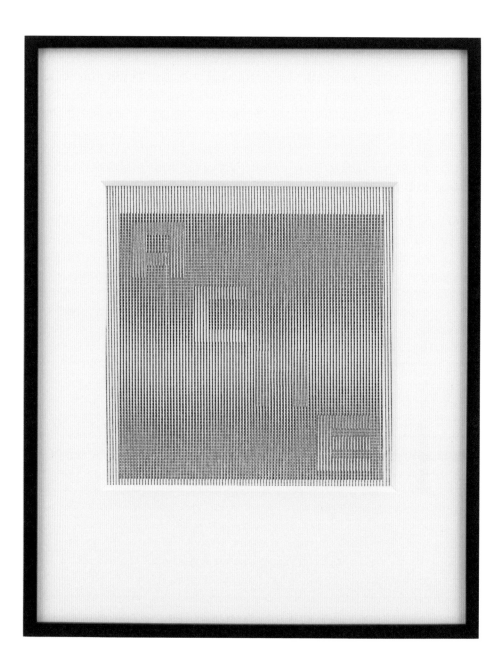

Dom Sylvester Houédard's output on his Olivetti typewriter embraced modernity in its execution, but the solitary pursuit of planning and then typing such dense and involving concrete poetry evokes the contemplative, repetitive life of the monkish scribes of old.

syllable 'e' (picture) and 'moji' (character).[23] Even so, the closeness of 'emoji' to 'emotion' certainly helped in the uptake of the term in English, where the 'e' could also be read as a signifier for 'electronic', as in email.

These coincidences helped to embed the use of emoji in emergent online culture, where easy neologisms were needed to bridge the gap between the complexity of the computer code making all the new stuff work, and the need for the public to adopt these new tools of communication. The name was easy to remember, and the meanings of these little typographic and iconographic tricks also helped greatly with their adoption and spread.

Ferdinand de Saussure was a Swiss linguist whose contribution to the understanding of 'the sign' in linguistics helped lay the groundwork for the discipline of semiotics. Saussure's assertion was that any sign requires a referent, and the relation between what is signed and what is meant by the sign depends on a matrix of contexts. The conditionality of meaning ranges from the literacy and sophistication of the reader to the means of delivery, and all points in between. As unlikely as it may seem, and without fanfare or any obvious need, the communication of emotion via semiotic means has risen without trace in the developed and connected world to be a go-to keystroke, thumbed with alacrity on the touchscreens of smartphones the world over.

If the brushworked originality of the rén character mentioned above contains the character (in the sense of a being) of animated humanity in its simplicity, then the origins of the neatly named 'emoticon' are aptly rooted in a different kind of invention. Emoticons hinge on the repurposing, development and corruption of some of the characters in the modern version of the Japanese katakana syllabic set of characters, together with elements of hiragana and kanji sets. Unbidden, the culture pulled together some characters and created something of character.

For instance, this: (ˉ∧ˉ) is the kaomoji (literally 'face character') for smug or snooty. The central character ∧ is pronounced 'heh', as in the first element of the word 'head'. With the correct inflection, such a word could be made to sound smug. But it's the nose in the air, the closed eyes and the bracketing forming the 'face' that create the meaning and emotional hit of this clever little sign. The skeuomorphically complex emoticons that come in the character menu loaded onto the average smartphone these days belie the simplicity of their origins on ASCII-net in Japan in the 1980s.

ASCII stands for American Standard Code for Information Interchange.[24] Scott Fahlman's ASCII programming, and the early work of programmers on the Programmed Logic for Automated Teaching Operations (PLATO) computer system working at the University of Illinois in the early 1970s, are the foundations of today's lexicon of emoticons. Gretchen McCulloch states that 'emojis didn't succeed because they were a language but because they weren't'.[25] It's a good point. The arrangement of existing characters to create pictogrammatic sign systems of the facial expressions of emotion is, in effect, an open-source system rather than a language.[26] Arguably such a system would not have emerged were it not for the freedom of experimentation with type forms, the page and meaning that occurred much earlier in history, as soon as poets, designers and writers got their hands on the means of production.

Users did not need to understand that ASCII created a common set of numerical codes relating to particular characters, building a bridge between different types of devices. They just needed to know that if you found two brackets, two hyphens and an '^' on your keyboard and then pressed send on your DoCoMo phone, the person at the other end would see and understand your rudimentary face drawing. 'It looks like a bit like a face with its nose in the air!' thinks the recipient. 'I wonder why my friend thinks I'm smug and snooty?'

Gesture, the hand and contemporary communication

It was the ease of use, the ease of transmission of meaning, together with the capacity for the range and scope of emoji and then emoticons to be expanded and democratized by users, that turned their production into an industry in its own right. The orchestration of simple keystrokes to organize characters into emoji sits at the point where a history of cartoonish shorthand for the rendition of facial expression meets the rapid, radically transformative influence of digital culture. That the glue binding these things together is the seeking out of the means to express human emotion is telling: it's simply what we tend to do with technology, as we shall continue to see.

Perhaps one of the most interesting points to make about the phenomena of the emoji and emoticons is the way in which their widespread use has, as it were, bridged the gap between pre- and post-typographic humanity.

Let's examine that idea for a moment. What we might call the cultural and conceptual threshold created by the organization of letterforms into moveable type in the mid-15th century created the conditions for a slow shift from oral and tribal traditions (knowledge and narrative spread by word of mouth) to literate and scribal traditions (knowledge and narrative spread, and to some degree fixed, by the written word). We've come a long way: now we are both tribal and scribal.

In simple terms, the difference between speaking aloud to transmit information and listening to the 'internal voice' when reading demarcates two different human states. The 'speaking state' persisted and was perhaps dominant from the time of those Neanderthals in the cave, spitting paint over their hands, or the unknown Chinese artisans carving out the siltstone in the Longyou Caves some 2,000 years ago, up until the start and the spread of mass-produced and mass-consumed written words. When reading to ourselves became the norm, the human state changed to an internalized and intellectual self, a state which arguably did not solidify into societal effect until the age of mass literacy and the birth of large-circulation newspapers in the late 19th century.

Parallels are found in song and music, where for most, until the mechanical reproduction of music became possible, the only way to experience the power of music was by hearing it played live. As a song, hymn or tune unfolds to its resolution, it's experienced by the listener note for note in a linear procession of related 'sound signs', which, because of the rules of harmony or the scales in which they are made, have encoded within them the direction of travel and their eventual resting place in harmonic and narrative resolution. (I make this point aware of atonal, microtonal and other ancient and modern musical forms.)

Words work a little differently. To paraphrase Kierkegaard, spoken narratives can only be understood by looking back, but must be experienced by moving forward.[27] When spoken, each word is a distinct revelation, making sense only in relation to what has gone before. When listening, we humans have to remain avid and present in order to make sense of the detail and, if it's there, the resolution.

When reading, things work differently. Not only do we listen to ourselves, sometimes as various personas, as internal narrators, but we are able to move freely across the page, through the sentence or book. Back and forth. Indeed, the eye scans the page in a distinctly non-linear fashion: pages are read through a combination of eye movements called saccades and fixations. Saccades are rapid movements of both eyes, used by a reader to cover the page; fixations are when the eyes rest for 200–300 milliseconds on a particular word or object. All saccades and fixations are measured in milliseconds.

With a printed book, the internalization of the process of reading to oneself is a direct function of the externalization of the means of producing the visual code in the form of the letters that go to make up the words. The simultaneous bridging of the inside (anima) and the outside (public self) with the narrative voice, via the elision of letters into words into internal sounds, is a phenomenon little short of miraculous in its power and its presence. Arguably, the progress of humanity as we know it rests upon the development and adoption of this mechanized visual mode of the transmission and communication of ideas. Reading and writing, as two of the 'three Rs', have long been rightly regarded as the core skills of a basic education.

Thumbs up: a gesture for now

We began this part of our exploration of visual communication with a discussion of the direct translation of gesture into mark. By way of a quick journey past medieval lettering and rose windows, via typewriters, typography and lime, we have come to the shared codes of character recognition across networks, and ultimately to the point where a small gesture on a smartphone keyboard generates a symbolic representation of emotion that can be instantly transmitted to friends and enemies alike.

It could be argued that a caps-lock Twitter missive like those once favoured by the 45th POTUS, Donald Trump (banned from Twitter in 2021), also conveys emotion. In Trump's case, basic anger and outrage, wounded self-righteousness or an off joke prevailed. The communication lacked the subtlety of the myriad facial expressions that can be drawn by combining the more arcane elements of the alphabet as emoji. However, technology always seems to drive complexity. As screen resolutions became higher across the first decade of the 21st century and object-based computer languages allowed for interaction via capacitive touchscreens, the development of emoticons and icons changed. They moved away from the simplicity of creating a line of characters that didn't require the reader's head to be tilted to an awkward angle, and gained greater detail and skeuomorphic qualities.

Whether, at the same time, emoticons gained greater power in their ability to transmit emotion or feeling is open to debate. Certainly the ability to render tiny pixellated icons replete with shading and seemingly three-dimensional detail became, in the 1990s, a seductive element of user experience and interaction design.

There is an apocryphal rumour around the battle of skeuomorphic versus flat design of icons in the genesis of the iPhone. Few would deny that the iPhone, under the design guidance of Jony Ive, boasted a minimal engineered aesthetic that married materiality with function in a way that nodded emphatically to the principles of 'good' design. The machined aluminium casing of silicate glass, the tactile feedback of discreet buttons and the satisfying heft and scale of the device all worked well. But under the tutelage of Scott Forstall, who was head of software until 2012, Steve Jobs's alleged love of dimensionality and shading in IOS environments took the software interface in the opposite direction to the device. Diaries were stitched in faux leather (unsubstantiated rumours suggested this was inspired by the seat stitching in Jobs's private jet); bookcases for the newsstand app looked like cheap flatpack pine veneer; specular highlights adorned the clapperboard that signified the video button. But why?

Perhaps, in terms of our collective ability to interpret an interface, we were not yet ready for a completely new visual environment. Better to make a button look like a button in terms of its dimensionality – something to press down on, something that exists in the flat world of the phone screen and yet looks as though it belongs in the 'real' world, too. In truth, the disconnect in the user experience between the physicality of the iPhone and the aesthetics of the interface were probably due to two different design philosophies at work in the same environment. When Forstall left and Ive was given responsibility for the interface, iOS 7 (launched in 2013) boasted flat buttons, a modern interpretation of Helvetica and a 'Swiss-derived' grid. Quite why the Swiss should figure so strongly not only in the interpretation of the meaning of signs (cf. Saussure), but also in their organization in space, is something that we will be looking at later on.

At the time of writing, emoticons seem to be resisting the trend for flatness and maintaining their progress towards a kind of 'illustrator's reality'. Shading and highlights abound. But although they are growing in complexity and graphic subtlety, they only occupy one extremely dedicated channel. Corporate logos, by contrast, are going the other way. As the channels through which brands have to communicate proliferate, the complexity of maintaining a coherent brand presence via logotypes is not helped by designs that feature lots of gradation, gradients, drop shadows and highlights. You cannot easily move through three shades of blue, for example, when you only have ten pixels in which to do it. Consequently, major corporations have moved back to solid colours and scalable designs that could have been penned by Peter Behrens or Saul Bass.

The transmission of emotion via emoticons, emoji and kaomoji has grown as a phenomenon. A recent expression of this can be found in the development of Memoji. To quote Apple's own support website: 'Create a Memoji to match your personality and mood, then make as many alter egos as you want in Messages and FaceTime.' These Memoji, as well as Animoji, bridge the gap between the simplicity and wit of the well-constructed kaomoji and the animated world of gaming and avatar-based internet presences. The naming of Memoji evokes the idea of the meme, as well as of the 'me'.

Mimesis is a concept familiar to students of Aristotelian philosophy as well as psychologists and literary critics. Its roots lie in mimicry and imitation. It's an extraordinary feature of modern life that the devices on which we have come to rely have become tools with which we are able to mimic ourselves for the sake of communication. It's almost as if the computational power of the modern smart device has created the conditions for a Boyle's law of culture: the given volume of what is possible in terms of communication will be occupied. Actually, let's call it Horsham's law.

For many users, the lure of being able to recreate ourselves as mimetic representations is strong, and it's further strengthened by what we might call the physics of empathy. There is an equation at work and it goes something like this: that's an expression of me, replete with the mood-signalling characteristics of facial movements and animated human or animal characteristics. The character is multiplied by its presence on networks. The common denominator is the ability (for all of us with access) to communicate emotion without divulging our true state. The final expression of the equation is in the convenience of the avatar, a now common shamanic form we inhabit to enable us to cross into the digital world, where ever new wonders abound.

The idea of representation in the digital sphere has moved on to encompass elements of the work of traditional commercial artists, in terms of the rendering of cartoonish faces with dimensionality, shading and highlighting that looks as though each might have started life on a draughtsman's board with gouache and ink at hand. Instead, the process of constructing your anime-friendly avatar is undertaken via a sequence of push-button choices of skin tone, hair, brows, noses and ears. Emotion is conveyed via a series of poses, facial expressions, hearts-for-eyes and rain clouds overhead. Remarkably, the pathetic fallacy has been harnessed in the service of the text message, and visual communication has become more and more simple by means of its underlying technical complexity.

There are programming, artistic, conceptual, organizational and corporate skills underpinning this deceptively simple tool. It represents a natural point of evolution in humanity's continuous development of technologically derived channels through which to communicate. Mimetic technology drives consumers to ownership of phones, fills the hours with amusing digital tittle-tattle and the back and forth of self-validation, thumbs-up 'like' gestures, hearts, praying hands, debates, information and argument. The corollary is the burden, or newly defined job, of maintaining a social media presence. There is money – lots of money – to be made from the new culture of visual communication.

In the decade from 2010 to 2020, tech companies emerged that had a symbiotic relationship with the burgeoning ownership of the smartphone, at least in the developed economies of the world. Now a panoply of corporations, setups, startups and outfits are creating the scaffolding within which we are encouraged to communicate visually with each other on a daily if not hourly or minute by minute basis in order to monetize their platforms. In order of users worldwide, as of 2020 they are Facebook, YouTube, WhatsApp, Messenger, Weixin/WeChat, Instagram, Douyin/TikTok, QQ, QZone, Seina Weibo, Reddit, Kuaishu, Snapchat, Twitter and Pinterest. Pinterest has 366 million users, while Facebook has around two and a half billion.[28]

The culture moves extremely quickly. The Facebook 'thumb' is now a sub-brand of the parent entity (renamed 'Meta' in 2021), whose new logo is a droopy blue shape evoking an infinity symbol and, if you strain the eye, the elements of an 'M'.

The reach of these platforms is vast: most inhabitants of the Earth, even those with absolutely no interest in using it, will have at least heard of Facebook. The ability to post images and have people react with a 'thumbs up' or 'thumbs down' provides an instantaneous hit of approval or disapproval. Depending on the cultural context, it links back to the gestural support of linguistic development – or rather, replaces the language of the gesture with an avatar of gesture.[29] So far has humanity come.

In some ways, the raised thumb and other reactions used on Facebook are simplified digital throwbacks to the hand silhouetted on the cave wall – but they are simulations rather than real products of human action on materials in time. It seems now that the language of gesture transmitted by the hand has gravitated towards the thumb, in the form of the thumbs up and the flying thumbs of the expert texter; even as we activate our handheld machines, though, gesture continues to underpin our communication with each other. It encodes our humanity using sign systems we all can share (albeit at a distance, with simulation, over networks) with the flip of a digit.

In the space of a few thousand years, the role of gesture in communication has mutated from a measured skill applied to a purposeful outcome, to the unthinking action of millions on their smartphone screens. We still gesture in space to let other people know what we think, but these days, most of us don't leave a physical mark, just an emotional one.

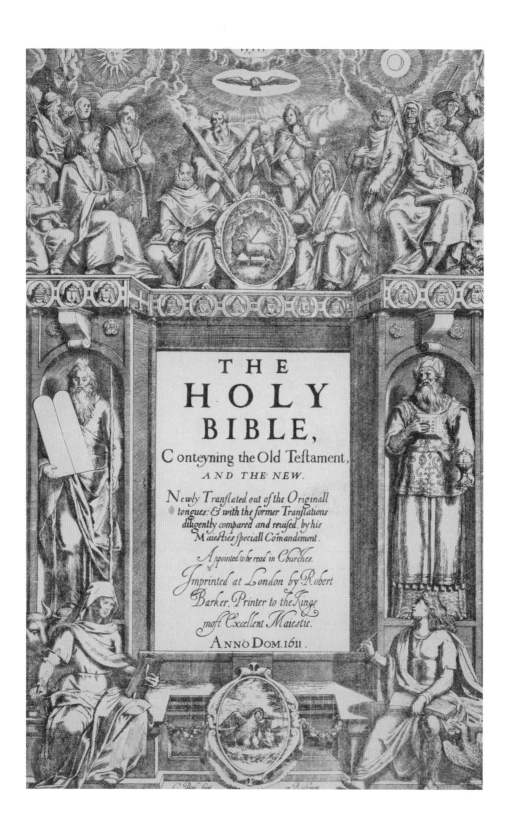

THE
HOLY
BIBLE,

Conteyning the Old Testament,
AND THE NEW.

Newly Tranſlated out of the Originall
tongues: & with the former Tranſlations
diligently compared and reuiſed, by his
Maieſties ſpeciall Comandement.

Appointed to be read in Churches.

Imprinted at London by Robert
Barker, Printer to the Kings
moſt Excellent Maieſtie.

ANNO DOM. 1611.

Part Two

Mechanization, Machines and Messages

Scribal, tribal, Bible

In trying to get a handle on visual communication, I've talked a bit about God and the power of religion, and yet I am not particularly a person of faith. I see nature as a wonder, and we humans are a part of that. At times we transcend and illustrate our humanity by making things of beauty and utility. We make in order to help ourselves and communicate with each other. In extremis, we make things, too, that may destroy us.

Our ability to design, our ability to think abstractly, to think 'if...then' as a process, has been key. We experiment, improving and manufacturing complex machines and tools in the service of our anthropocentric lives. We've shaped the world and it's shaped us. What we do is not always for the good, though latterly, some of us have been thinking about how we might better manage our impact on the planet and the other lives that depend upon it.

These qualities set us apart from most of our fellow Earth-dwellers. *Homo faber*: man or woman the maker, space traveller, artist, inventor, destroyer of worlds and other lives...ordained as such by a higher power? I'm not so sure. It's easy to write this now, to express this view, but doubts such as these within printed pages were not always allowed or encouraged. Instead, the heavy lifting designed to ward off apostasy such as mine was delivered in book form; and, as I originate from a Christian culture, the Bible is and was key.

So that's why, so far in this exploration, I have used some religious texts and the manifestations of religiosity as exemplars of visual communication. There is, I hope, good reason for this. In the early part of the Common Era, before the rise of Protestantism in Europe and well before the industrial revolution, religion drove economies. As well as ontological certainty, religion was busy creating justification for wars, concentrating learning and

OPPOSITE The engraved frontispiece of a 1611 King James Bible; the prolix description and complex engraving adds to its gravitas and presence. This is one of a multiple edition, identical to the others in the print run – a novel phenomenon at the time.

authority in abbeys and monasteries along with castles and fortifications, defining cities and legitimizing civilization through the connection of God to kings and queens via the concept of divine right.

The legacy and symbolism of the scribal Bible tribe persists to this day – it's powerful ju-ju. I remember distinctly as a child in our local cathedral – St George's in Southwark, where I was briefly a choirboy – the aesthetic hit of ecclesiastical purple on the robes of the priest, archbishop or canon; the stoles edged in gold, the brocaded silk; the towering gothic presence of the monstrance and the waft of incense from the swinging censer. All of these had been designed to communicate visually in ways that were, by then, based on centuries of tradition. The communication was of authority and certainty but also mystery, ritual and the magical act of transubstantiation.

The Bible on the lectern in the pulpit was a part of this staging, and its presence at school and in church was constant. Masses I went to in the 1960s were conducted in English. It seemed natural enough and, save for the odd *hallelujah* (Hebrew) and the *kyrie eleison* (Greek), everything was easy to understand, if not believe. But we were never apprised of just how it came about that we spoke in our mother tongue at church, rather than in Latin. It turns out that this all centred on the production of a book. The Bible: as key a piece of designed visual communication as has ever existed.

I cannot claim to have read the Bible in its entirety and I find the argument of the ascendancy of one apocryphally derived text over another difficult to accept. So, I want to look at the Bible not out of any liturgical fealty, but because as a piece of encoded visual communication there are few books to which greater power, history and meaning are attached. Seldom has any book caused nations to change direction or empires to teeter in the same way. Seldom, too, has a book resulted in as much martyrdom and even posthumous burning. (In 1428 John Wycliffe, declared a heretic for his work on translating the Bible into English, had his bones exhumed and burned with his books forty-one years after his death, just to make the point to his presumably everlasting soul.)

In the Church of St Mary the Great in Cambridge is a 1611 first edition of the King James Bible.[1] It is printed with an engraved frontispiece, and its subtitle has that prolix tendency you find in the explanatories and forewords of the period. 'Newly translated out of the Greeke', it reads, 'and with the former Translations diligently compared and reused by his Maiesties special Commandement'.

When I embarked on this project, I felt I needed to see a King James Bible in the flesh, as it were. My postgraduate work instilled in me not only a love of material culture but a belief that we can better mine, use and understand the essence of things by being in their presence and handling them. As the

Robert Barker's work on the King James Bible evokes the blackletter columnnular organization of a page hand-lettered in a scriptorium. The Roman-style headings, based on letterforms found on plinths, elide two important design traditions.

lockdown of 2020 eased, I duly went to the website of the British Library to book a table and get my hands on a first edition. But COVID had created a situation where there were no available seats in the library until well after the deadline for submission for this book.

What to do? A bit of digging, and I found out about the copy in Great St Mary's Church: they had discovered it on a shelf sometime in the last couple of decades. It was a first edition in a 19th-century binding. I called the church and spoke to a man called Richard, who, when I told him I wanted to smell his Bible, helpfully suggested I come to Cambridge and do so.

I took up the invitation on a jewel-bright day in May. The book was kept in a lockable glass case at the west door, open at the frontispiece of the New Testament. Richard unlocked the case and carried the hefty volume upstairs, placing it on a low coffee table on its Perspex stand.

I leafed through it. The paper was a heavy laid wove, in exceptional condition for something four hundred years old. I turned page after page. The Bible smelt a little musty; the text had texture, where the printer's galleys had been weighted into the forme. I leafed further through until I reached the final pages...and found they were missing.

Richard was as surprised as I was to discover that blank pages had been glued in, inscribed with columns in pencil, and an unknown scribe had attempted to replicate the printed metal type in ink by hand. This had proved unsuccessful and the unknown scribe had given up after two lines, underlining perhaps the way the invention of the printing press had helped to marginalize scribal culture. It's hard to write like that.

When that King James Bible was printed and published in England in 1611, it marked a turning point in the common understanding of the liturgy and in the meaning and power of the book. Written in common English, but with a turn of phrase mined from everyday idiomatic language that would resonate with the ordinary churchgoer when read aloud, the Authorized Version in some ways democratized the Word.[2] How so? Well, the book was composed and composited to resemble the manuscripts of old, so there was a familiarity in at least the form of the text for the mostly illiterate churchgoing population. It combined a form of blackletter with a roman typeface in the headers.[3] Its design signified 'religious book', whether you could read or not.

The King James version was printed by Robert Barker, the king's printer, so this was what we might call today a 'top-down initiative'. To look at a first edition is to see mechanical reproduction in its relative infancy, but to read a first edition is to experience the cadences and nuances of the English tongue at its most powerful.

In this case, emotion, empathy and understanding are triggered in the reader via turns of phrase that are still used in conversation today, such is

The illegality of translating the Bible into English meant William Tyndale had to take his translation to Germany. Forced to abandon the print run, he went into hiding, but was arrested and executed. This 1526 edition is small, allowing for easy concealment.

their connective and evocative resonance. An overcooked meal can be a burnt offering. We still may give up the ghost; we know that a leopard cannot change its spots, and that some ideas are akin to a double-edged sword. In the twinkling of an eye, we may escape by the skin of our teeth. You get the idea. The deft, poetic and incisive use of language achieved by translator William Tyndale and incorporated into the Authorized Version carries an empathetic, suggestive power that brings the text alive.

The experience of hearing the word of God delivered in language akin to the way the common people spoke in day-to-day life, with readings inflected with the dialects and local accents of Britain, would have engendered a sense of ownership and belonging in congregations. With the introduction of the Authorized Version, the impenetrable Latin muttered behind rood screens as a secret incantation, with its roots in far-away Rome, no longer held absolute sway. The King James Bible is a paradigmatic example of how the

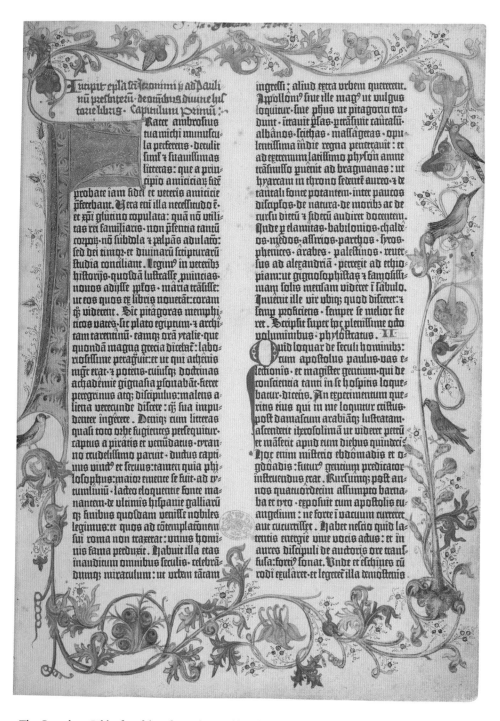

The Gutenberg Bible, first folio of 1455, featured hand-painted illuminations – the better to ape the qualities and appearance of illuminated manuscripts.

development of precision in repetition in the printing process created the framework within which we can find ways to effect societal, cultural and political change through human connection.

It's fair to say that this level of precision in production was a long time coming. Much had to be invented and many elements had to be aligned to make it possible. A book does not come into being on its own – the chain of command linking authors to readers is now formed by editors, picture researchers, proofreaders and fact-checkers, paper merchants, printers and binders. Then logistics companies, software developers and distributors take over. These techniques and organizational principles (particularly the latter ones) were necessarily still in their infancy and of course some were non-existent in 17th-century England, resulting in numerous errors and an approach to making books that was at times haphazard and random. In a subsequent edition of the Authorized Version, the lack of a clear production process incorporating a proofreading stage resulted in the notorious 'wicked Bible', published in 1631, which contained an error in the ten commandments by omitting the word 'not' from the injunction on adultery. The Bible containing the commandment that 'thou shalt commit adultery' resulted in a £300 fine for the printers.[4]

Back to the form of the book for a moment. The decision to ape the power and precision of handwritten text by using a blackletter typeface can be seen as a deliberate attempt to create a page that would resonate with readers, evoking religious books of a greater rarity. This mode of storytelling, of presenting the written word as columns, is contained within a carefully constructed grid, itself the result of the need to align the print precisely on the page before trimming and binding it between covers (though the Authorized Version was also available in an unbound edition). Thus, margins, slug, bleed, type, ink and processing come together to create the structure within which the humanity of the text, rendered as type, can shine.

The Authorized Version was not the first attempt to democratize the Bible via translation and the power of print. In the 14th century, John Wycliffe – an Oxford scholar with unorthodox views, whose followers were derisively nicknamed the Lollards – worked on a translation from the Vulgate, the only version of the Bible recognized by Rome at the time. (Later, when Tyndale took on the task, he used Greek and Latin texts as well as the Vulgate.)

We can leave aside the influence of the book in terms of instilling a moral compass in the faithful, or representing the word of God on Earth. The scholars' work was theoretically heretical, as any departure from the Vulgate in Wycliffe's time signified the desire for a liturgical and, given the power structures of the Roman Church, a political shift that the powers that be could not tolerate. So symbolically and linguistically powerful was the idea of a Bible in English that anyone found in possession of such a thing would be put to death.

By the time Tyndale was working on his translation, however, the status of scholarship and the effects and impact of its output had changed significantly. Tyndale found himself the author of texts that on the one hand argued for the head of state, the king, to be the head of the Church rather than the pope – and, at the same time, argued that the annulment of marriage was against scripture. This was a difficult position to maintain under the reign of Henry VIII, for obvious reasons. Tyndale's translation used words that set the text directly against the orthodoxy and power of Rome. As a consequence he had to flee to Europe, into the heart of an explosion of literacy, literature and visual communication supported by new technologies.

By the early 16th century, it has been estimated that there were up to 200 million printed items in circulation in Europe.[5] Hundreds of 'arithmetics', merchants' manuals and how-to guides vied with lives of the saints, Bibles and editions of prayer books, schoolbooks, stories and a whole variety of other incunabula. In 1500, there were between 200 and 300 moveable type printing presses in the historic cities of Europe, where in 1450 there had been only one: in the city of Mainz, run by Gutenberg and his collaborators.[6]

The spread of printing as an occupation for entrepreneurs was aided by a number of technological advances. An important factor, too, was that the relatively new art and craft of typography – the act of making and setting moveable type – fell outside the influence of the guilds and companies who tended to control apprenticeships and articles, and thus access to trade.

Allied to this was the complex web of technologies and material sciences that supported the manufacture and use of moveable type. Consider for a moment what the makers of moveable type had to achieve. Not for them the certainties of hewing a page from a familiar material such as a block of wood, or hacking from end grain and boxwood the type used by xylographers (the precursors and forebears of the printers using moveable metal type). No, metal type had to be cast from alloys that could survive the pressures of the screw press, maintain a straight-sided form when cooling after casting, maintain definition and edge after multiple uses, be non-permeable to ink, and be stackable, sortable and moveable. The mixture of tin, lead and antimony (an element relatively new to Europe) that was used to harden the alloy was a trade secret of sorts.[7]

Trade drove the growth of printing. The accountancy and business manuals, how-tos, ledgers and a flourishing book trade meant that printing and the use of printed materials was, initially at least, a mostly urban phenomenon. The increase in the number of towns with presses was necessarily supported by density of population, education and ease of transport. So, in

IMPRESSIO LIBRORVM.

Poteſt vt vna vox capi aure plurima: Linunt ita vna ſcripta mille paginas.

This late 16th-century engraving depicts the small factory of a printing press: typesetters, proofreaders and the accoutrements of printing. The grimace of the printer operating the screw press suggests the physical effort required for the making of books.

Europe, port cities and larger towns became early adopters of the new technology, as the output of the new presses could be supported by authors, publishers and consumers of new printed materials. This economic model sustained the growth of the press and printing as the primary means of information dispersal and what we might now call knowledge exchange. On the back of that, a book trade grew: ships, sloops, barques and barges with cargo holds of bound and unbound books travelled between Antwerp and London, Rye and Calais, Genoa and Trieste, and all points in between.

The very presence, and hence the ownership, of books was underpinned by growth in the trades supporting publishing. These included paper-makers and merchants; the makers of vellum and parchment; leatherwork-ers; toolmakers; makers of cord and thread; needle and bodkin makers; knife-makers; ink factors; manufacturers of presses; typographers; wood-workers; booksellers and brokers; librarians; authors and editors; carters; ships' captains; teachers; churchmen and women. Each individual trade had its subsidiaries, like tributaries feeding the great rivers of literature that sprang from the cities and states of Europe. For example, the bookbinder's art encompassed other trades, depending upon the value and importance of the sheaf or folio being bound. The jeweler, the embroiderer, the gilder and in some rare cases the ivory carver could all play a part in the manufacture of a rare or expensive volume. The development of any skill or craft necessarily creates its own arcana.

The language of printing is complemented by equally arcane terminology describing the activities of the binders. Bookbinding is first and foremost a protective act, involving nipping and smashing, rounding, trimming, edging, sewing, sectioning, cloth starching, decorating and tooling, embossing and debossing. Slipcase manufacture and belly bands speak of a set of skills rooted in the neologisms of almost 600 years ago, and they persist today.

But where to put all these books, all these products of the human drive to visually communicate?

Libraries gave us power

The book as a cultural artefact has acquired a power and symbolism through time underpinned by its function as a physical repository of knowledge. The adage that knowledge is power could, with the acquisition and display of books, be codified and presented to the world in the form of a library.

The power of the library persists as a signifier and symbol of learning and erudition. During the COVID-19 pandemic that began in 2020, politicians and pundits who appeared on television via conferencing platforms such as Zoom and Skype often chose their bookshelves as a background. Commentators noted with interest the details of what was on those shelves; for instance, much was made of the fact that the then Cabinet Secretary Michael Gove's collection included titles by Holocaust deniers and dubious 'political science' topics, as well as a variety of niche studies leaning somewhat to the right of the political spectrum.

What's interesting is not only the lack of balance evident on a shelf like Gove's, but the alacrity with which many individuals' bookshelves were studied and commented upon as evidence of learning. The decision to be interviewed in front of book-laden shelves can also be regarded as a deliberate attempt by the interviewee to be seen as a person of learning and gravitas. Of course, in the age of social media it should have been obvious that the content of the shelves could be captured, freeze-framed and analysed at leisure by the twitterati and those whom Sarah Vine, the journalist who was at that time married to Gove, characterized as 'trolls'.

Clearly, the symbolic weight of book ownership remains undimmed, even if the content and so the context, meanings and interpretation of libraries and collections of books have changed over time. The display of books has become in itself a form of visual communication, a meta-symbolic statement of wealth, power, learning and literacy. The trope persists because of how it came into being.

I had the opportunity to use one of the oldest libraries in England during my postgraduate studies. I was researching the idea of 'taste' as the term entered common usage in the 18th century, and as part of my background reading I discovered that the Bodleian Library at Oxford held various ledgers and accounts of England's landed families. I thought a trawl through some ledgers might reveal how much a household would spend in a year on objects of taste such as busts, paintings, books and plate. Primary research using primary sources was an important facet of the process of gaining an MA. The experience of using the Bodleian felt simultaneously exciting and fusty: ancient walls loomed, floors creaked and books were chained to

The Bodleian Library evolved from a collection of 'chained' books started in *c.* 1320. Chained libraries speak of the power and value of books as possessions, signifying knowledge and therefore power.

shelves. I think I wore white gloves to handle the old manuscripts; I made my notes in pencil on index cards. But each page I turned revealed a new insight.

The Bodleian, one of the oldest libraries in England, was founded by Sir Thomas Bodley in the early 1600s. His largesse was partly funded by his marriage to a widowed heiress whose fortune had been built on pilchards. Bodley created a model for the building of a library that involved an agreement, made in 1610 with the Stationers' Company, to receive a copy of every book published and registered with them in England. The original 2,500-volume bequest was destined to grow to the 13 million-plus objects, manuscripts and books that the library boasts today.

Other libraries built their connections in other ways. In Alexandria, in the 3rd century BCE, ships entering the harbour were routinely searched for books and if any were found they were taken to the library. If they were deemed worthy, copies were made and handed back to the ship. These acts of literary piracy bolstered the city's book collection until the fortunes of what is now Egypt declined, and with them, the power and status vested in its library. The book, whether manuscript or printed, bound or unbound, scroll, palimpsest or folio, assumed the status of a fetish object. The concentration of cultural and monetary value in book collections helped in turn to concentrate knowledge, research and authorship in the universities, monasteries, abbeys, palaces and castles of the world. This remained the case until the mechanization of production and the ramping up of methods of distribution of the written word, along with growing literacy, brought education within reach of the masses.

While I was researching this book, the pandemic meant that libraries were closed for long periods and access to travel was severely limited. I came to rely, to some degree, on the wonders of the internet, not only to pin down facts but to reveal some of the more obscure artefacts I was hoping to uncover. One way of achieving this was to avoid Google as much as possible.

Google aggregates the most common questions. The first few pages of results it offers in response to a typical query are determined through the relevancy of keywords, and page rankings. Links to websites also count. It can be tricky to 'game the system' and find things others have not found. Websites that are able to invest in quality content to generate views and links are more likely to be higher up in the rankings determined by Google's patented PageRank algorithm.

Google has grown big as a result, and with scale it can do many things. It's unclear why the company removed the injunction 'Don't be evil' from its employee manual back in 2018. Perhaps they were just doing good things anyway. For example, Google Books had a project, begun in 2003, to digitize

The Uncensored Library within *Minecraft* is a repository for writing that might be censored in the real world. This imaginative use of digital space is not reflected in the library's design, which resembles a hybrid of the British Museum and the Pantheon.

every book in the world: a noble project, but one which has stalled due to wrangles over copyright and ownership. More than 25 million books have been digitized to date, but many remain inaccessible. In some ways, the collection resembles a library like Alexandria's – books plundered and copied, bolstering the image and presence of Google as a cultural force.

But what happens should Google fail? However big it is, it's just a subsidiary of a larger company called Alphabet. It may be that we have to go back to the beginning and start again. Knowledge of the chain of interconnected skills and services that brought books into being in the first place would, perhaps, be useful. The 1958 essay 'I, Pencil: My Family Tree as Told to Leonard E. Read' is perhaps a useful template for understanding the complexity of how everyday things come into being.[8]

One of the world's newest libraries has been built within the multi-user online game *Minecraft*. In an unexpected and revolutionary act, the programmers behind *Minecraft* – realizing its popularity and its status as 'just a game' (to the uninitiated as to what lies within) created the opportunity for users to navigate their way unobserved and with stealth to a repository of investigative journalism, some of which would be suppressed in countries in which *Minecraft* is free to access. They called it the Uncensored Library.

It's a brilliant concept, and an interesting take on the power of the book and of the library: decentralizing the repository. Visually, however, the library rendered in *Minecraft* is redolent of traditional libraries from Alexandria to the old British Library to the Bodleian: a rather grand, clichéd classical marbled hall replete with staircases and pillars (see page 77). It seems however virtual the expression, we cannot escape the semiotics of civilization when libraries are rendered as visual communication.

Towards the modern, via the old

Texts of all sorts have often been accompanied by illustrations. With good reason – it's a powerful combination. From a chapbook of executions at Tyburn showing a woodcut of a disembowelled heretic, to newspaper reports and all points in between, the pictorial representation of a story underpins and reinforces meaning and sometimes adds a vicarious thrill.

The earliest illuminated manuscripts had within them images of religiosity and veneration, stories and parables. The process of getting an illustration into a book changed as the technology for pictorial representation developed. Aside from hand drawing, that process of development included the carving of wooden blocks or woodcuts. Albrecht Pfister of Bamberg, an early adopter of Gutenberg's moveable type printing techniques, also

Albrecht Pfister of Bamberg pioneered the inclusion of wood-blocks with hand-coloured elements in books. This was a painstaking process, conferring on each copy a uniqueness which subsequent print technologies would remove.

innovated in the inclusion of wood-block illustrations in his books.9 Like almost everything else we are looking at, the process of making a wood-block illustration is the connecting point for a variety of different crafts, skills and techniques. It's the same with wood engraving – although because engraving involves the incision of an illustration into the end grain of a hardwood such as box, or a fruitwood like pear, apple or cherry, the tools differ. We'll come to the toolkit in a moment.

Wood-block printing uses the plank side of the wood. It sounds simple when put like that, but let's pause for a moment and consider how a plank would have come into being in the 15th century. A tree in Europe – oak, ash, beach, hornbeam – would be cut from the forests that dominated the landscape. Planking in the age before the circular saw (incidentally invented by the Shaker religious sect in rural 18th-century America) was a matter of brute force. The tree, once felled, would be planked with a two-handed saw. Saw-making from mild steel was the realm of the blacksmith, but saw setting, working the alternating angling of saw teeth that made the tool efficient, was that of the tinker or the carpenter. Once planked, the wood would be seasoned by stacking it in the forest with air gaps created with pegs to encourage circulation. Although a wood block can be made from new or heartwood, the process of carving is easier once the moisture content of the wood has decreased or reached equilibrium. Then, with adze and spokeshave and box plane, the plank could be flattened and made good, ready to receive the artwork.

On to the equipment. The tools for carving a wood block are, with practice and training, relatively simple to handle and wield, but immense skill and advanced metalworking techniques had to be developed in order to make the chisels, blades and gouges that a skilled wood-block carver would use. Most carving tools are made from a single piece of extruded metal, beaten to form and then finished with an edge that could be sharpened on a whetstone. In other cultures – such as Japan and China, where wood-block carving became a highly popular and advanced form of visual communication – it generated different toolsets. A Japanese wood-block carver might have used a gouge of high-carbon steel that could take and maintain a finer edge. That steel would have been hand-forged onto a softer lower-carbon steel shank for support. The better the edge, the more versatile the tool and the greater detail in carving could be realized. The quality of the image was conditional on the quality of the tools and the skill of the carver.

Part of the art of the woodcut was in the transference of the image to the wood, as those involved in carving were not usually the originators of the image. Instead, an artist's image drawn in ink would be transferred to the plank side or end grain of the wood, either by whiting the wood and drawing the image onto the block, or blacking the verso of the drawing and again drawing over it, leaving an impression on the wood. Either way, the artist's original would be destroyed in the making of the woodcut. Woodcut images rely on the relief principal of printing: the area not to be printed is cut away below the print surface, leaving the parts to be inked in relief. The wood is then inked with a roller or pad – a brayer, in the parlance – and the print taken by applying pressure on the reverse of the wood block to ensure an even impression on the paper, vellum or parchment.

Wood blocks made in this way offered printers a kind of prototypical system to experiment with colour separation. Indeed, modern offset printing relies on the same principles, the key to a good colour print being the register, or alignment, of the different colours to avoid overprinting or gaps between different colours that butt up against each other. Printers today would call this process 'trapping' – where steps are taken to make sure the alignment of colours is correct. It's only the case with spot colours, and applies to woodcuts because when printing with a wood block, all colours added are effectively spot or separate colours. In other cases, printed line images could be hand-coloured, a lengthy and laborious process.

In Japan and China, the processes of wood-block printing predated their adoption in Europe by some 400 years. The genre of art known as *ukiyo-e*, the 'floating world', created the cultural conditions in which the act of making a print was an exquisite craft of execution and reproduction. Such was the investment of human skill in the process that the work produced came into its own not only in the process of conception and production, but also when the viewer spent time contemplating the synthesis of craft, skill, material and subject matter in the finished object. Humanity is embedded in the object by dint of the way it came into being, and we seem to be able to recognize and value this quality in the handmade almost instinctively.

Back to lime, back to lithography

The processes of making colour prints with wood blocks using spot colours in register persisted through the 18th and 19th centuries. But in the mid-19th century, the invention of lithography changed the scale at which visual communication could be rendered as single-sheet posters.

Lithograph City, in the American state of Iowa, came into being because of the discovery of lithographic limestone in the area by the geologist Clement Webster while he was out walking one morning in 1903.[10] Until then, the fine-grained quality of lithographic stone had come principally from deposits in Bavaria in Germany and southern France, and the

Utagawa Kunisada, 'Artisans', from
the 19th-century series 'An Up-to-Date
Parody of the Four Classes', Japan
(Metropolitan Museum of Art).
Triptych of polychrome woodblock
prints; ink and colour on paper.

lithographic process, popular in Europe, was in the USA and elsewhere an
expensive way of getting large-scale colour print to the masses. This was due
to the cost and complexity of importing fine-grained limestone of the necessary quality.

In order for a piece of visual communication to be created using a lithographic stone, the stone had to have been quarried from beds free from the
ancient fossils of tiny creatures, which served to corrupt the smooth surface from which a print would be taken. So static, fetid prehistoric ponds
of silt, places where no life could exist, produced the best type of stone for
use in lithography.

The step-by-step process of lithography is painstaking and time-consuming,
involving the preparation of the stone to receive the artwork in many stages.
A lithographic stone can be used several times to print different images, and
each time it is reused it has to be ground down and all traces of the last lot
of greasy lithographic 'tusche' (essentially, grease suspended in water)

removed. Then the artist can draw directly onto the stone in an echo of where we started in the cave with our Neanderthal, bringing the gestural power of an artist's hand directly into contact with the ink and the stone. Each colour used needs a new stone.

Gum arabic reappears here, too, used to separate the printing and non-printing areas of the stone and create a thin layer that will absorb ink. The chemical change that then occurs fixes the image in the stone, and the stone is washed down to remove the drawing medium (the tusche, or crayon, or other mark-making medium). It is then re-etched with gum arabic and buffed down, left to dry and then inked, and the first proofs taken from the image on wetted paper. The first few prints are proofs: the true detail of the drawing emerges in the sweet spot after the proofs, but before the inked surface wears out.

The *belle époque* of lithographic poster design is generally regarded to have occurred in Europe and later the USA at the turn of the 20th century.

Toulouse-Lautrec's entire output used between five and eight colours. The image at the top speaks to the minimalism that could be engendered by the lithographic process, on the right is a more complex image by Chéret.

Examples abound. The process of drawing onto lithographic stone favours broad expanses of flat colours, carefully keyed outlines and a small number of 'spot' colours. In some ways this technique follows the traditions of Hokusai and Hiroshige, the acknowledged masters of the wood blocks of the floating world.

As with wood-block printing, each colour in a litho poster is made on a separate 'plate', block or stone. Henri de Toulouse-Lautrec, whose reputation was catapulted into fame by the 3,000 litho posters advertising the Moulin Rouge that were plastered across Paris, only used between five and eight colours in his whole output of 'lithos'.

The creative restrictions inherent in this way of printing, caused by the lengthy production process and the expense it involved, were a spur to the origination of a graphic sensibility that appeared suddenly and undeniably modern. Economy of line and expression in the best of the litho prints prefigured the stripping back of ornamentation and the move towards abstraction in the service of direct communication that was to follow in the 20th century. Lautrec alone, in his short ten-year career, produced no less

In this Ibels lithograph, the different colour passes are relatively easy to spot. The cummerbund of the pipe-smoker shares its colour with the trousers and epaulettes of the soldier in the middle distance, as well as the factory roof in the background.

than 368 prints including menus, illustrations, invitations, song covers, greeting cards and magazine covers. He was not alone. Jules Chéret produced more than 1,000 designs accompanied by, across Europe, the likes of Pierre Bonnard, Maurice Denis, Edouard Vuillard, Henri-Gabriel Ibels, Alphonse Mucha and Jacques Villon.

The effectiveness of the lithographed display advertising print, its success in promoting cars, magazines, restaurants, lubricants, travel, liners, champagne and wine, aperitifs, exhibitions, housewares and foods, perhaps lies in its direct connection to the hand of the artist. The poster's power is in its recording of the gesture in space and time, fixing the human mark made by a brush or lithographic crayon.

The central theme of this exercise, this book, this thought journey, is contained in that last observation on the power of the human-made mark. The further away we humans get from the action of the hand in the rendering of marks made for human communication, the more technology amplifies, converts, translates and anticipates the hand. Subsequently, the greater is the potential for the absence of the empathetic triggers we seem to need.

The shape of water

If you have the opportunity to watch any film involving ships and the sea made before the advent of digital effects in the mid-2000s, I recommend you do.[11] Like fire, water is impossible to scale, and so no matter how good the model ships, how over-cranked the film speed, how inventive the rendering of the cyclorama, in these films the sea always looks...well, unrealistic.

The flourishing of computer-generated imagery (CGI) in the mid-2000s changed that. For a while now the measure of an animator in the digital effects industry has been how well they can render water, particularly the sea in motion, as an animation. I would argue that Hokusai rendered the sea as a fixed thing with more humanity, dynamism and skill than any of the 3-D versions of waves in films from James Cameron's *Titanic* through to Wolfgang Petersen's *The Perfect Storm* or Roland Emmerich's *2012*. Perhaps it may seem that we are comparing apples with oranges – a wood-block print of a great wave with a highly polished digital simulation of storms at sea – but it's the subject matter and intention that bind them together. Both types of depiction rely on the mastery of the technology of their time to connect with viewers on an emotional level, through the depiction of a natural phenomenon designed to produce awe and empathy.

The technologies in the floating world were basic in comparison to the render farms, NURBS nets and relighting software behind CGI animation.

As basic as the technology was, creating colour separation for wood-block printing like that in Hokusai's great wave still presented a range of challenges. The chemistry of colour drove innovation. Traditionally, the main colours in Japanese prints were tones of indigo: the blue of the ink derived from *Persicaria tinctoria* (the Chinese/Japanese indigo plant) or from the petals of the *Commelina* (day flower), a flowering weed. Until the introduction of Prussian blue – a chemical pigment imported from England and Holland to Japan in the 18th century – indigo in various concentrations was the principal source of blue and the only colourfast pigment derived from nature.

The plant-derived blue colour was common in Japan and shot through the fabric of society. Sumptuary laws in the Edo period (1603–1868) stopped ordinary people from wearing clothes made of luxurious materials, such as silk and fine wools. The colour palette was severely restricted for the lower-status citizens who were subjects of the ruling classes. Plebians had to rely on what would now be called a capsule wardrobe. The predominance of indigo blue in Edo culture helped to maintain the social order, but also embedded a recognizable visual sign of belonging into clothing, in woven fabrics and in the *noren* used to divide rooms or hung with three or four slits

Much has been written about Hokusai's *Great Wave*. Its inclusion here is on several counts: the use of Prussian blue, the precision of the woodcut, but most importantly the narrative power of the wave rendered as a being with anima, soul, intention.

The *noren* is a curtain over the threshold of a Japanese dwelling. This blue wash, derived from plant sources, was widely used owing to the sumptuary laws that helped reinforce the social hierarchy under the shogunate – visual communication shot through society.

over the thresholds of doorways. A weak blue wash was an omnipresent visual reminder of the stratification of life lived under the shogunate.

The arrival of Prussian blue in Japan at the hands of Dutch merchants in the mid-18th century created the possibility of greater depth and vibrancy of colour. The convention in art is that the perception of depth in an image can be enhanced by making objects at the front of a composition darker in hue, and those in the distance lighter or fainter. Prussian blue or Berlin blue (so-called because of its origination in Germany), with its blue/black ferro-cyanate derivation, allowed for a depth of colour that could not be achieved with traditional indigo dyes and inks. The new pigment's lightfast qualities meant that with its adoption by wood-block artists and printers, its use and visibility spread. Inherent luminescence enhanced the perception of its colour to the human eye, so much so that something approaching a mania for the new colour occurred, and the market for wood-block prints using the new deep blue grew. The technology behind the creation of the pigment effectively expanded the market in visual communication.[12]

Words and images, continued

I was lucky enough, aged about fifteen, to go on a school trip to Fleet Street organized by one of our English teachers. Fleet Street was at that time, in the 1970s, still the epicentre of the UK's newspaper industry.

The news desks were dull. Typewriters clattered as men (and it was mostly men) hunched over their writing work in shirtsleeves. Cigarette smoke hung in the air. Next was the typesetting room, which was much more exciting. We gathered around a man sitting at an enormous black machine, one of many in the room. The mechanisms at its back clanked and whirred and there was a smell in the air of molten metal. Lead. The noise in the room was a constant cacophony of machinery in motion.

The man's hands moved over a keyboard that was not set out like the usual typewriter keyboard – no QUERTY here – instead the keys were arranged

The skill of the highly trained operators of linotype machines redefined working practices, so predictable was the speed of their output.

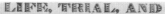

LIFE, TRIAL, AND
EXECUTION!
WILLIAM LEES,
FOR THE MURDER OF HIS WIFE.

December 17, 1839

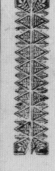

OLD BAILEY SESSIONS.

Friday, Nov. 29, William Lees was placed at the Bar, charged with the Wilful Murder of his Wife Elizabeth Lees.

The first witness examined was Elizabeth Fraser who stated that she kept a school next door, at 9 o'clock on monday morning she saw the prisoner and his wife pass her door on very good terms, at three in the afternoon of the same day she was standing at her door when she saw the prisoner leave his house, lock the door and put the key in his pocket. The prisoner appeared to be very fond and attentive to his wife when sober, but when tipsy they very often quarrelled.

Mrs. Rhoda Hall said she kept a shop opposite to the prisoner and had been intimately acquainted with him and his wife.; about Half-past 2 on Monday week the prisoner sent a boy for her, and on going into the shop he said his wife was very ill, and desired her to go up and see her. She went up stairs and found Mrs. Lees lying on the floor crying, and appeared as if recovered from a fit. Witness saw no more of the prisoner until 5 o'clock, when an alarm was given that she was murdered, and on going into the shop saw her on the ground covered with blood

The next witness called was Mrs. Sarah Bailey, sister to the prisoner stated that she resided at 53, York Street, Saint Luke's, that about 4 o'Clock on the evening before, the prisoner came to the house and said he was a Murderer, and wished her to accompany him to his house.

John Lees, a brother to the prisoner stated that he has at the house of the last witness on the evening before, when the prisoner came, and on entering the back-parlor, the prisoner caught hold of Benjamin Bailey's hand and kissed it and said "I'm a Murderer," but did not say who he had murdered.

Mr. Garratt, Surgeon, No. 3, New Road, deposed that about half-past 5 on Monday evening he was called to the house of the prisoner, and on examining the body he found about the throat, face and head eight different wounds, but the deepest and most extensive was on the left side of the throat, and caused instant death.

Other witnesses were examined whose evidences corroborated the above.

The Judge having summed up the evidence, the Jury retired, and after a short deliberation, returned the following Verdict **Guilty of Murder.**

Mr. Baron Parke having put on the black cap, addressed the prisoner, and told him that the Jury who had just pronounced their verdict had done so, he

was sure, with very great pain, but they felt, no doubt, that consistently with the oath they had taken, and the duty which they owed the country, they could not arrive at any other conclusion than that of pronouncing him guilty of the murder of his wife ; and the solemn duty now devolved upon him (the Learned Judge) to tell him that he was to die an ignominious death on the public scaffold. The barbarity of the act admitted of no excuse, and only one circumstance could possibly be suggested as to the cause of the dreadful crime—namely, that he was intoxicated at the time. The law, however, could never admit intoxication as an excuse for such a henious offence ; for if it did, the most dreadful crimes, many of which were committed under the baneful excitement of drink would go unpunished The Learned Baron then pronounced sentence of death upon the prisoner in the usual form. The prisoner, who remained unmoved to the last, was then taken from the dock. When he was taken below, his first remark was, "What b—infernal liars those policeman are !" He was very desirous to procure some spirits or beer, which Mr. Cope refused to supply him with any thing but the prison allowance, with the exception of a pint of porter, which was considered necessary after standing so many hours at the bar. The trial lasted nine hours, and the court was crowded to excess during the day.

Copy of a Letter to his Mother.

Dear Mother,

I scarcely dare presume to adress you and I wonder that I have sufficient nerve to Write, being fully impressed with the knowledge of the dreadful Crime that I've commited and the shame and disgrace which must for ever be a stain on the character of my Family and Friend; Oh how do I wish that the Sinful World knew what I now suffer, knowing well that I shall shortly die an ignominious Death, which I sincerly pray may be a warning to all others, do my dear Mother compose yourself endeavour to see me soon as possible, remember me to all my relations and beg of them to forgive me, tell them all to abhor Jealousy and intemperance as the last Dying wish of your unworthy and Unhapyy Son,

Wm. LEES.
Newgate, Dec. 1839.

At an early Hour this Morning a large assembly of spectators had assembled, about Seven o'Clock the Sheriff's ar-

rived at Newgate, and proceeded with the Gaoler to the condemned cell, and after the usual melancholy preparations having been completed Lees was brought from the cell to the room where he was to be pinioned. The solemn procession then proceeded towards the Scaffold, which he mounted firmly, the executioner after having adjusted the rope and the Ordinary had concluded his address, the fatal bolt was drawn, and he soon ceased to exist.

Copy of Verses.

Come listen to my mournful tale,
　　You tender christians all,
And kindly shed one pitying tear,
　　Unto my sad downfal.
My name is William Lees,
　　In Chapman Street did dwell,
And there the horrid deed was done,
　　As you all know full well.

My parents dear, with tenderness,
　　Endeavour'd but in vain,
To keep me from all wickedness,
　　But their souls I've filled with pain ;
I followed sin as you do know,
　　Which brought me to this place,
Thro' drinking, and bad company
　　I'm cover'd with disgrace.

O how, could I so cruel be,
　　To a wife I loved so dear,
To take her precious life away,
　　And cut her throat from ear to ear ;
Twas jealousy that prompted me
　　To take away her life,
Fulwell I know, she was to me
　　A most endearing wife.

When I had done the wicked deed,
　　I was filled with fear and dread,
I unto my relations went,
　　Told them my wife was dead,
And that, I was her murderer
　　But that they'd not believe,
But when with me they did come home,
　　Their minds were undeceived.

Then listen all, who now are gay,
　　Unto my dreadful fate,
For the dreadful crime that I have done,
　　I alas repent too late ;
Twas jealousy and drunkedness,
　　Caused me her life to take,
I hope you'll all shun wickeness,
　　And ne'er meet my sad fate.

Good people all, a warning take,
　　Before it is too late,
For if you dont repent in time,
　　You'll surely meet my fate ;
Ne'er give your mind to jealousy,
　　Intemperance, quick give o'er,
Or else like me you soon may be,
　　In the prime of life "no more".

Printed and Published by *J. MARTIN*, 13, Little Prescot Street, Goodman's Fields.

in order of the letters most often used: ETOIN SHRDLU. A strip of paper with the copy to be typeset hung from a peg on one corner of the machine. The linotype operator's hands moved quickly, touch typing his way across colour-coded keys through the journalist's words, as slugs of metal miraculously appeared in a chute. Lines of type. These lines would then be sent to the compositing room, where the page would be laid out and stereotypes made ready for the presses to roll.

I can clearly recall this visit to the newspaper partly because, as a memento, the linotype operator made each of us a slug to take away. We just had to say the words. My guitar- and music-obsessed teenage self opted for 'Michael "Hot Licks" Horsham'.

News and technology

Here is an essential truism: technology is, and always has been, the motor driving the expansion of visual media and communication. Now clickbait news feeds have their newsrooms staffed by journalists who get real-time feedback on how many clicks their headlines are generating. If we are not careful, this could lead to an unstoppable race to the bottom for 'cut-through' and clicks. Oh, hang on...

Technologies of reproduction are developed and come on stream, and illustrators, artists, art directors, engravers and printers develop in turn the mastery of these tools and techniques. Ideally, the more honed the mastery of our channels of communication, the more powerful the resulting resonance and power of the work. But resonance and power are, of course, not always deployed in the service of good.

If we look at the history of the newspaper, we can see how it sits at the intersection of many technologies that combined to change not only the course of visual communication, but the course of human civilization and history. Handwritten broadsheets were in existence in major cities in Europe throughout the 16th century, featuring commodity prices, news of war and commentary. It was not until the early 19th century that presses that could run more than 1,000 copies an hour were introduced. *The Times* of London cleverly adapted its machines to print both sides of the paper at once, so by 1814 what we now recognize as a 'newspaper' – with columns, close-set type, a masthead and logo, and, crucially, advertising – was in existence.

OPPOSITE This 1839 broadside was sold at the foot of the scaffold outside Newgate prison, where on 16 December William Lees was executed. *The Times* reported that his 'last dying speech' was a selling point of the broadside before he had even mounted the scaffold.

The next great shift in the newspaper as medium came with the introduction of engraving, and then the halftone image. Early newspaper illustrations were made by engraving onto the end grain of hardwoods such as box (*Buxus sempervirens*) or fruitwoods such as pear, apple or lemonwood (not of the lemon tree, but so called because it emits a citrus note when freshly cut), and occasionally seasoned oak. Box was once a plentiful wood in the hedgerows of Britain, where the craft of engraving to illustrate newspapers and broadsheets first took off.

The end-grain block would be made from many other blocks of end grain glued together and then planed flat. The toolkit of the engraver would include, of course, burins and gravers, the essential tools of the craft; other tools such as spitstickers for engraving straight lines; and a set of round

The most affecting thing about this image, for me, is not the rather sentimental treatment of the lyre player, but the evidence of the hand-working of the plate with cross-hatching. The entire image has been built up via this laborious technique.

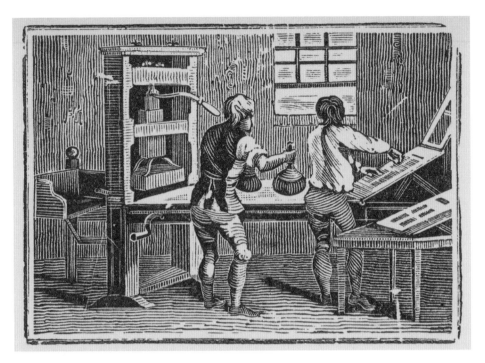

An end-grain engraving can take many more impressions than its copper, zinc or steel counterparts. This printer is holding inking balls: sheepskin sacks stuffed with wool, with cupped wooden handles. They are used to work the ink and beat it into the type.

scorpers. Round scorpers are made with a section in the shape of a 'U' and so make an incision in the surface of the wood of a line with a rounded end. Scorpers are also good for creating a stippled effect, a series of dots to create tonal effects – a precursor of the halftone process. A leather sandbag would be used to steady the block, and the whetstone would be ready for honing the edge.

The technological advances that combined to make engraving possible include the creation of high-carbon steel, the forging capabilities of blade-makers and the development of reliable oil-based inks. Even tanning, for the making of the sandbag, is in the mix of technologies supporting the explosion of the print. But again, it's the mastery of muscle memory, the human connection to the medium through the gestural work of engraving, that determines the quality and hence the emotional punch that an image can convey.

The block is turned to the light as the engraver sits at his desk making microscopic incisions across the glued and squared sections of boxwood, with the segmented annular growth marks of the tree visible as a geometric reminder of the material's origins. The engraver takes up his tools, reflecting on the tonality that is to be achieved through the build-up of hatches and dots and the power of depiction through the precision of line.

That such a product of artisan skill should find its way into the burgeoning world of newspapers – at the time (the late 18th/early 19th century) a quintessential expression of modernity and modularity in terms of the use of types and paper – can be explained by the properties of the material with which the wood engraver worked. A wood engraving on end grain can take many more impressions than a copper or steel engraving. As presses ramped up their capacity, the hard-wearing nature of end grain – the ease with which such engravings could be made to sit with type on the forme prior to the platen being lowered, pressure applied and the print being made – made them an indispensable element of visual communication. This remained the case up until the mechanization of reproduction by photographic and electronic means. So Thomas Bewick, the Dalziel brothers, and all the other engravers who translated the designs of artists to the end grain were, in effect, human machines of reproduction of images, before the age of mechanical reproduction.

Because the work of the engraver was essentially interpretive, standing between the artist and the reproduction of the work, the treatment of the subject matter would vary depending upon the market. The ownership of prints for display was restricted to the privileged few at least until the mid-20th century; although a wide variety of prints, from small black-and-white for a few pence up to full-colour engravings, could be bought, the dissemination of information was in part taken care of in major European cities by print shops. Print shops would display in their windows a constantly changing array of images that the general public could see and buy. With more than 20,000 satirical prints published between 1770 and 1830 in London alone, and countless prints on other subjects, from natural disasters to executions to biblical and classical allegories, the visual culture expanded rapidly, driven by the idea and technologies of the reproduction of images.

There exists in the British Library a print entitled *Spectators at a Print Shop in St Paul's Churchyard, London*. Dating from 1774, it shows a macaroni in full fig, wig and make-up and a lady observing the prints in the shop window, while a gentleman in a blue frock coat appears to be issued with an arrest warrant by a bailiff. (The bailiff's nose is poxed.) Presumably the subject

OPPOSITE The popularity of prints available through London's 18th-century print shops helped drive the technologies behind their manufacture, distribution and sale. This explosion in the consumption of visual communication was accompanied by the growth of satire and the visual literacy of the population.

SPECTATORS at a PRINT-SHOP in St. PAUL's CHURCH YARD.

matter of the print the lady gestures towards with her fan is something with which 18th-century Londoners would have been familiar. They would have been familiar, too, with the debt structures that made London at that time the engine of the developing world. The print shop and the debtors' prisons were within walking distance of St Paul's Cathedral, whose colonnades and cloister had long served as a meeting place for gossipmongers and news vendors, entrepreneurs and deal-makers.

The place features in what is known as the Agas Map (a possible misattribution to the surveyor Ralph Agas, born *c.* 1540), which was printed from wood blocks in the mid-16th century. It shows the old 'Poles Church' at the centre of the old city. The church was the locus of so-called 'Paul's walking' – the activity designed to glean information and news. A 'Paul's walker' would be assailed by the sights and sounds of early modern London: the vendors and visitors vying with the spectacle of the church and its crowds; the sewers competing for the attention of the senses with, at certain times of the day, the cacophony of bells and bawling cries. Within this seething cityscape would be the sellers of chapbooks and prints, lurid tales fixed in print for the telling in taverns and inns; lists of shipping and cargoes would be available, as well as the aforementioned cartoons and caricatures; and by the late 18th century, the first broadsheet newspapers were being sold on corners and read in coffee shops.[13]

The power of print as a means of visual communication was well understood. In London, after the restoration of the monarchy in 1660, an Act of Parliament was passed named 'An Act for Preventing the Frequent Abuses in Printing Seditious, Treasonable, and Unlicensed Books and Pamphlets; and for Regulating Printing Presses' (1662).[14] The act, commonly called the Licensing Act, prevailed until 1695, when its demise coincided with increased efficiency in mail delivery. Subsequently, printed newspapers (which had once been limited to London) could by that time be found in numerous cities throughout Europe and North America.

Terminology and technology: a deeper dive

We are all familiar with the term 'stereotype'. It has come to mean a recognizable repeated behaviour or set of signifiers, an unthinking copy – but its origins lie in the print industry and the escalating demand for news. Once a newspaper page had been set on the forme with metal type and perhaps a wood-block-engraved image, *papier-mâché* or a similar material, a thick card saturated with water, would be spread over the forme and an impression taken. This impression could then be used to create a hot metal cast of the page, so allowing for multiple presses to run taken from the same page – *voilà! La stereotype!* Later, when vast rotary presses were rumbling away in the basements of newspaper offices in Fleet Street, or West 43rd Street in New York (just off the eponymous Times Square), or Karduansmakargatan in Stockholm, stereotypes were used to cast in lead semi-cylindrical versions of newspaper pages. These roughly 10-kilo half-pipes were then bolted onto the drums of rotary presses fed by great webs of paper running at up to 40 kilometres an hour, producing thousands of pages from a coldset machine to feed a circulation of hundreds of thousands, often in a first and then a late edition.[15]

The transition of the idea of the stereotype into the world of psychology and social sciences, to describe behavioural tropes, came later. Equally, we are all familiar with the idea of the cliché. The past participle of the French verb 'to click' (*clicher*) became an onomatopoeic noun for the objects containing the pre-set phrases journalists would use to introduce news items, court circulars and the like. The cliché – a pre-cast hot metal slug of a line of type – could be dropped into a column on the forme with a satisfying 'click' and hence the cliché, the oft-repeated phrase, initially without its negative connotations, was born.

The technologies driving the explosion in newspaper production and readership were underpinned, at the beginning of the 20th century, by the growth in mass education and hence literacy. In the UK at the beginning of the 19th century, London boasted more than fifty newspapers. The tax structures around the production of news and print were constantly revised across the century until, by 1854, all duties and taxes on the production of print were removed, creating the necessary conditions for a self-sustained take-off into growth for the trades and technologies around print and printing, writing and image-making. Channels of visual communication expanded from gazettes, chapbooks, ballads and broadsheets into newspapers, posters and magazines. The need for speed in the turnaround of news meant that once technology had been developed, systems of typesetting were, like many other methods of production, partly mechanized and automated.

Let's look at how a newspaper page would come into being with the newly invented monotype and linotype machines at the end of the 19th century. Monotype machines would produce slugs (individual words cast from antimony, lead and tin, and air-cooled) while the Linotype machine – invented by Ottmar Mergenthaler and trademarked under his name – set lines of type, rather than individual words, in a single font, and was perfect for compositing large amounts of type in columnar configurations.

Backed by a consortium of newspapers, linotype became the standard. The clever marrying of typographic units with automatic functions created reliable and reproducible outcomes. Mechanization took command, but the

The left-leaning French newspaper *Le Monde* did not feature any images on its front page until 1972. Here the presses are rolling in Paris and the webs of paper can be seen passing through rollers overhead as a printer checks the quality of the broadsheet.

machine, initially, still had to be driven by skilled operators. Linotype machines used an ingenious method of creating their lines of words: the keyboard divided into white for upper-case letters, black for lower-case and blue for numbers, special characters and punctuation. With letters on the keyboard arranged by how often they would be used, each line of type came into being by brass matrices being used to create the mould from which the 'line o' type' would be made, from a continuously molten hot metal pot. The advantage of creating a fresh slug of type each time, rather than wearing out the types stored in the usual letterpress frames, was obvious. Word spacing was controlled by wedge-shaped spacer bands that automatically justified the line of type to the width specified by the machine operator.

When the patents ran out on the Linotype machine, the prospect of improving the technology beckoned. The early 20th century saw hot metal machines from new companies such as Intertype able to use multiple magazines of type, opening up the possibility of changing font, italicizing and creating captions for images. Now a whole newspaper could be composited on one machine comprising roughly 5,000 parts and selling, in 1900, for something like a thousand dollars.

The specialization involved in operating a hot metal compositing machine also had its impact on the skill base and the separation of labour. A journalist – press ticket in hatband, wire-bound notebook and Pitman shorthand skills at the ready – would produce copy for sub-editing and then it would be passed to the typesetters. This process separated the act of writing from the process of printing even further than the innovations of Gutenberg and his followers. The principle of establishing distance between journalists and compositors led to the formation of print unions, journalists' unions and compositors' unions, often with the express purpose of maintaining the distinction – or, in the jargon, the demarcation lines – between the professions. A linotype machine, when used at full chat, also helped compositors to bargain for their nine-hour day, so reliable and predictable was the output of the machine from a fully trained operator.

The methods of illustrating newspaper articles also progressed during this period. The progenitor of the halftone process, which replaced illustrations delivered by wood engraving, metal plate engraving or, more rarely, lithography, was the inventor Frederic Ives. Through an interest in photography, Ives developed a number of ways to get a photographic image onto a printing plate before alighting on the process of direct photographic transfer to a sensitized plate. His breakthrough was in the halftone process, where dots of varying sizes could replicate to some extent the gradations of shade in an image, fooling the eye with as few as fifty-eight dots per inch into seeing the tonal variation of a photograph.

By the end of the 19th century, photography and journalism had combined to bring visual representations of people, places and things to an ever-increasing audience. The culture of what was possible within the realm of visual communication had irrevocably changed.

The mechanized mastery of light (and chemicals)

The invention of mechanical and chemical processes for the reproduction of images shifted the required skill base from the manipulation of tools to the framing of the image at the point of capture by the photographer, and then to the editorial and reproductive processes. The roles of the photographer, picture editor and printer came into being as the technologies developed – the invention and adoption of the halftone process was the turning point.

'A Scene in Shantytown, New York', appearing in the 4 March 1880 edition of the New York *Daily Graphic*, is often described as the first photograph printed in a newspaper. It was subtitled 'reproduction direct from nature'.

This is in some ways a direct nod to the idea of 'nature's pencil' – a term derived from the first photographic book, *The Pencil of Nature*, published by Longman's of London between 1844 and 1846 in six instalments. Each calotype – an early photographic process invented by Henry Fox Talbot, involving the sensitization of the paper with silver chloride – was pasted into the book by hand. Of course it was: mechanical photographic reproduction had yet to be invented. What's intriguing is that what we now regard as a process derived from scientific experimentation, chemistry and engineering was initially described as 'photogenic drawing'. There was a classical allusion within the term 'calotype' (a compound from the Greek, meaning 'beautiful impression') and the general idea was that this was the bringing together of a system of image-making inherent in nature's bounty: the great watchmaker providing us with the components to reproduce nature via nature, in extraordinary and realistic detail.

To modern eyes, 'A Scene in Shantytown, New York' is an unprepossessing image of some wood-built dwellings behind what appear to be piles of earth or slag heaps, with a brick-built tenement and a rudimentary sidewalk in the foreground. To the 19th-century viewer, for all the hideous mundanity of the subject matter, it was a wonder: reality transcribed to the page by mechanical reproductive means. No artistic licence, no human hand, just the sublime thrill of the truth of depiction in the raw. We can almost hear the well-heeled readers of the *Daily Graphic* exclaiming to themselves: 'People actually live in places like that!'

Stephen Henry Horgan, a graphic artist, designed the line screen that was laid over the photo image that had been printed on the engraver's plate. The production of halftone images evolved via the rotation of line screens over each other, creating distinct 'dots' with which to make the final variation. The differently sized dots in the halftone mesh determined the percentage of white versus black ink that would be used to make up the different parts of the image. The shifts in density between black and white transitions smoothly and imitates the continuous tonal range of photographic grain, meaning that, perceptually, the eye creates the interstitial information so that the broken-down image is reassembled by our brains as an approximation of a photograph.[16] The dot is the key: it's the modular expression and translator of the stochastic qualities of photographic grain.

The little dot had a tremendous effect on the speed of visual communication and transmission. It changed not only the nature of how the world was represented, but the pace at which images came to rival words in importance within those representations. Arguably we are still living with the consequences today. The 'Insta' of Instagram has democratized the instant in the same way that the Box Brownie camera and, later, the Kodak Instamatic democratized the capture of the moment. The principal difference between

A SCENE IN SHANTYTOWN, NEW YORK.
REPRODUCTION DIRECT FROM NATURE.

The first halftone image reproduced in a newspaper was an unprepossessing shot of a house in New York. Note the caption – 'reproduction direct from nature' – although, in fact, the image was a product of the first truly photomechanical process.

The cropped version of Nick Ut's famous image from Vietnam retains its extraordinary power to shock and inform. Visual communication via news media, despite the evidence of recent times, can be a force for good.

the technologies is in the collapsing of the time lag between capture and display, or, as we now call it, 'sharing'.

The explosion in the effectiveness and presence of newsprint meant that a variety of means of production rapidly had to scale up. Paper mills would need to pulp and produce huge amounts of paper for the webs that fed the new rotary offset presses that appeared in the early 20th century. The rotary presses 'offset' the print image; that is, the impression was not taken directly from the forme of a plate cast by a stereotype, but instead, a mirror image of the page was transferred onto a rubber 'blanket' around the printing cylinder. This in turn implied a rapid scaling up of the technologies of the rubber industries, an uptick in output that would not have been possible were it not for the colonization of the parts of the world where rubber trees grew. Also essential to the whole process were the growth of the steel industry, for the machine tools and parts for the presses; the tin and lead mines, for the type; the chemists and metallurgists, for antimony; the oil and coal industries, for the ink and the power that drove the presses; and the training of engineers, to maintain them. Further down the line were the railways, for distribution; the shipping of timber, for wood pulp; the increase in the numbers of dockers and warehousemen. Within the print industry there were the journalists, typists, editors, sub-editors, compositors, photographers and administrative staff. Out in the wider world, the numbers of people consuming stories and imagery grew and grew.

Harvesting the crop

In terms of the history of visual communication, the power of a photograph reproduced in a news context is evidently a rich and modern phenomenon. Nick Ut's 1972 image of a nine-year-old child, Kim Phúc, running towards the camera, naked and crying with arms outstretched as she tries to escape from a napalm attack, has been reproduced *ad infinitum*. It was designed and destined to be so.

Ut, a Vietnamese American, was an Associated Press photographer. The Associated Press is an organization that dates back to 1846, when five New York City-based newspapers banded together to fund a Pony Express delivery of news from the Mexican–American War. The speed of newsgathering and delivery coincided with the rise of the image and headline as the driver of newspaper sales in the 19th century, so it makes sense that the AP found itself in another war zone more than a century later.

The crop of Ut's photograph is significant. The original image includes a soldier to the right of the frame, apparently concentrating upon the task of rewinding some film in a camera. He is looking down, intent on his job, not running but walking. His presence changes, maybe even dilutes, the urgency and drama of the famous published image.

Ut's crop was arguably a political decision, turning a *vérité* moment into a construct. It served to make a more powerful point about life in a country where America was deploying napalm, a gelatinous compound designed to burn while sticking to human skin. Ut's purpose was to highlight the conditions and the effects of war. The crop is an effective editing tool that grew in use in tandem with the role of the picture editor, the idea of reportage and documentary reality and 'truth'.

The power of the press gave rise to its characterization as the 'fourth estate'. This is attributed to Edmund Burke by Thomas Carlyle: when, at the end of the 18th century, reporting on parliamentary proceedings opened up, Burke reportedly recognized in Parliament the three 'estates' – the commons, the nobility and the clergy – and acknowledged, in the press gallery, a fourth estate perhaps more powerful than them all. At that time the idea of a fourth estate residing in journalism, with the power to affect and steer the country, must have seemed fanciful to some.

Fast-forward to the 20th century and, in the wake of the United Kingdom's 1992 election result that saw John Major unexpectedly returned to power, the red-top tabloid newspaper the *Sun* (owned by Rupert Murdoch) carried the headline 'It's The Sun Wot Won It'. Leaving aside the faux-working-class 'wot' for a moment, on the previous day – election day – the paper had run an underlined headline in sentence case on a blue ground, which read 'If Kinnock wins today will the last person to leave Britain please turn out the lights'. There was no question mark to punctuate the request. The headline was accompanied by a crude and bizarre photomontage of the Labour Party leader Neil Kinnock's balding head encapsulated within the glass of an incandescent light bulb. Depending on how you looked at it, the fourth estate had either reached its nadir in terms of the quality of visual communication, or its zenith in terms of self-congratulatory triumphalism and effectiveness.

To get there – to be able to create and publish photomontages, however unsubtle; to have headlines reversed out of bright blue grounds; to have full colour throughout the newspaper, commanding the attention of the masses with the power and presence of the comic book rather than the greyed-out traditional broadsheets of the newsstand – huge changes had taken place in the way images and words were brought to the public.

The crudity of the photomontage on this famous front page belies the leaps in technology – and reorganization of labour within the printing industry – that had to take place before it could come into being.

Lithographic stone took the drawing of the artist directly from the hand. Like Japanese *ukiyo-e* prints, each colour 'pass' required a different stone, but the lithographic process also allowed for detail, highlights, shading and, in tone lithography, a 'wash' of colour.

The highly specialized, mechanized and technical nature of print production for newspapers had led to a strong unionization of the labour force wherever newspapers were in production. An unwritten rule meant that there should always be two pairs of hands between the journalist and the newspaper, in the shape of the sub-editors and the typesetters. The idea that a journalist could type directly into the newspaper was at the time a no-no of some magnitude. Demarcation lines between journalists and workers on the print shop floor created what was effectively a closed shop.

In the UK, technological advancements were accompanied by a drive towards new working practices. Under the influence of an attitudinal shift engendered by Thatcherism, one Eddy Shah, a publisher of local newspapers, took on the print unions in Warrington in 1983. Depending upon where your political sympathies lie, his aim was either to modernize and streamline the industry or to crush the unions, depopulate the industry, remove closed shops and restrictive working practices, drive down costs and increase profits. Somewhere between those two positions lies the truth. More importantly, by the time of the disputes around News International's Wapping print works three years later – triggered by the sacking of 6,000 print workers at Rupert Murdoch's News International Group, which took place on Friday, 24 January 1986 – the shape, content and means of production of the visual representation of news had changed irreversibly.

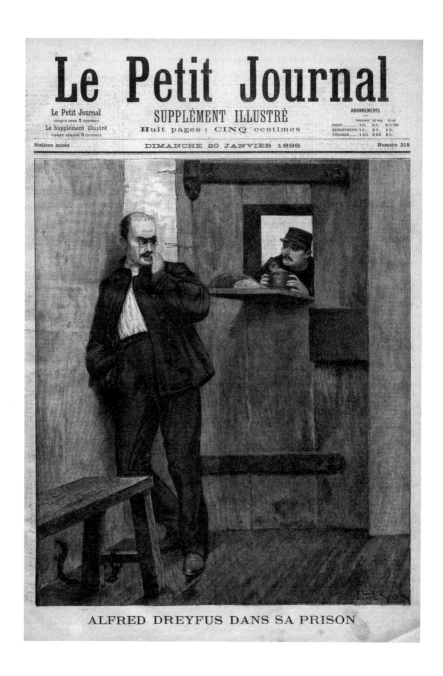

The Dreyfus Affair, which split the French Republic, was ideal fodder for the new mass-circulation magazines. Technology was driving public interest in politics and the functions of the state.

Colour and tech

By the late 20th century, newspapers looked different from their early predecessors, were made differently and were gradually assuming a role that went far beyond reportage. Underlying this change were further huge shifts in technology.

The processes of colour separation and registration that allowed for full-colour reproduction relied on the assignment of different colours to specific screens composed of halftone dot matrices. Benjamin Day's 1879 invention of small ink-efficient dots (Ben-Day dots) didn't really come into its own until they were used in the mass-produced comics of the mid-20th century; but the arrival of these dots in the late 19th century coincided with advancements in the understanding of colour theory, and the application of that theory in the painterly pursuits of divisionism and pointillism.

The stippling used in engraving foreshadowed the use of continuous-tone techniques, fooling the eye into seeing gradation and in turn, with colour separation, a full range of tonalities based on colour passes overlaying each other and the density of the dots. Colour lithography used the Ben-Day process at this time. Around 1890, the first rotary colour press was invented by Hippolyte Marinoni. Marinoni's mastery of colour techniques in fin-de-siècle Paris contributed to the success of his tabloid publication *Le Petit Journal*, an early forerunner of today's tabloids in its emphasis on the lascivious and the gossipy, the tragic and the accidental over hard news.

The techniques of colour reproduction rely on a now-familiar breakdown of the visible spectrum (for print purposes, at least) into four colours: cyan, magenta, yellow and black. CMYK seems obvious as an initialism until we get to the K, which stands for 'key'. The colour plates for the other colours are aligned or 'keyed' to the black, and this registration is what allows the colours to blend subtractively with each other and replicate the visible spectrum. Any print material works subtractively, cancelling out wavelengths of the overlayed colours, ultimately to create black; whereas light (in photography or in film) works additively, wavelengths building upon each other to create white.

The documented beginning of the understanding of colour in terms of light goes back at least as far as Francis Bacon, whose musings on the rainbow predated Newton's experiments with prisms. Colour reproduction using dot screens relies on the precise geometric alignment of photo-etched mechanical screens to create a good four-colour image. The time spent creating each screen, and the precision required of the printing process, meant that the skills of the printer were closely allied to their understanding of the machinery and the effects of running paper at high speed through offset rotary or plate presses.

Breaking down colour in a painterly way, in the way that artists like Georges Seurat and Paul Signac did with their divisionist and pointillist approaches, required a degree of randomness in execution if not in intention. The nature of the gestural art of painting meant that absolute precision in the rendering of the image in this way was necessarily impossible. The human hand and eye do not work in the same way as machines. Interesting, then, that as the capture and reproduction of imagery became digitized, so the reproduction of photographic imagery via digital print media became stochastic, or random: where the interpolation of coloured dots is distributed in order to make the closest approximation of 'true' colour by randomizing the angles and density of the dot screens. A bit like a pointillist painting.

With a stochastically printed image, because the dots are not precisely aligned on grids, there is reduced moiré patterning or rosetting. Less ink is used, and the eye reads the image as more detailed and precise. Digital stochastic printing uses a print head that ranges across the print surface and distributes the dots quasi-randomly. Because the technique does not rely on physical screens for colour separation or the method of offsetting the image to a rotary drum or plate to a print surface, the direct transmission of ink to the substrate (or material to be printed upon) frees up the scale at which images and text can be reproduced.

Size matters

The design journey undertaken to make large-scale images has changed since the first billboards were invented and installed. Just as the naming conventions of billboards illuminate the scale at which they were designed to work. In the UK, the home of imperial measurement, 'crown' posters measure 15″ x 20″.

A 'quad crown', or door panel, was oriented with four crowns vertically on top of each other. The 'sheet' is perhaps the module on which we should concentrate. A sheet measures 20″ x 30″ and it's multiples of this module that to this day govern the print sizes used in outdoor or 'out of home' advertising.

The dominance of these sizes has been challenged by the ways in which images can be transferred to various new substrates – most notably those made from long chain hydrocarbons, or 'vinyls'. The rise of digital stochastic printing allows for the production of large-scale digital prints, limited only by multiples of the size of the print bed, the scanning range of the print heads and the length of the substrate roll.

Peter Behrens's 1909 design for Allgemeine Elektricitäts-Gesellschaft transmits certainty and unity in its design. Now, in the age of social media, logos are once again becoming flat, crisp, minimal and easy to reproduce at small scale; see Volvo and compare.

Print with huge impact can now be designed, specified and hung to cover the sides of entire buildings. Previously, advertising or communication on this scale would have had to be put in place by teams of painters working from small-scale gridded artwork, either projecting onto or mapping onto the larger surface in a painstaking and time-consuming application of technique harking back to the gestural precision of the medieval monk.

The visual impact of large-scale graphics on buildings has not only been deployed in the domain of commerce and advertising. The *Organisationsbuch der NSDAP* is a 500-page-plus guide to the organizational principles of the Nazi Party, published first in 1937. It details everything from the hierarchical structure of the party and its operatives to the scalable insignia, uniforms, flags and crests that would adorn its buildings, and the lapels and collars of its Hugo Boss-designed uniforms. (The Hugo Boss of today is not the same entity as that which gave the Nazis their distinctive style, bolstered as it was by the threat of violence and death.)

That the techniques and tools of commerce should be co-opted by politics is not necessarily surprising. The ground rules of corporate identity that we recognize today were laid down by designer Peter Behrens in his work for the Allgemeine Elektricitäts-Gesellschaft (AEG) from 1907, though the idea that corporations should have a consistently recognizable visual presence with which to flag their activity had been in play for some years. The logotype predates Behrens's work, but Behrens and his team were among the first to codify and condense the rules into what we now understand to be corporate identity.

Arguably, the nexus between politics and easily recognizable visual communication could be traced to the military, where bold uniforms were used to distinguish warring sides on the battlefield. This propensity for colour-coded conflict held sway until camouflage shifted the focus to the silhouette in the First World War. Scarlet tunics and white webbing, royal blue greatcoats with polished brass buttons became ceremonial, while khaki, sand and green or grey solid serge became the functional tools of soldiering. The silhouette, of course, communicates visually.

Propaganda

When the skills behind advertising come into contact with politics, the result is propaganda. The ability of this kind of communication to connect with the feelings rather than the rationality of the audience is well known. Examples range from the aspirational imagery of revolutionary communism to the demonization of queues of people by Hitler in the 1930s – and by the advertising agency Saatchi & Saatchi in the 1970s, on its infamous 'Labour Isn't Working' poster. The latter is an interesting example. It depicts a snaking line of 'the unemployed' that was in fact made up of Young Conservative volunteers. The resulting image, used for the 1979 UK general election, is credited in part with securing the election victory of Margaret Thatcher. The impact of such carefully crafted imagery serves to reinforce the unattributable maxim (though some say it originated with Goebbels) that a lie, or a fabrication, can get halfway round the world before the truth can put its boots on.

It's rare, however, to have the creators of such material go on record about what they think they are actually doing. In 2019, in an interview on the national UK radio station LBC, the now ex-Brexit Party leader and former

Pithy three-word marketing slogans, when applied to politics, swiftly become propaganda. Take Back Control, Get Brexit Done, Drain the Swamp and Lock Her Up are recent examples. Here, the queue of 'workers' were actually Conservative activists.

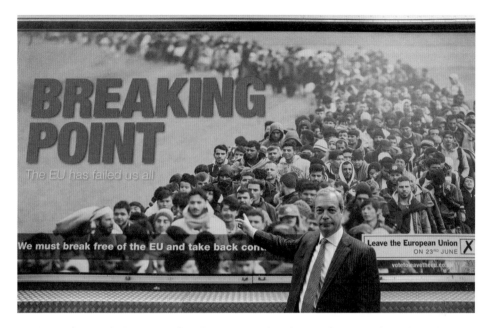

Nigel Farage stands before an equally infamous queue-based piece of propaganda. He later claimed it was not a design but a photograph of what was actually happening: a slippery assertion belying the emotional force of such deliberately deceptive messaging.

MEP Nigel Farage found himself quizzed on the equally infamous 'Breaking Point' poster of June 2016.

During a discussion with presenter Iain Dale, and in defence of the 'truth' he was claiming the billboard depicted, Farage made the following point: 'The inference was that somehow this was, you know, a design...it was a photograph of what was actually going on.'[17] There is indeed a photograph involved, and we'll come to that. But to deny the design decisions made in putting together this extremely powerful piece of communication places far too much emphasis on the efficacy of the photograph alone.

This is not to say that the photograph was not a legitimate depiction of factual events. It was sourced from Getty Images and had been shot by Jeff J. Mitchell on the Slovenian border in October 2015. Mitchell is a documentary photographer whose work contains a strong seam of this kind of imagery, and it's important to say that he was vocal in decrying the use of his image for this poster. It's a quality documentary image that is indeed a truthful depiction of Syrian refugees crossing the border from Croatia into Slovenia as a result of the ongoing conflict in their home country.

The image, like many of Mitchell's, uses depth of field to emphasize the scale and drama of what we are seeing. In isolating the foreground with this technique we register faces and see the real people involved, while the defocused queue in the background is read as a mass of humanity. The selection of the photograph is, in itself, a design decision. Although not doctored to any high degree, the image has been judiciously cropped so the queue drifts perhaps infinitely off the boundary of the image. This is a design decision, too.

Equally important to the design is the use of type. The red headline is set in Helvetica Neue Black Condensed – a typographers' choice of typeface – and on close inspection, the headline has been carefully kerned. Furthermore, a drop shadow has been added both to lift the text from the background and mitigate the 'beating' effects of the contrast between the red and the grass-green background.

The strap at the bottom of the poster has around an 80 per cent black transparency added and more type in Helvetica Neue. For the avoidance of doubt, and to counter the idea that this highly effective piece of propaganda

The famous moment in 2012 when Boris Johnson got 'stuck' on a zipline. It seems that mendacity and buffoonery are no longer a barrier to high office. The clownish public persona developed by Johnson – the toddler haircut, the fake bumbling, the aping of supposedly Churchillian mannerisms, the photo-ops from the dressing-up box – is little more than a distraction.

was not designed, it was produced, allegedly, by an advertising agency in Scotland – and, as we all know, ad agencies design communication. Furthermore, whether or not you agree with the purpose of this exercise in design and copywriting, the empathetic emotional jolt it delivers is undeniable. Despicable, but undeniable.[18]

Events that flow from propaganda cannot be pinned with any causal certainty to the propaganda itself. However, it is doubtful whether the events of 9 November 1933, later dubbed *Kristallnacht* after the myriad shattered windows of Jewish businesses in Austria and Germany, would have taken place were it not for the highly propagandized activities of the 'anti-Jewish' and 'spontaneous' protests carried out by members of the *Sturmabteilung* under the command of Josef Goebbels. As another example, the murder of the British MP Jo Cox on 16 June 2016 arguably would not have taken place were it not for the atmosphere of hatred, fear and division in the country being stoked by propaganda like the 'Breaking Point' poster. Simple images are powerful things and can transmit multiple meanings, or open the door to multiple interpretations.

On the day that Heather Stanning and Helen Glover won Team GB's first gold medal in the coxless pairs at the 2012 London Olympic Games, the then mayor of London, Alexander Boris de Pfeffel Johnson – ex-Bullingdon Club member, *Spectator* editor and *Daily Telegraph* columnist, and future prime minister – chose to upstage the rowers by mounting a zipline in order to slide down it waving a small plastic Union flag in each hand. It is not known whether the zipline (which had been malfunctioning earlier in the day) seized by accident or by design, but Johnson hung there for around ten minutes. This was long enough for the image to be tweeted, and for the sparse crowd and Johnson himself to become bored of the spectacle. The image persists, however, as a cursory search of the internet turns up 10 million results in under half a second.

On 1 June 2020, while the fallout from George Floyd's murder by Minneapolis police officer Derek Chauvin was raging around the US – particularly in Lafayette Square and H and 17th streets in the heart of Washington, DC – officers used methods of riot control forcefully to clear the area of protesters. In doing so, the law enforcement officers effectively cleared and maintained a path so that Donald J. Trump, 45th POTUS, could walk to St John's Episcopal Church with some of his acolytes, pose and solemnly hold the Bible aloft for a photo opportunity. Trump was playing to his God-fearing base of Middle American MAGAnistas with an image constructed to be decoded as politically loaded visual communication. A tweet claimed that he held the Bible upside down, too. This rumour spread like wildfire across social media, but turned out not to be true. The Bible in his

Donald J. Trump holds a Bible aloft during a photo opportunity enabled by the forcible clearing of protesters from the streets. His intended message is probably only clear to his radically faithful evangelical Christian base. What would Jesus do? Not this.

hand was the right way up, even if the globe's moral compass was spinning and for a while, the world itself seemed upside down.

Photo opportunities such as these are both a modern phenomenon and a phenomenon of postmodernism. The generation of imagery for the purpose of communication remains modern as the contemporary entrepreneurial world opens channels – Instagram, Facebook, Flickr, TikTok – and creates new spaces for image-savvy users to fill. The flow of images is a stream that can be read as data, or as a cultural phenomenon, or both. The anthropologists and historians of the future will, should the servers and corporations sustain, have a mineable source of tagged, flagged and geographically specific imagery with which to understand the ways in which we live now.

We are in the process of unconsciously mapping our culture via the making of visual communication. Furthermore, the seductive immediacy of image-making has benefited from the aforementioned shortening of the sequence between making an image and sharing it. Before the digital, things were different. Once, film had to be loaded into the Brownie or the Instamatic, exposed and advanced 12, 24 or 36 times, then either sent for processing or processed as a hobby in the darkness of your bathroom. The prints would arrive perhaps weeks later, to be shared with friends and family via albums. You were lucky to get three or four 'good' photos from a batch. Contrast that process with the avalanche of 'likes' driving the ever-growing cache of images and posts from Instagram's one billion users. Then think about the exponential growth of server capacity, and its energy usage. If that continues at the present rate, in the case of a country the size of Japan and in the absence of any material better than silicon for data storage, it will use the entirety of the country's energy production by the year 2030.[19]

Notwithstanding the Microsoft Corporation's innovative sinking of server farms into the cold waters off the Orkney Islands with Project Natick – which has been running since 2014, and builds on the fact that most people in the world live within 120 miles of a coastline – the technology underpinning our current obsession with image-making and sharing, with visual communication, needs to change and grow. Project Natick is, on the face of it, a neat initiative. The idea is that Microsoft will manufacture these farms and drop them into the sea near cities where more capacity is needed. Such is the present-day thirst for visual communication and stimulation that fully 25 per cent of all downstream traffic on the internet is occupied by video streaming platforms, with Netflix occupying half of that on its own.[20] Clearly, the human appetite for visual communication has accelerated and been buoyed by technology enabling what seems to be instantaneous image-sharing between everyone, all the time.

For example, Instagram launched in October 2010. By December 2010, it had one million users. Within a year, the startup had 10 million users. By the end of 2016, there were 600 million monthly active users. Artificial intelligence, machine learning and algorithms are facilitating this surge in sharing visual communication across the planet; later, we'll examine this phenomenon more closely. For now, consider this: more than 90 million images are shared on Instagram every day. Since its inception in 2010, more than 40 billion pictures, videos and pieces of visual communication have been shared. The coldly engineered brilliance of the networks and systems of Insta, Facebook, TikTok, Twitter and the like constitutes a seemingly infinitely expanding infrastructure that can be filled and refilled with our emotionally loaded stories, experiences and humanity. Births, holidays, experiences, places, views, weddings, music, lockdown, farewells, festivals, food and faces: all are captured and shared with minimal textual description, or overlaid with emoji and animations.

We are in the heyday of visual communication, it seems.

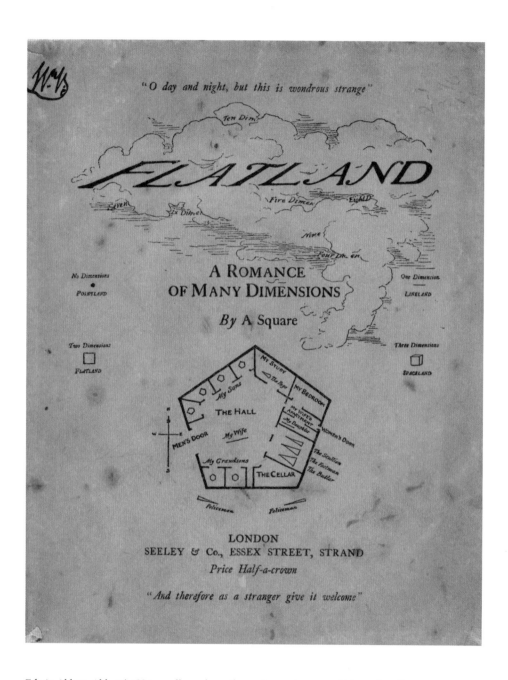

Edwin Abbott Abbott's 1884 novella explores the notion and nature of dimensionality as a philosophical and political subject. Published on the cusp of the dawn of the first truly modern age, the book attempts to codify dimensionality as an expression of social hierarchy and stratification, but also, significantly, as a signifier of enlightenment and modernity.

Part Three

The Third and Fourth Dimensions

Towards the representation of the real

Perhaps the journey to our current orgy of visual communication, our continuous representation of the real, did not start in the ordinary world but, in part, in the abstract imagination of a Victorian theologian and geometry fan. Edwin Abbott Abbott published his novella *Flatland* in 1884.[1] Its first-person narrator, an inhabitant of Flatland, describes the differences between it and Spaceland (where we, the readers, live).

Flatland has a hierarchy of form. The lower orders are simple, one-dimensional triangles while the nobility, the older families, have many sides to their geometry. But, unsurprisingly for a place called Flatland, everything is flat – everything is 2-D. Leaving aside what is, to us, the gender discrimination at the heart of the story, *Flatland* is presented as a 'romance'. (Women are not held in high esteem in Flatland. They are described as 'needles': invisible and dangerous when turned to the side. While moving through Flatland, women must maintain their 'peace cry' on pain of death. They must make this noise lest they accidentally pierce and damage a male piece of geometry. In spite of Abbott's pioneering work on female education and satirical tone, his contemporary Sigmund Freud would have had a field day with him.)

The romance in the title occurs between dimensions. The genius of Abbott's visionary tale lies in its grasp of how powerful the lure of dimensionality is to humans. Visual communication has always romanced dimensionality. In *Flatland* the concept of dimensionality arrives in one fell swoop, delivered by a visitor (like Klaatu, 'from space') in the year 2000. In reality, the development and use of dimensionality is rather more complex and took rather longer, as we shall see.[2]

What do I mean by 'dimensionality'? Here I am using the term to describe how we endeavour to capture, represent and show the world in all its dimensions as seen by the human eye. The urge to fix a moment in time and, crucially, in space has driven the development of the technology, techniques, tools and materials with which to reproduce the world in such a way that it should, to the observer, feel real.

How to make things look real

How we represent the world in all its dimensions involves an understanding of the way that light works on objects and how we perceive them.

I have had the opportunity a couple of times to be involved in the conception, making and direction of fully CGI TV commercials, both of which turned out to be steepish learning curves. Having pitched the idea of creating a world of 'morphing objects like living buildings' (to Microsoft, of all people), we found ourselves in the strange position, together with a highly skilled team of programmers, particle experts, 3-D builders and skilled lighting technicians, of designing and directing a commercial that we could not see. Until each element was built, skinned, lit and animated, rendered and then relit and graded, we were flying blind. There was no budget for a meaningful pre-visualization. For the first few weeks, in progress meetings with the client, we showed simple grey boxes floating in grey space as placeholders for the pace of the commercial, with some reference images/photographs and wireframes and a bit of reference music. As a client, they were extremely patient. The problem was that making things appear real, when they only exist within the binary code of a computer, takes time and technology.

To be fair, makers of visual communication have always had to deal with the problems of time, tools and technology, be they painters, graphic artists, filmmakers, architects or, latterly, visual effects artists and technicians. With the tools we now have at our disposal, it's clear that we have come a long way in our mastery of the effects of light and its perception by the human eye; and yet we still have some way to go in the perfect reproduction of reality.

The pursuit of realism has driven innovation. Innovation has driven the development of new tools and techniques. The use of these tools and techniques has in turn encouraged the crossover of what are usually described as discrete cultural phenomena such as art and design, photography and painting. These thresholds are often crossed by practitioners in pursuit of the real, intrigued by why such divisions exist in the first place.

Take the artist Chuck Close, for example. His monumental paintings such as *Big Nude* (1967) are extrapolated from photographs that have been broken down into tiles, like pixels, and then scaled up using a grid. Predating Close's 'pixellated' work is the work of Leon Harmon and Ken Knowlton, whose *Studies in Perception #1* (1966), a computer-produced mural, was shown in the 1968 MoMA 'Machine' show. Measuring 5' x 10', the wall art's title demonstrates its purpose.[3] It's the earliest reference I have found to a computer having been used to break an image down into its constituent parts. It's pixellated, but the pixels are huge.

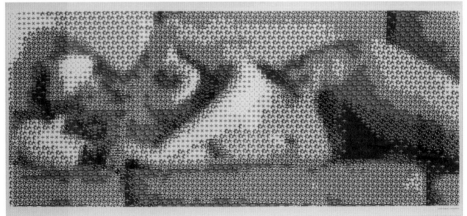

TOP Chuck Close's technique for *Big Nude* broke the photographic image down into 'pixels', attempting to reproduce with paint the accurate sensation of seeing an image that has been processed through a lens. Photorealism is an intensely meta undertaking.

ABOVE Harmon and Knowlton's approach differs from Close's in that the computer is the interlocutor between what is processed, represented and seen. The crudity of the pixellation represents a first step towards today's ultra-HD image-making.

Close used a similar technique. The super-realist paintings that resulted from his process appear finely detailed and, apart from their size, have a photographic quality to them. Most people experience them on the printed page or online, rather than in the flesh. Consequently, their appearance is mediated via photographic reproduction, perhaps reinforcing the perception of them as photorealist. What is achieved with a painted hyper-realistic Close image (he also worked with Polaroids and daguerrotypes) results from the artist's careful reproduction of the way light refracts through a lens, creating specular highlights and the effects of detail and depth of field determined by the combination of focal length and aperture.

At this point in the evolution of visual communication in the 21st century, we tend to know what photographic realism should look like. Seeing the effect of light through a lens is a common experience. This was not always the case.

Optics and the processes of reproduction

Sometime in the mid-13th century, Roger Bacon stood beneath a great anvil-shaped thundercloud that had just dumped inches of rain onto the muddy streets of Paris. Bacon had travelled all the way from Oxford with the aim of developing his experimental interest in optics, the science of how we see and how light works.

The storm may have been moving eastward; the grey-purple clouds banked up on the horizon. Behind Bacon, as he walked, the morning sun broke through the ragged cloudscape and illuminated the storm cloud. A rainbow formed as light, refracted, split into the constituent parts of the visible spectrum. Bacon was fascinated by the natural world: legend has it that the rainbow sparked his interest in optics, but his purview was wide. His *Opus Majus* (*c.* 1266) references an extensive list of topics, from the 'golden number' and natural phenomena like rainbows to arithmetic, music, perspective, the organs of vision, experimental science – and the list goes on. The impulse to understand how we perceive the dimensions of 'the real' is an ancient one; the mastery and understanding of optics were at the heart of Bacon's efforts. But of course, significant as he was, he was not the first.

In the ancient city of Basra in what is now Iraq, Hasan Ibn al-Haytham, also known as Alhazen, constructed an innovative optical device. He made a dark space with a pinhole – acting as a lens – in one wall, and used it to create an inverted projection of the sunlit city on the opposite wall. The *camera obscura* built by Alhazen is the first recorded example of such a device. He was well placed to explore the mysteries of optics: his *Book of Optics*,

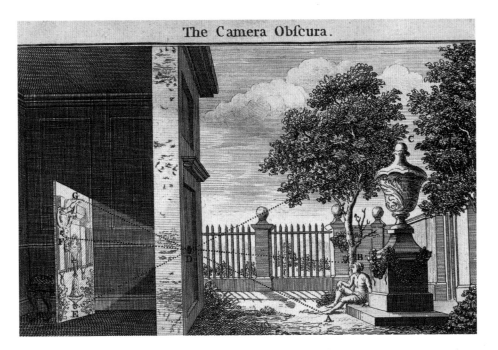

The *camera obscura* was for centuries the only way of seeing a full-colour moving image projected onto a wall or screen. It developed from a hole in a curtain or wall into elaborate systems using lenses and periscopes.

authored between 1012 and 1021 in Cairo, is a primary scientific text on the behaviour of light.

Alhazen knew what he was doing. The spectacle created by his *camera obscura* would not only secure his credentials as a scientist but elevate his status as a thinker and man of renown. Imagine, for a moment, the impact in the 11th century of seeing an inverted moving image projected onto a wall, filled with colour and detail: people moving through the streets; birds flying to roost at the top of a minaret; a pack mule being unloaded in a busy market. The impression would have been of watching an inverted film – a real-time panorama of dimensionality rendered, human life in bright colour with the multipoint perspective of the real world – all presented in front of the wondering eyes of the scientifically uninitiated.

The urge to capture this experience and make it repeatable drove the development of new technology. The journey from Alhazen's *camera obscura* to a *camera lucida* illuminates the process by which humanity brought itself to the threshold of the photographic representation of the dimensional world.

Henry Fox Talbot, holidaying in Europe in the mid-19th century, took with him a *camera lucida*: a clever arrangement of prisms and lenses that

The Reading Establishment: the first photographic printing firm. It was here that prints for Fox Talbot's *The Pencil of Nature* were produced. Talbot is shown operating the camera at the centre, while at the right his assistant Nicolaas Henneman photographs a sculpture.

would project a real and erect image onto a drawing surface, enabling an artist to replicate the scene with perspectival and detailed accuracy. Anecdotally, it was his dissatisfaction with his prowess at drawing using the *camera lucida* that prompted Fox Talbot to seek a way to transfer and fix the image it cast directly onto paper.[4]

The use of optical devices in the creation of portraiture, history and religious painting, landscape and the interior realism of the Dutch masters remains moot, in spite of the spirited argument that forms the backbone of the Hockney–Falco thesis: namely that by around the early 15th century, optical devices were in use by artists in order to make paintings appear more 'real'. David Hockney famously constructed a wall of printouts and postcards in his California studio that spanned the entire history of Western painting. Jan van Eyck's painting of Cardinal Albergati (*c.* 1435) was placed at the point where Western painters suddenly seemed to 'get' how to create something approaching, for the 15th century, photorealistic portraiture.

Analysis of the preparatory sketches for the portrait does not necessarily support the idea that optical devices were involved. Van Eyck changed the ears and some proportions of the seated figure. The physicist Charles M. Falco scanned and layered the preparatory drawing and the final portrait in Photoshop, convincing himself and Hockney that a lens had been used. Some years after the publication of their book (in 2001), it's still worth questioning what the point would have been in Renaissance artists keeping such knowledge 'secret'. But it was the existence of such lenses and optical devices that primed the public eye, pushing science to explain just how the brain could process what the eye could see and transfer that information to the hand of the artist – who, guided by grids and rules, horizons and vanishing points, could replicate the world.

Orthographics, modernity and representation

Dimensionality was not always used in the pursuit of real-looking pictures of things, people and places. What Hockney called 'the tyranny of vanishing point perspective' did not, for example, hold the same sway in China. A Song Dynasty (960–1279) image of a hydraulic grain mill has particular qualities shared with other scroll paintings of the medieval period in China, where a different approach to dimensionality in the image plays with the idea of perspective; but to what end? The evocation of depth in this kind of image is an orthographic projection, or at least as close to it as the anonymous Chinese artist could get. The primary tool used to create this 'ruled line painting' was a split ruler that could be parted to create a guide for the brush or stylus, in order to create parallel lines.

The difference in approach to orthography may be a function of the medium. Scrolls do not have the advantage of the rectangular boundary of a frame or wall, which seems to suggest the possibility of a singular vanishing point – a bit like looking through a window. The approach to perspective in these Chinese scrolls is not a single or simplistic approach: there is a complex weave of composition and depiction at play in the use of perspective, although some traditionalists in art history have cast Chinese artists of the medieval period as having no interest in it.

It is possible to use an optical device for the transference of accurate perspective to paper –
the drawing machine shown here, the pantograph, and later, lens-based devices.

Often, the vanishing point for the perspectival rendering of this period can be found outside of the image – indeed, so far outside that the convergence of perspectival elements is so subtle as not to be noticeable. In other cases, our human propensity for wanting to see perspective informs what we *think* we see. The brain will predict convergence where no convergence exists.

The evocation of depth and dynamism is there in the grain mill image; but look closely, and the image lacks true perspective. The workers and bosses are the same size whether they are in the foreground or the background. There are no shadows. This is less an attempt to render reality than an attempt to codify and depict the power bases of the Song Dynasty.

By depicting industrial endeavour via the mastery of geometric drawing techniques and tools, we are transported to a world of modernity. Any medieval image where orthographic projection replaces the accurate rendering of perspective is in service of the modern. Just as the grain mill is a bustling, busy factory rendered in what was then the most innovative and revealing of graphic techniques, so has that technique retained its currency as a signifier of contemporaneity today. The geometric precision demanded by any orthography absolves the maker from the aforementioned tyranny of multipoint perspective.

This Song Dynasty image of a hydraulic grain mill uses orthographic projection to give all the elements equal prominence. In applying the rule of projection, it expresses the visual cues of modernism.

The use of dimensionality and orthographics can signify a certain kind of contemporaneity. These Zaha Hadid sketches have dimensionality but use a relatively free, subtle and human form of projection to convey architectural and spatial ideas.

So, the adoption of orthographic projection is not a recent phenomenon: but it has been and still is used, for the same reasons as its ancient Chinese progenitors, by the likes of Walter Gropius, Theo van Doesburg, El Lissitzky and later Zaha Hadid and Conrad Shawcross. All these practitioners play and have played with a particular kind of contemporaneity.

Perhaps part of the atmosphere around isometric and axonometric drawing comes from its association with industrialization. The great gold rush of inventors seeking patents for engineering and equipment relied to some degree on the work of William Farish, who developed isometric principles while lecturing to his Cambridge students on 'manufacturing engines' during Great Britain's take-off into self-sustained growth in the industrial revolution of the early 19th century. Modernity, industry, contemporaneity, progress and power became wedded to the use of iso- and axonometry. In tandem with technology, the pursuit of contemporaneity drives visual innovation in communication.

From reality to abstraction

I took my degree in design history in the mid-1980s. It was a relatively new subject then, and the narrative of just how design had evolved as a discipline was necessarily Eurocentric. We were exploring our own back yard at a time when Europe was still divided between East and West, communist and democratic. The powers that be were still planning for tank battles on the plains of Germany. When I visited my uncle who lived in Mönchengladbach at the time, we were continuously overflown by warplanes exercising out of RAF Wildenrath. Our Design History field trip behind the iron curtain to Poland in 1986 coincided with both the bombing of Libya by American planes – an event we learned of from BBC News on shortwave radio – and the Chernobyl disaster. Naturally, we didn't hear about Chernobyl until we got home to the UK. It was an eventful trip, opening our eyes to strands of history that had been hidden to us, and underlining the cultural complexity and unfamiliarity of the European mainland.

Europe then had about it an atmosphere that was coloured in my twenty-something head by music (Kraftwerk's 'Trans-Europe Express' and 'Europe Endless'; Ultravox's cheesily romantic 'Vienna') and the post-war film languages of Reed's *The Third Man* and Fellini's *La Strada* and *8½*, and Godard's *Pierrot le Fou* and *À bout de souffle*). For me, the discovery of European modernism and its roots was akin to being seduced. I loved the heroic vision of

Gerrit Rietveld's Schröder House is almost a century old, although it looks newer. In eschewing traditional form and ornament, if not materials and techniques, Rietveld and his collaborators pointed towards a neoplastic future that would never be realized.

the 'white architecture'. I loved too its representation in magazines, angular high-contrast photography, beautiful sketches and line drawings, architectural plans and orthographic projections. I spent a good deal of time in the library at the Royal Institute of British Architects, poring over reports of newly built houses of the 1920s and 30s in the *Architectural Review*. Then I took to travelling around London, the home counties and even abroad, looking at houses like Six Pillars in Sydenham, or High and Over in Amersham; the Tugendhat House in Brno; and some little brick houses with concrete porches near Crawley, designed by the Tecton architectural group. The latter led me to look up Berthold Lubetkin in the phone book, ring him up and visit him at home in Bristol and – well, just listen to him.

I'm aware that this fascination I had, and still have, with modernism is an orthodox male enthusiasm for 'heroic' revolutionary thinking. I find the aesthetic and the philosophy seductive and it's a habit I have not been able to break. (This in spite of growing up in a system-built duplex with bad aluminium windows and a propensity for growing black mould.) So when, a couple of years ago, I found myself collaborating with a landscape architecture practice based in Utrecht, I could not help but take some time to explore one of the weirdest examples of architecture as visual communication.

If you walk down the Prins Hendriklaan in Utrecht, just before you get to the underpass with its Delft-blue tiling featuring images of other De Stijl designs, you will come across Gerrit Rietveld's Schröder House. It's still a startling structure in the context of the quiet suburban street in which it has stood since 1924.

Leaving aside for a moment its reliance on traditional tools, skills and materials (wood, paint, brick and plaster, worked by hand in ways the De Stijl fellows' grandfathers would have recognized), the visual expression of the new, the contemporary, came to life in a spatial projection using Cartesian nodes and primary colours in the form of chairs, light fixtures, shelving and ultimately the Schröder House. On the one hand, the house is a rich person's indulgence in avant-garde sculptural play; on the other, it is a bold exercise in the three-dimensional communication of the idea of the new. On a third hand, it's just a house. But a house that signifies a different way of seeing and representing the world.

The De Stijl approach was at once progressive and reductive. Piet Mondrian's path to abstraction – taking the verticals of trees, buildings and windmills and the wide horizons of the polders to their logical place of post-pictorial painterly orthogonality – laid the intellectual and geometric groundwork for the move into neoplastic three-dimensionality. The schematization of the world into a Cartesian cage, within which the universe and humankind could be both implied and described and human experience

Theo van Doesburg and Cornelis van Eesteren, *Contra-Construction Project (Axonometric)* (1923, MoMA). The use of axonometric projection confers a sculptural dimension, implying architectural thought and spatial organization.

shaped and lived out, found its expression in the tectonic experiments of Van Doesburg and Rietveld. Van Doesburg's tesseract was an attempt to visualize the fourth dimension in a three-dimensional medium.[5] But there was madness afoot, too.

When Theo van Doesburg and Nelly van Moorsel toured Europe in the early 1920s as part of a De Stijl-inspired Dadaist tour, Kurt Schwitters would sit in the audience making animal and Dadaist noises, interrupting Nelly's renditions of modernist composers like Erik Satie. No doubt he was eyeballing Tristan Tzara as he did so. Together, they were all creating a moment of modernity and madness. They were giving form and presence to actions and words in time, evoking and using the fourth dimension.

The momentum of modernity carried forward a certain moneyed, experimental elite in their pursuit of new languages of form and expression in a Europe recalibrated by war. By 1923/24 an exhibition of De Stijl architects was running at Léonce Rosenberg's Galerie de L'Effort Moderne in Paris.

There is a photograph of this exhibition that shows a room filled with extrapolations of cuboid orthogonality and, from what we know of the De Stijl palette, primary colours. Although there are some architectural models perched on wooden stools, the effect is of a unified proselytizing for neoplasticism, a reductive sculptural approach which the De Stijl-ists proclaimed as the inevitable destination of art. Of course, we now know that they were wrong – but revolutionarily so.

The drawings, and to some extent the models, in that 'Les Architectes du Groupe "de Styl"' exhibition emphasize the nature of the geometric planar relationships between elements of the architecture. In so doing, they imply that any isometry drawn from the geometry is infinitely extendable. The drawings, models and photographs do not adhere to perceptible vanishing points, as in conventional perspectival drawings. Instead, De Stijl evokes the possibilities of the infinite while invoking the adoption of a way of building and making at the human scale. It's a clever nexus of big and small. Sit in a Rietveld chair or stand in the Schröder House and imagine its wooden lathes or walls extending into infinity, and you quickly get the idea. The act of sitting becomes an abstract art event. The signal is the visual communication of the idea, transmitted by a chair.

Saul and Elaine Bass and modern movement

In terms of visual communication, the shorthand of the orthogonal continued to work its ju-ju after the Second World War. Isometric projection connects De Stijl to one of Alfred Hitchcock's finest thrillers.

Elaine and Saul Bass (though only Saul appears in the credits) were hired by Alfred Hitchcock in 1958 to create the title sequence for his feature film *North by Northwest* (1959). The beginning of this sequence is famous for the way in which, perhaps for the first time, graphic elements, type and the *mise-en-scène* of the film move and combine with Bernard Herrmann's score to produce a truly contemporary and yet future-facing title sequence (see page 130).

It could be argued that the essence of its modernity lies in its suggestion and use of the Z axis (where X is vertical and Y horizontal), where elements appear to move into (and out of) the screen towards a vanishing point and seemingly follow some of the rules of perspective.[6] The title sequence is dynamic and kinetic for sure, but the effect is more akin to trompe l'oeil than a true use of the Z plane. Italicized Franklin Gothic Condensed sans serif type is oriented along fine lines that follow the orthography of the facade of the CIT building in Manhattan, where the hapless Roger Thornhill's (Cary Grant) advertising agency is located. But it's clear the type

The *North by Northwest* title sequence achieves dimensionality and dynamism almost by a trick of the eye. Close inspection shows that the fenestration and perspectival grid almost match, but the effect, combined with Herrmann's score, was revolutionary.

does not follow the rules of perspective; the capitals do not decrease in size as they march into the distance. It's not *Star Wars* (1977). Instead, the type slides in and out of the frame. From where it originates we do not know, nor do we know where it goes. Outside the frame, the type could be flying still into the infinite, like the Pioneer 10 spacecraft or the intersecting lathes of the Rietveld chair.

Perhaps by dint of the novelty of the technique, the letterforms are imprecisely aligned on the fenestration, and when the solid green ground dissolves through to the building, we can see that (possibly due to the effect of the spherical VistaVision lenses) there is little in the way of diminishing perspective in the building's frontage. But it is vestigially there. The type, on the other hand, is italicized and set so that the upper-case ascenders appear to be truly vertical, thus creating a kind of orthographic projection into space. It's a brilliant trick: a neat manipulation of Morris Fuller Benton's 1910 American Type Founders addition to the type family, creating a powerful sense of creativity and modernity underpinned by the emotional punch of Herrmann's frantic orchestration. All this through the simple deployment of a consistent angle governing the composition of parallel lines – or, in other words, orthographics. (This consistency may be questionable when the image is closely examined – the orthographics aren't that precise.)

The other kind of modern movement

Thanks in part to the self-mythologizing efforts of the mostly male cohort of modernist visionaries who emerged in Europe between the two world wars, we have a Eurocentric canon of works that, in their eschewing of traditional ornament in favour of the signifiers of functionality, have become a shorthand for the idea of modernity. The salience of the visual codes sanctified by various art, design and architectural histories has bolstered the undeniable influence of modernist design engineering on visual communication today. But in proselytizing for the removal of ornament and going for form derived from functionality, the modernists both succeeded and failed. The setup is glorious in its simplicity, the execution dubious in its complexity and compromise.

When Adolf Loos's polemic 'Ornament und Verbrechen' appeared as a full text in German in 1929, there was already a long history of functionally derived architecture and design that in its way transmitted the idea of purity of conception and execution. Of course, as with any cultural artefact, be it a chair, a piece of typography, a poster, book or building, the idea that objects made by humankind could transcend their time through eschewing ornamentation has proved to be false. Loos's mistake was not to factor in the inevitable changes and progress in material science and its relationship to technology, and the shifting sands of people's taste. How could he have known? Instead, it seems he preferred to backdate his polemic to 1908, to get one up on ornamentalists and what he saw as the decadent decorative impulses of the Secessionists of Vienna prior to the First World War.

So bound up in the tacit visual communicative qualities of modernism are the products of the creed that it is often difficult to find the humanity in their execution. The rhetoric of the use of machine-age materials and techniques was powerful, and it still resonates. The list of 'modern' materials and techniques is long and well known: tubular steel and plywood; climbing shuttering with which to build a concrete house; plate glass; typography that refuses the traditional serif ornaments on ascenders and descenders and terminals; photography that is collaged or printed directly from light onto photosensitive paper. Then there are the legendary experiments in machine art conducted by László Moholy-Nagy, whose instructions sent directly to the printer sought to remove the interpretive dimension of what it is to design communication (see page 132). All these things were deployed in service of the modern and modernism.

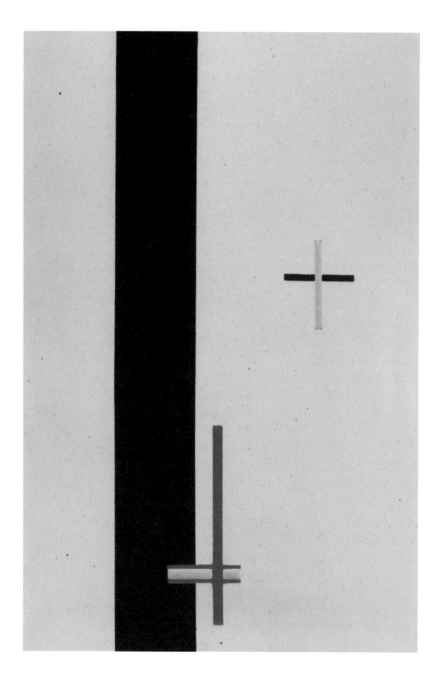

László Moholy-Nagy's machine art experiments disrupted the model of making visual communication. As telephone and print technology evolved together, his ideas opened up a new role for the communicator (see page 131).

We need to talk about Charles (-Edouard Jeanneret-Gris)

Perhaps one reason I find it hard to escape the pull of modernism is that there is a dense gravitational field at the centre of the story. Of the canon of European design thinkers whose work communicated how the uses of the modern can show us how to live, it's arguably Le Corbusier whose impact on the ordinary lives of people was, and is, most felt. Crucially, however, the true impact of his 1923 essay collection *Vers une architecture* did not come to full fruition until some time after the Second World War had ended, when young, mostly male architects looked to his concepts for the basis of the construction of mass housing in post-war Europe and beyond. My aforementioned childhood duplex, with its black mould and ill-fitting windows, was partly the result.

Leaving aside my lived experience of modernism for a moment, the rhetoric remains persuasive. Modular forms, universal living standards, the grid derived from human dimensions: all played their part in the architectural inspiration for the planning and erection of housing estates from Ursynów in Warsaw to Highcliffe in Alton West in London, and to Buenos Ares, Chicago and Hong Kong.

It may seem here that we have strayed from visual communication into architecture, but we should remember that the birth of almost any modern architectural phenomenon lies in the making of drawings. The transmission of an idea through the medium of visual communication is key both in the origination of the idea, the excitement around the birth of an architectural language and its execution in the act of building.

There are apocryphal stories around the origination of buildings by so-called 'starchitects' using the most basic forms of visual communication – the casually folded and crumpled piece of paper that becomes the destination art gallery; the three strokes of a black felt-tip pen on the back of a napkin at the end of a long lunch that becomes one of the tallest buildings in London; dynamic large-scale geometric sketches in chalk that have to wait years for the right engineering technology to be developed before their seeming weightlessness can be cast in concrete and steel. (Gehry, Piano and Hadid, in case you are wondering.) The connection between the idea and the reality of any communicated concept is in the human propensity for mark-making and form-giving; consequently, the projection of a design philosophy or idea into the spatial realm can occur in many ways.

The visual communication inherent in the formal language of modular construction espoused by Charles-Edouard Jeanneret-Gris – better known as Le Corbusier – is a case in point. He was a visionary who, some have said, could not bear to see his ideas developed by anyone other than himself. His behaviour around Eileen Gray and her E-1027 house seems to back this up, but as ever, the story and the motivation behind his actions are more complex than is first apparent. Spanning sculpture, polemics, architecture and art, Le Corbusier was a true product of the male dominance of the *beaux arts* at the pinnacle of which stands the work of the architect. And Le Corbusier loved to express himself.

E-1027 was conceived as modern dwelling with white blank walls and well-organized space. Once Gray had split from her partner, Jean Badovici, and the house she designed had come into Badovici's ownership, Le Corbusier was driven to make marks and painted vivid murals onto its white walls. The architect performed at least part of the task naked (apart from his spectacles, of course), in his most animal state. The sight of a naked man mark-making on the wall of a modernist villa has echoes of where we started in the caves of Puente Viesgo, with the significant difference that the shelter being decorated with wall art by Le Corbusier is a dimensional extrusion of a drawn plan, a modernist building made in concrete and glass.

The visual codes of modernism sprang from an obsession with what it meant to live as a modern human being in time, light and space. As we've seen, Theo van Doesburg, Gerrit Rietveld and their De Stijl acolytes sought to frame and capture humanity within the rationality and proportionality of a Cartesian cage. Alternatively, the naked and bespectacled Le Corbusier created his own avatar – from which the proportionality of his architecture reputedly sprang – in the shape of the Modulor Man.

The ambition in both approaches is breathtaking and the egoism undeniable. Jeanneret's Modulor Man (with the emphasis on 'man') recalls too our point of origin in terms of visual communication: the greeting, the raised hand, the humanity of a simple gesture. To invent a system of proportion to govern the way that buildings should be proportioned – and hence shape the way that we should live – from an imaginary male form ostensibly waving 'hello' or 'goodbye' is both hubristic and inspired. Derived via attempts to bridge imperial and metric systems, incorporate Fibonacci's sequence of numbers and find some divinely inspired system of human proportion, with a nod to the cultural plunder of what was seen as the 'primitive' African continent, the idealized and stylized image of a six-foot-tall man is a logo for ego.

With the Modulor and its expression in quasi-human form, Le Corbusier created an avatar with which to inspire and occupy his world of ideas and the world itself. Standing on the well-proportioned shoulders of Vitruvius, da Vinci and Alberti in an implausible *castell*, Corbusier's Modulor Man represents a shamanic form, an inhabiter of an identity that allows him to both be seen, and be seen to shape the world in his own image.

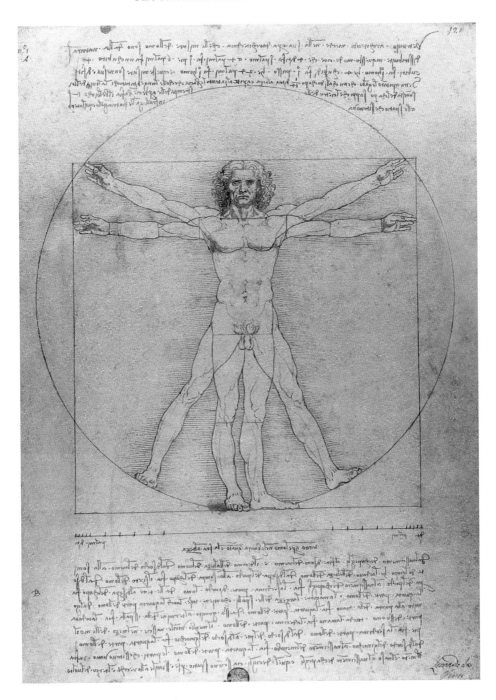

Leonardo da Vinci's *L'uomo vitruviano* (*c.* 1490) depicts the ideal proportions of the human body using systems created by the Roman architect Vitruvius. Le Corbusier's Modulor system builds on a long tradition of relating human (male) proportion to architecture (see page 134).

Although it was derived from a variety of sources and inspirations I still find the Modulor Man, his hand raised in greeting, strangely affecting. Perhaps in 40,000 years he will provoke the same reverence as the painted hands on the cave walls of Europe.

The Unité d'Habitation residential block in Marseille is
a coolly engineered grid within which humans can express
themselves – not unlike Instagram, Weibo and TikTok.

Amid the cold rationality of the architectural grid, the stark modernity of
Le Corbusier's Ville Radieuse project, the brute facts of concrete, shuttering
and glass, Modulor Man was and is the signifier for empathy in modernist
iconography. In the same way that Corbusier's murals occupied the white
space of E-1027, he visually communicates the humanity that might otherwise be hard to find. At the Unité d'Habitation in Marseille he is set as a
bas-relief in the wall, human in size and, presumably because of his location,
standing with his arms by his side. The message he delivers is clear: a system
derived from the human must be suffused with humanity. It's contentious,
but the oddest thing about the Modulor is that it seems to work. (As I think
we've established, though, I am a critical fan.)

The Unité d'Habitation is on the Boulevard Michelet, Marseille, where
the combination of a sunny climate, proximity to the Mediterranean Sea
and, perhaps, the collective spirit of being a *citoyen* rather than a subject
makes for a building that feels good when you are inside it and looks
impressive from the outside, with its combination of colour and shuttered

concrete. The place seems to function as intended, either as a radiant city or, depending on your point of view, as a magnet for a self-selecting group of architecture aficionados who are almost pre-programmed to live well within its bounds.

The composition of the facade works as a grid within which the people living there express themselves through the artefacts they use and choose as they dwell in their apartments. The differences glimpsed in the windows – the blinds, the curtains, the odd vase, lamp or chair – depict and define the variety of human life. They are the ornamentation in the stark visual code of the modern that helps to bring the place alive, adding human nuance to the clear visual communication and signification of modernity in the architectural, gridded form of the building. In some ways, the engineering of the Unité's infrastructure echoes that of Instagram, Facebook and the like: systems coldly and brilliantly engineered to allow humanity to express itself within clearly defined parameters and rules.[8]

Reorienting the purpose of visual communication

If the Unité d'Habitation sits at the end of a particular trajectory of the definition of 'the modern', it might be worth backtracking a little to examine other examples of how dimensionality in modernity helped to shift the orthodox historical hierarchies of form and meaning into new modes of visual communication. The intention here is not to reinforce the canonical approach of European modernism, but the idea that the *Mitteleuropean* experience between the wars was something of a crucible of creation and expression is difficult to deny. This is not to suggest that other modes of invention and innovation weren't occurring elsewhere in the world, or that powerful and privileged European elites did not continue to travel and to plunder and appropriate other cultures' material and visual cultures, dubbing them 'historical', 'primitive' or 'inspirational' whenever it suited, as they always had done.

Consider Frank Lloyd Wright's sojourns in Japan, for example. He was inspired and drawn there by the wood-block culture of *ukiyo-e* and found himself significantly influenced by the visual codes and the architecture he discovered. Many of his compositional traits can be traced back to the traditional languages and lateral planar forms of Japanese building and the atmosphere of the prints of the *ukiyo-e*. Perhaps the mythology of European creativity persists because the conditions for experimentation, play, education, manufacture, publication and critical discourse were bolstered in the period between the two world wars in Europe in a way that had not occurred before. Conditions created by the need for economic and societal renewal – not to mention the restoration of parts of the built fabric of war-destroyed cities – met the psychological change in perception of what was possible in the world experienced by a generation who had just come through humanity's first fully mechanized, fully mobilized and fully propagandized world war.

It wasn't just the war, though. Many areas of science and culture were developing along paths of their own making, with only a vague sense of where they might lead. Einstein had, in 1905, laid the groundwork for the general theory of relativity that emerged in 1915 and formulated the idea that space-time was a physical thing. The work of Freud and Jung placed the ideas of individuated experience and the collective, inherited unconscious in counterpoint; Schoenberg and Berg moved music from recognizable harmonic form to a different kind of tonality; Mallarmé, as we have seen, broke the relationship of the word and the page; and the German writer Hugo Ball did his best to divorce poetry from accepted linguistic form, relocating to Switzerland in 1916 while the 'war of cousins' was fought elsewhere, in order to concentrate on his non-sense.

The Cabaret Voltaire café in Switzerland, founded in 1916: Dadaist outriders determining new forms of cultural expression, or daft students having a laugh? The truth must lie somewhere in between.

One evening, in front of his friends in the little café they called the Cabaret Voltaire (see page 139), Ball read out his poem 'Gadji beri bimba', including lines such as: 'zimzim urullala zimzim urullala zimzim zanzibar zimzalla zam/elifantolim brussala bulomen brussala bulomen tromtata/velo da bang band affalo purzamai affalo purzamai lengado tor'. These ejaculations, although they now seem rather tame, were based on an approach to refining the word and the word form in order to repurpose the very building blocks of communication. As Ball put it: 'With these sound poems we should renounce language, devastated and made impossible by journalism. We should withdraw into the innermost alchemy of the word, and even surrender the word, thus conserving for poetry its most sacred domain.'[9] But this is a justification that arguably dresses up standard art student daftness in the cloak of intellect. What is not in doubt is that the Dadaists threw themselves into their art, demonstrated a genuine love for the breaking of convention in the making of their work.

Everything communicates, and the negative and nihilistic associations of the desire to shock and destroy the structures of the bourgeoisie that had led the world into war – the pelt merchants and profiteers, as Tristan Tzara had it – were the drivers of the Dadaists, notwithstanding their joy in performance and the fun of making something new. They created in order to

David Bowie in triadic costume, carrying on the language developed by Schlemmer and his acolytes. The meaning of such appropriation by the Thin White Duke is perhaps deliberately unclear.

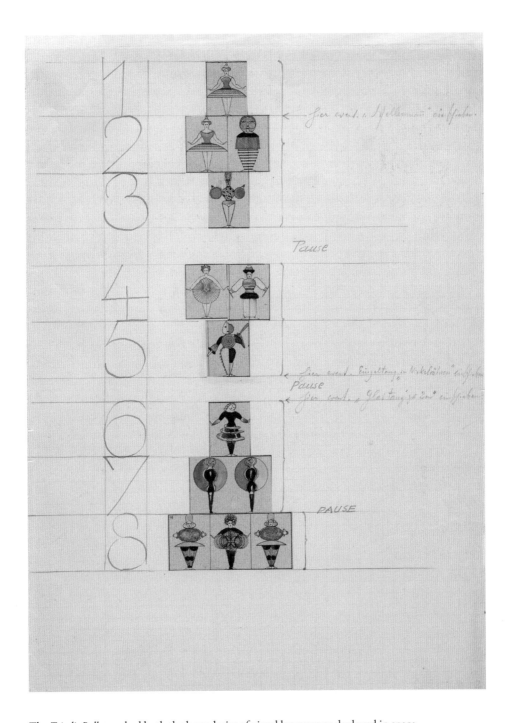

The *Triadic Ballet* pushed both the boundaries of visual language as deployed in space, and the patience of its audiences.

destroy perception, convention and the status quo – and, crucially, to have fun. What took place may sound to many people today like an average night out: 'Tzara is wiggling his behind like the belly of an Oriental dancer, Janco is playing an invisible violin and bowing and scraping. Madame Hennings, with a Madonna face, is doing the splits. Huelsenbeck is banging away non-stop on the great drum, with Ball accompanying him on the piano, pale as a chalky ghost.'[10]

The performative nature of what this group was doing nightly at the little café, and their desire to replace the rational madness of warfare with their own version of rational madness, in a party atmosphere, was hamstrung by its own studied ignorance of convention and practicality. According to member Richard Huelsenbeck, the Cabaret was bankrupt, as – appropriately enough for a group dedicated to overthrowing the usual way of doing things – no one ever sat on the door to collect an entry fee, and visiting students had destroyed the fixtures, fittings and furniture.[11] Again, standard art student behaviour.

If Dada aimed to rearrange the relationship of words to meaning, of action to intention and of spectacle to communication, it had to do so through its members' assumption of performative identities as Dadaists, replete with costumes and alter egos. But away from the Cabaret, they still had to eat, defecate, wash and live. The manifestation of the shamanic spirit-selves in which they occupied the performative space (witness Hugo Ball's costume of truncated conical hat, stiff cape and what look like lobster claws) prefigured today's avatars of the internet and echoed the shamans of other prehistoric cultures. Transcending the real and crossing the veil into the surreal became a trope of the avant-garde, and it persists today.

The Bauhaus *Triadic Ballet* (see pages 140 and 141) suffered a similar fate to the Cabaret Voltaire, in that despite its capacity to entertain with its own shamanic, costumed performances, the troupe was forced to beg for money to pay for the petrol to get them to the few performances they managed to deliver. Inexplicably (or perhaps obviously), even in the ferment of ideas we are led to believe was reshaping European thought in Weimar, the general public was reluctant to turn out to see a plotless three-act ballet based on the concept of 'multiples of three' and suffused with Bauhaus colour theory, music and the desire to remake traditional art forms anew.

Undeniably, the formal language devised by Oskar Schlemmer and his students has persisted down the years. It has been reframed by David Bowie in full triadic costume, then by Philippe Decouflé in his 1987 video for New Order's 'True Faith', repurposed by the Bavarian State Ballet to celebrate the Bauhaus School's 100th birthday in 2019. The Getty Educational Foundation has a lively, exploratory website fusing animations of choreography with costume and music on which you can make your own *Triadic Ballet*.[12] In spite of its intention to challenge the bourgeois expectations of going to see a ballet, it's intriguing to consider that the imagery of Schlemmer's ballet has both been subsumed into and maintained its difference from the culture at large. As visual communication goes, it's powerful stuff.

Perhaps the agency to challenge expectations wielded by the *Triadic Ballet* came from its abandonment of traditional story structure and resolution. Divided into three colour-coded acts with music, the rule of three referred to the primary colours; space, height and width; the Platonic solids of ball, cube and pyramid; twelve dances; eighteen costumes; and so on. This structure, though it boasted a beginning, middle and end and was redolent with geometric predictability, lacked narrative resolution. The three acts were yellow, pink and black. The music was atonal. It would seem that humans are programmed, somehow, to expect and enjoy resolution, be it harmonic, structural or narrative. In order to truly *épater la bourgeoisie*, any hypothetical instruction manual for disruption of the status quo would have to suggest the suspension of logic, reason and resolution in the conception and execution of cultural phenomena – including, but not limited to, visual communication.

MIDDLE TAR As defined by H.M. Government H.M. Government Health Departments' WARNING: CIGARETTES CAN SERIOUSLY DAMAGE YOUR HEALTH

In Alan Waldie's Benson & Hedges campaigns, meaning was abandoned the better to hook and intrigue the viewer. What does the image above mean? Perhaps simply that advertising will always find ways to subvert regulation via invention and appropriation (see page 144).

The contemporary reliance on the surreal

Visual communication in all its forms functions predominantly in the service of commerce. This is equally true in the art world and the world of design. Art raises questions around the intentions behind communication where, broadly speaking, design attempts to answer and service them. What has become known as the Duchampian impulse so coherently expressed in 'readymades' – the bicycle wheel on the stool, the urinal – has generated more than a century of debate around the meaning of such works of art: the self-mythologizing impulse of the artist obscures the intention, multiplying the potential for myriad interpretations.[13] No one knows what these things mean. The lack of resolution is the grease on which conceptual art continues to slide into the future.

Art that communicates visually always has the potential to feed commerce. But when visual communication is made at the instigation of and in the service of commerce, the outcomes are different and rarely transcend their purpose, though there are areas of crossover.

Arguably, without the work of the likes of Schlemmer, with his synthesis of space, time and colour, the visual languages of commercial art would not be what they are today. Equally, without his contemporary El Lissitzky and his conception of 'das zielbewußte Schaffen' (the goal-oriented creation) – where the purpose of art and life found expression initially in the form of abstract dimensionality and then in terms of photomontage and typography – the everyday surreality of advertising imagery would not be able to identify its wellspring.

The phrase 'goal-oriented creation' could have been coined to describe commercial art and its antecedents in advertising. For example, in the UK in the 1970s, restrictions on tobacco advertising were brought in as a way of reshaping people's attitudes to smoking and creating a beneficial effect on the health of the nation. The restrictions stopped advertisers from showing people smoking and enjoying cigarettes. Alan Waldie, an art director at the London agency Collett Dickenson Pearce, was responsible for the creative work behind the Benson & Hedges campaigns, which took montage and a Daliesque disregard for reality into new spaces and realms of non-meaning. Of his award-winning ads Waldie said: 'I thought the harder to understand they were, the longer people would stand and look at them, which is the result you want from any ad.'[14]

The photomontages that formed the backbone of the B&H and other campaigns needed Dada and the surrealists to pave the way. Crucially, such large-scale out-of-home advertising also needed its own technologies to come into being, most notably photomechanical transfer.

Technology in the service of the surreal

A photomechanical transfer (PMT) machine was, at the time of its inception, a thing of wonder, enabling the creation of print-ready artwork from a range of sources including photographs, paste-ups and drawings. Although individual machines differed in terms of what they could handle and how the output was made, the principles of photomechanical transfer remained the same.

The PMT process was developed by the Eastman Kodak Company in the early 20th century, to speed up image-making for the graphic arts and printing industries. The process uses an opaque 'negative' sheet on which an image is exposed. This negative sheet is then placed in contact with a positive sheet, with the image sides touching each other. The two sheets, sandwiched in this way, are run through a processor, absorbing chemicals, and then 'rested' so the chemicals can take effect. After this, the sheets are separated and the image is left on the receiver sheet. The negative sheet is thrown away and the receiver sheet is washed and dried.

The PMT process confers speed on the production of the final product. It requires fewer man-hours and, if the instructions are followed, the usual method of exposure – processing an exposed negative, exposing a print and then processing the print – is rendered obsolete. A PMT should take minutes. At the time of its invention, this was revolutionary.

PMT was one way of creating the film from which a printing plate could be made; the other was with a special camera called a 'stat' or copy camera. These were huge affairs, using special film and filters to mask and create special areas for four-colour print reproduction. If oriented vertically, they consisted of a tabletop and a bellows camera, while a horizontal orientation for a copy camera was for the creation of larger pieces of artwork and could occupy extraordinary amounts of space, occasionally requiring whole rooms. There, then, is the means by which a pasted-up bit of artwork could be made 'camera-ready', a term still in use today.

Artwork, not works of art

A word on the artwork itself. The advent of desktop publishing (DTP) created a much shorter workflow from origination to print. The industry-standard digital programs have changed over the years, both in the detail of their functionality and also in their pricing structures, but from Quark to InDesign, or Freehand to Illustrator, the principle is the same. The designer originates artwork and delivers it to the print.

The true revolution in this process came in 1991, when John Warnock, one of the co-founders of the software giant Adobe, started the rather grandly named 'Project Camelot'. The stated aim of this project was Arthurian in its ambition to unite. The vision was to enable anyone to capture a document from any program or application, send it electronically and print it on any machine. Within a year, Camelot had morphed into the Portable Document Format project. Now PDFs are a staple in the making of visual communication and are maintained by the Geneva-based International Organization for Standardization, the ISO (who, incidentally, also look after the standards for paper, board and printing inks. ISO/DTS 19857, in case you are interested).

Before the advent of the PDF, camera-ready artwork was pasted onto art board in a painstaking process using scalpels, cow gum and 'magic tape', which becomes more transparent when pressed onto the artwork. Typesetting was delivered as galleys, which would be trimmed and set by hand on the artwork, then masked appropriately in order to sit on top of or be reversed out of the picture or ground. To the untrained eye, a piece of camera-ready artwork seldom looked like it was ready to be photographed. It would typically be festooned with small pieces of paper carrying type; black marker pen would be used on the tissue paper covering the artwork

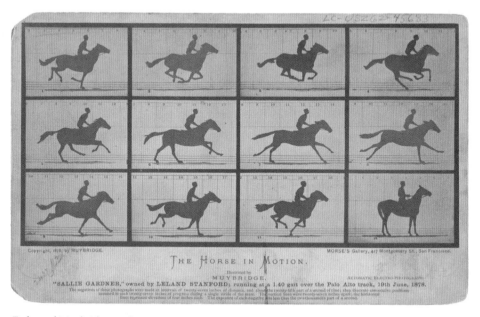

Eadweard Muybridge used 24 cameras, triggered by tripwires, to photograph a horse, perhaps unwittingly prefiguring the standard frame rate of motion-picture cameras. The experiment took place in 1878 in Palo Alto, now the epicentre of Silicon Valley.

with instructions for the printers, as well as in the slug area around the art-work. Bleed would be marked up by hand, as would the guides to the artwork in colours that the camera's orthochromatic film would not register.

There could be bits of tape holding things in place, great swathes of *impasto* or objects attached to the artwork to be photographed, or a paste-up copy of an image, drawing or photograph. With printed media, the world is col-lapsed into 2-D. The substrate or surface to be printed upon is itself a flatland of our making, whose geometries and rules are determined by our human technological prowess and filled with our stories, our humanity, the form of our lives.[15] Now there are technologies on the way, and in part already in existence and use, that will take the world of information as we understand it and create a new paradigm of visual communication in the shape of 3-D printing and the elision of live graphics and information with a view of the world through a lens.

More 3-D than 3-D

So-called AR, MR and XR (augmented realities, mixed realities and cross reality) take a view of the world and lay information upon it, either via the screen of a smartphone or via headsets. Naturally, Google was among the first to this party with its Google Glass project, which in the early teens of the 21st century looked briefly at the future and then, just as quickly, looked away again.

There are many reasons for the slow gestation of Google Glass since 2012. The widespread denigration of early adopters as 'glassholes' is one. The doubtful readiness of the world to accept digital wearables as normal fashion, rather than a badge of nerd-dom, is another. At the moment, Google Glass is not a realistic way of blending 2-D info with the 3-D world in real time.

Even so, Google Glass is still going as a development project. And because it seeks to overlay information on the world, in what could be seen as a con-temporary real-time version of what Saul and Elaine Bass achieved with the titles for *North by Northwest*, or the chyron-heavy news feeds of so-called mainstream media, it's hard to imagine Google pulling the plug. Indeed, with the announcement by Facebook of its tie-up with the sunglasses man-ufacturer Ray-Ban to manufacture sunglasses called Ray-Ban Stories replete with cameras, speakers and microphones, or Snapchat Spectacles, which at the time of writing are in their third iteration, Google would be ill-advised to drop out of the race to make futuristic face furniture just yet.

Whichever company comes to the fore with a workable and wearable solu-tion, the ability to look through a field of type, symbols, images and infographics that float between our eyes and the world remains the holy grail of wearable tech. The real-time titling of the world with a never-ending scroller of AR possibility will appeal to some. Labelling the sequence and simultaneity of real life in this way perhaps became inevitable once time was added to dimensionality in visual communication.

Time-based media

Visual communication of various kinds has been toying with time ever since the sequential possibilities of film were explored by the likes of Eadweard Muybridge (see page 146), Emile Cohl, the Lumière brothers and William Friese-Greene. Film, in the sense of moving pictures, developed across the late 19th and early 20th centuries as an art form in its own right. The beauty of the fixity of print, the ease of reading a well-set page, the directness of a well-designed poster, the destination boards of trains and buses, the dense legibility of a newspaper page, the experimental liberation of the page achieved by advertisers and artists, the precision of the typographer's art: all these elements were designed to be locked into the forme and fixed on the page. The advent of time-based media as mass communication meant that the possibility of moving and animating typography could take root. John Barnes Linnett's 'kineograph' of 1868 post-dated the various zoetropes and phenakistoscopes and praxinoscopes that had been in existence since the early 19th century – it was a flick book, or flip book.

The same principle was shared between all these devices: still images in sequence, passing before the eye at a such a speed that the human brain either creates the interstitial frames or is unable to discern the gaps, and full motion is seen. In 1872, when Muybridge arranged his array of cameras and tripwires in Palo Alto, California, to determine for Leland Stanford whether a horse's hooves all leave the ground at some point during a gallop, he used twenty-four cameras. Unwittingly, perhaps, Muybridge set the standard for the 24 fps (frames per second) rate at which films were shot and shown until digital took over.

Mastery of the pixel

There is argument around what was the first film to be shot entirely on digital cameras, but by the mid-1990s films such as *Windhorse* were shot digitally by prototype and prosumer Sony cameras. Famously, *Star Wars, Episode II: Attack of the Clones* was the first major film to be shot and post-produced entirely on digital formats, though the finished film had to be transferred onto 35 mm for showing in some theatres. Prior to mainstream film production coming to rely on the pixel, digital post-production was where the true innovation in image-making and visual communication lay.

I had the luck and privilege of starting to work with the Tomato studio around 1993/94, when it was located on the top floor of a narrow building in D'Arblay Street in London's Soho. At that point there was a true reliance on analogue techniques, but an excitement around the adoption of the new digital.

It was not unusual to arrive at the studio to find a bunch of people grouped around a large piece of paper spread out on the old parquet floor, all making marks on each others' marks. A hand print, or a random ink-rollered slab of solid black. A sheet of acetate would be scrubbed across the floor and then scanned to create a one-off 'grain' that could be overlayed on some letterpress. Dyeline machines, used by architects to create blueprints, would be repurposed with drawings and photographs fed through to create complex, multilayered, blue-tinged long graphic pieces, once ostensibly as an unfinished project based on the *Epic of Gilgamesh*. Lastly, in the studio, the fax machine was repurposed. Its thermal paper could be 'drawn' upon with any appropriate heat source, or alternatively, marks made could be fed through the machine and the paper speed varied (with a thumb on the roller, or by pulling the paper) to create original, unrepeatable analogue markings. One member of the studio, I forget who, claimed to have made a 1-km-long drawing using fax paper.

Outside of the studio, other opportunities offered themselves for making graphic marks like no others. The glass in the gate of the camera could be manipulated; torches could be shone directly into rostrum cameras; odd materials like spaghetti, string and wire could be photographed. Prisms could be rotated to create specular flares. The output of the studio was remarkable both for the way it looked and the ways in which it was made. Rough-edged, in motion, unfinished but composed, typographically dense or classically set. These people knew what they were doing. However experimental the methods, they were underpinned by a solid training in making visual communication.

I didn't know what I was doing at the time, but I was an enthusiastic experimenter. My input initially was mainly in the form of the written word, but inevitably, as is often the way in a busy studio, opportunities arose to join in and cross boundaries and, above all, to learn. It took a while before I made anything worthwhile in terms of the execution of visuals, but conceptually, narratively, I was OK. Conversation and collaboration were key.

There were everyday mysteries to be unravelled as the studio moved into making more and more television commercials. Prior to the development of

Mechanization defined modernity in many areas of culture, from music to science to entertainment. Mastery of machinery, and the techniques needed to make machines work at their optimum, drove the occupation of channels of communication.

Adobe's After Effects program and other software available to all, how was type made to glow, drift, move or glimmer; to build itself against a shifting backdrop of light?

The suites in the post-production houses of Soho seemed to me at the time to be akin to a flight deck, or the bunker control room of a world domination enterprise. They were softly lit places, with Aeron chairs and arrays of high-resolution monitors. Runners arrived with drinks and food while the director worked closely with the operator, or rather Flame artist, on the footage. Relighting, moving, rebuilding. Tape or film would be digitized and transferred into the machine. A workflow would be created on screen that looked something like a mind map, except the elements of it could be picked up and joined to each other. Below was an edit line in which the sequence was composited. The Flame artist used what looked like a pen to control and create everything, accessing the interface by 'drawing' on a pad. In the mid-1990s, this was revolutionary stuff. Rendering, heavy relighting or CGI would take place overnight.

The strapline of the software company Autodesk is 'Make Anything'. This is the company that was behind the invention of the technology – a suite of software designed for compositing, correction, design and VFX – to control the qualities and perception of each pixel in an image, on an individual and collective level. It was, and remains, a revolutionary innovation. Something similar had been happening with Adobe Photoshop for some time; Adobe actively promoted a 'Masters of Photoshop' nomenclature in the 1990s. Indeed, I remember being on a judging panel in Tokyo some time in the late 20th century with someone holding that title; their work seemed mainly to consist of depictions of unfeasibly proportioned women in the process of turning into motorcycles.

The difference between a dot and a pixel is an important distinction. Think back to how images came into being in newspapers and magazines. Colour separation and the halftone governed the reproduction of images in news, advertising and many other forms of visual communication. The dot in print is a physical manifestation of a mechanical process, whereas a pixel is a virtual/physical division of a screen area. The quality of an image, in print or on screen, depends upon resolution, or the number of pixels or dots in a given area. The human eye is an amazing thing, as is the brain. Given enough information, the brain will 'fill in' the missing information to create an image, invert it so we see it the right way up and make sure that our perception of colour is consistent. This is much like the perceptual trick that happens with film at 24 fps. The eye only needs 300 dots per inch (dpi) for there to be a crisp, richly detailed image. Even at 150 dpi – the resolution at which most magazines are printed – things look pretty good to us. The first dot screens were 58 dpi.

It's different on screen, though. Resolutions have been increasing in density since the pixel took over from the cathode ray tube in around 2008, when Sony stopped manufacturing its Trinitron sets. Trinitrons ran at 480i, meaning there were 480 vertical lines interlaced. Now, the standard 4k screen displays a minimum of 3840 × 2160 pixels. That's more than 8 million points of light. Resolutions climb still higher with the most recent screens, capable of 8k – 7680 × 4320 pixels. That's 33 megapixels, or more than 33 million pixels. The computational power needed to alter the relative characteristics of each pixel, to make things look 'real' to the eye of the viewer, has determined the speed at which visual communication can be digitally manipulated.

In the early days of Autodesk's Flame and Inferno suites, when rendering a relatively short sequence, the machine would be set to work overnight and

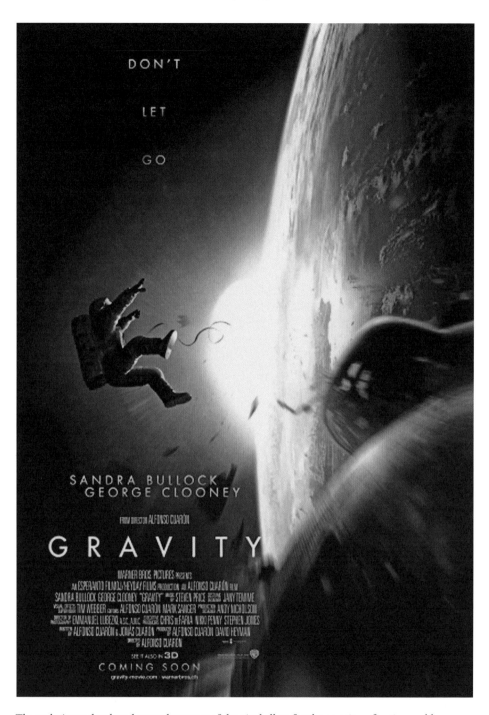

The techniques developed around mastery of the pixel allow for the creation of entire worlds. Chris Parks, stereographer on *Gravity* (2013), has noted that if they'd had to render all the effects for the film on one computer, it would have taken 7,000 years.

all concerned – save for those in the machine room – would go home, returning to see the results in the morning. Increases in processing power have shortened those times considerably. Chris Parks, the stereographer on Alfonso Cuarón's Oscar-winning feature *Gravity*, has noted that if they'd had to render all of the effects for the film on one computer, they would have had to start 7,000 years ago to meet the release date.[16]

Moore's law, framed in 1965 by Gordon Moore, the co-founder of Intel, and revised in 1975, states that computing power will double every two years. But there are physical limits to this exponential growth. There are only so many transistors that can fit on a chip, after all, and quantum and bio-computing are still ideas rather than functioning realities. It remains to be seen what this will mean for the generation of the images with which we communicate with one another. Our reliance on connectivity and computation seems, now, to be a given. But how did we get to this point, and where will we go from here?

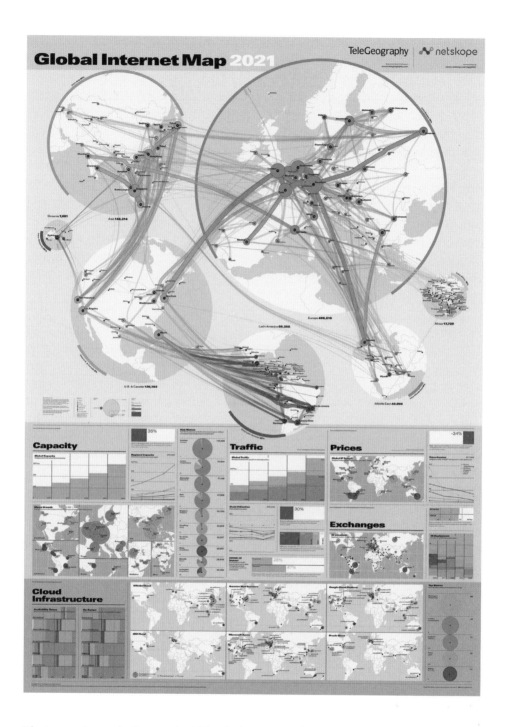

The internet is now the framework within which a torrent of visual communication swirls around the globe, some parts of which are more enabled than others to indulge. Look, for example, at the number of exchanges in sub-Saharan Africa.

Part Four

The Digital World

Amazing tales of information storage and retrieval

My first experience of international computer connectivity took place in 1988 in an upstairs room of either the National Art Library (NAL) or the British Library, during an induction into the workings of the place. As this was over thirty years ago the memory has faded, but I suspect it was the former, as this was during my time studying at the Royal College of Art and the Victoria and Albert Museum.

I had an odd relationship with the NAL. To supplement the student bursary (yes, we were paid to take a postgraduate degree back then), I took a part-time job there. If you haven't visited, I recommend it: it's a magnificent galleried room, with tall windows facing an internal courtyard and a large skylight diffusing sunlight from above. The gallery is lined with bookshelves and from up there you are level with the huge globe chandeliers, which are always illuminated. Down on the reading floor, leather-topped desks hold green-shaded lights mounted on the mahogany screen dividing you from the reader opposite. It's quiet in the room, and a great place in which to research.

It's even quieter backstage in 'the stacks', the bookshelves, which are not such a great place to work, read or research. Dimly lit, dusty and fusty, the seemingly endless runs of boxes, books and binders were a labyrinth made navigable by the Dewey Decimal System. I would end a day there with the acrid smell of book dust in my nostrils and its fine grain under my nails.

The process of book retrieval from the stacks was enabled by a system worthy of Terry Gilliam's 1985 film *Brazil*. A three-part carbon-paper docket would be filled out by the reader. Original retained at the desk, one retained by the reader and the third, the faintest copy, dispatched via a vacuum tube upstairs to the Library Assistant (me). The dockets would arrive in the tube with a hiss and a bang encased in a steampunk glass bullet, the top unscrewed and a fistful of thin papers withdrawn. Then off I'd go to the shelves for books, pamphlets and sheaves. Sometimes things were easy to find; at other times, perhaps a single sheet in a box that had not been opened for years, less so. Once retrieved, the books would go into the dumbwaiter with the docket, to be distributed on mahogany and brass book trollies by the librarians. At quiet times, though, I would disappear into the stacks and randomly open boxes, finding some Max Ernst drawings in one, a Cruickshank cartoon in another, a Wadsworth print in another. I loved the place and at times, mostly on sunny Saturdays, I hated it too. I detail this process of retrieval of information, a system that had been in place for centuries, because of what happened next.

Whoever it was inducting us students into the mysteries of the library and its uses concluded the tour with an introduction to a computer terminal. This, we were told, allowed for searches of resources 'outside the library'. To be clear, this was happening pre-internet. The internet did not come into being proper as a public domain until at least 1993, when Tim Berners-Lee, then researching at CERN, worked out how to link hypertext documents via nodes of accessibility, thus forming the world wide web.[1]

Searching outside the library: where, for example? Well, we were told, we can search American databases from here. At the time, I was working on researching the provenance of a Tschudi harpsichord, so any route into the history of 18th-century musical instrument manufacturers was welcome. I asked the librarian to access the 18th-century short title catalogue held in a library in California.

Remember, it often took a couple of hours to find and deliver just one book for a reader in the NAL, so when after a couple of minutes the dot matrix printer in the corner began to buzz back and forth over the sprocket-fed paper, lined with what looked like faint blue musical staves, I was amazed. Perhaps more accurately, I could not understand what had just happened. A computer I was looking at in London had communicated across the Atlantic and then across the entire continent of the USA to the West Coast, 'asked' for a catalogue, and here it was being printed in front of me.[2] It was explained that the files, the catalogue, remained over there some 6,000 miles away. I boggled. And later on, as I leafed through the concertina of paper (they generously gave me the printout), I boggled again.

Although I did not know it, I was being granted a glimpse of the birth of internet style connection as a useful tool – and although I wouldn't send an email myself for several more years, I would say that this early experience gives me a different view of the digital world from that enjoyed by a so-called digital native. Along with anyone else born prior to 1994, I have seen the internet grow from a distribution network relying on simple, text-based instructions to a torrent of visual content, communication and stimulus.

And yet the terminology used to describe this astounding technology remains archaic. Yes, we understand that there are web servers and that what we see on our screens and devices is the result of Hypertext Markup Language (HTML), cascading style sheets and Javascript enabling browsers to find and present web pages. But: *pages. Script. Sheets. Text.* The scriptoria of today, it seems, are occupied by coders.

The decision to call web pages 'web pages' harks back to the origins of web content and the difference between a static and a dynamic piece of content. Originally, web content was fixed – often a simple combination of text and images – or, in its earliest form, just text. The web was designed to be read, so: pages. Then, as the world wide web grew, web pages, each one with its own universal resource locator (URL), were 'bound' together to form websites. If a website is made from static content, the analogy of a website to a book – pages bound or, more correctly, linked together – just about holds. Things changed later, when two main events came together. Firstly, the main players in delivering the engines of experience driving the internet decided to collaborate and standardize rather than compete. This process of development continued throughout the 1990s.

Avoiding a 'Betamax versus VHS' type of battle in this way helped to ensure access to the internet via the world wide web using a common set of protocols. Secondly, this meant that the generation of rich content, or multimedia, could be enabled by dynamic pages; that is, environments where text, image, moving image and sound could be assembled on the fly with access to the servers via your web browser of choice. In an instant, the analogy of a web 'page' became obsolete. So-called 'runtime environments' made the web a time-based medium – a compositor and deliverer of multimedia.

Crucially, time on the web is not finite as it is in film or television or video. There is an infinite space in which the centre, to coin a phrase, is everywhere. The duration of user experience of the web is determined by the user.

Things we take for granted now were once revolutionary in terms of what this medium could deliver. Consequently, occupying the space and interacting with the world wide web demanded a new set of skills from both users and content creators. Some are more adept than others at using the network and generating content.

Secret channels that everyone knows

On 29 January 2019, the make-up guru James Charles was scheduled to open a new store for the Morphe cosmetics brand in Birmingham's Bullring shopping centre in England. His appearance was due to last thirty seconds.

Thousands of fans showed up for a glimpse of their idol. Traffic was stuck in huge jams around the centre of Birmingham, and the police and the shopping centre security teams found themselves managing a critical incident. Crucially, the authorities were taken by surprise. They had no idea who Charles was; no idea about the extent of his reach then or his direct connection to his audience, who that audience might be, or by what means his

Crowds gather for the opening of the Morphe store in Birmingham in 2019. The social media-inspired flashmob took the authorities by surprise.

following had been achieved. The gathering of the crowd had been enabled by social media. If you weren't subscribed to Charles on YouTube or following him on Twitter – and clearly the authorities weren't – you would have no way of anticipating what was about to kick off.

A lot has happened in the world of make-up since then. Early in 2021, James Charles's YouTube channel was temporarily demonetized while allegations of grooming and inappropriate texting to minors were investigated. Charles returned to YouTube some months later, but the rapidity with which such a prominent social media star can find themselves at the wrong end – or rather, trapped in the central reservation of – the information superhighway is itself a testament to the power of the network and its gatekeepers, even if much gatekeeping of the internet seems to happen *post factum*.

Charles seems to have been a longtime adept at more traditional media, too: not many high school students would think, as he did, to ask for a reshoot of their yearbook photo, and even fewer would bring their own ring light and make-up to what would usually be a workaday shoot. The effect of a ring light in portraiture is to give a soft, diffuse, even light. Importantly, the light creates a specular highlight in each eye, a kind of cartoonish, almost anime addition of vitality and character and a point of focus for the way humans read each other's faces. The almost 9 million images uploaded to Instagram every day, the further millions on Flickr, the others on TikTok,

Snapchat, Twitter, Parler, Twitch, Telegram and Periscope, are mostly the work of individuals. Consequently, huge amounts of data now flow around the planet; it has been estimated that 90 per cent of the world's data has been created in the last two years.[3] The drivers behind this kind of growth are rooted, in part, in the dopamine hit of the new,[4] and the new denizens of internet influence are experts at creating the kind of flow of image and speech that occupies the social media frame in a compelling way.

To watch one of Charles's YouTube videos from start to finish is to see in action a relatively new area of design culture, emerging from the collision of an unquenchable thirst for online content with the inevitability and now seeming ease of monetization of a digital presence. He is not alone: there is an occupation of the online space by influencers such as NikkieTutorials, Zoella and Olivia Neill that is hyper-photoreal, as 4k hi-def becomes the norm and the online screen image becomes ever more detailed. Faces are defined by make-up, flatness of tone, definition of eyes, lips and brows, moving the appearance of the human further towards that of the avatar or Memoji.

Other YouTubers like Markiplier occupy the world of games as a picture within a picture, making their way through first-person shooters and puzzles; and one of the platform's giants, PewDiePie, with his 110 million subscribers, can rack up 3.2 million views in a month for a video of himself watching and commentating on TikToks, in a circle jerk of internet interest. In every case, graphics appear as overlays, 'popping' and moving and glowing. This elision of the real with the augmented real behind the screen is a seemingly innocuous but, in fact, extremely significant development in our relationship with online visual communication. It represents a new type of screen experience, as the encoded use of elements originally used in apps on mobile devices and elsewhere migrates to the carefully controlled realm of the YouTuber. More importantly, perhaps, as YouTubers, TikTokers and Instagrammers invent and perpetually reinvent themselves on screen, the avatar and the influencer are becoming indistinguishable: a perfect hyper-real, digital, infinitely malleable, shamanic second-life rendering of self crosses into the real, emotional, internal world of the viewer. The presence of these outrider avatars prefigures the selves we may all have the opportunity to become, once artificial intelligence and the internet combine to create spaces in which we can be who we want to be: our own heroes, just for one day.

Joining the dots that led to the creation of deeply flawed internet supernovas like Charles, PewDiePie or their myriad fellow influencers is not so difficult. The Z plane, once the playground of constructivists, Dutch masters and Chinese engravers, has become a kind of bridge connecting the real world to the Asgard of digital space. The colonizers of the new digital space are the influencer and the 'new-verb' subcategories of vlogger, TikToker and

Instagrammer. These new content providers have become the users of a communication space in which empathy encoded as visual communication is the principal currency of engagement. Crossing the fourth wall of the screen is an emotional journey.

The rapid career trajectories of influencers herald a new chapter in the design of visual communication, one in which design is as much about the way individuals present themselves and occupy space as it is about art directorial, directorial or graphic elements (although these are also all present). As entities and occupiers of communication channels such as YouTube, which are technically determined and therefore as rules-based as any earlier channel we can name, such cultural icons are under pressure to create ever more engaging content. The race for cut-through and emotional connection can lead them, and consequently their viewers, to some dark places. For instance, in the case of ReSet (twenty-year-old Kanghua Ren of Barcelona), the desire to monetize, connect and create a profile led to him filling an Oreo cookie with toothpaste and paying a homeless man $20 to eat it. He then filmed the man vomiting five minutes later. ReSet earned advertising revenue from the thousands of views of the clip that took place before it was deleted.

The results of humans occupying online space as avatars are not always as indicative of our baser instincts. In February 2021, during a period of lockdown, lawyer Rod Ponton took part in a Zoom conference call for the 394th Judicial District Court of Texas under Judge Roy Ferguson. Ponton was using his secretary's computer, and had omitted to adjust the filters she had been using with the software. The result was that Ponton, a middle-aged white male, appeared at this judicial hearing as a rather worried-looking white kitten. The software he inadvertently used maps a cat filter onto the user's face, synching it with their lip and eye movements. On the Zoom call, the cat/lawyer appears to speak and utters the surreal, gnomic phrase 'I am not a cat.' René Magritte would have been proud.

The Snap corporation (developer of Snapchat) has created another app that speaks to the Zoom software, allowing users to explore an almost infinite variety of characters, animals and personas with which to inhabit the world beyond their screens. The Snap community of users is actively involved in creating these avatars with which people can alter their appearance on video calls. On the one hand, in the context of visual communication this is evidence of a democratization of image-making, showcasing the character development and digital skills that exist within a given group of users. On the other hand, the ease with which digital enhancement can morph into concealment – or worse, believable fakery – should give the world pause for thought. The cheap fake is potentially the precursor to the deepfake – more of which anon.

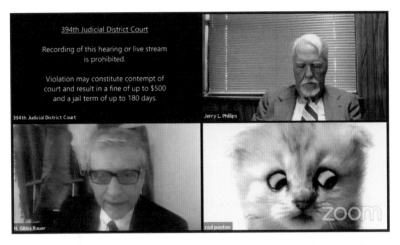

This Zoom mishap in 2021 went viral when a Texas lawyer appeared as a cat. Filters, plug-ins and software have created a new universe of possibilities for enhancing one's visual online presence. Digital natives seem to accept these, but older users can sometimes be confounded by the technology. In the future, Ponton's cat may rival Schrödinger's as shorthand for something existing in two states at the same time.

Break the Internet®

In late 2014, *Paper* magazine attempted to 'Break the Internet®' with a cover image of Kim Kardashian. The magazine's art directors commissioned photographer Jean-Paul Goude for a photo session showcasing the Kardashian rear end clad in glossy black with a champagne glass balanced on it, wine flowing into the glass in an impossible arc over her head.

This image had a long gestation, going back to the print media of the 1970s. Sketches in Goude's notebooks from that period, and his photograph *Carolina Beaumont, New York* (1976), are the direct antecedents of the scenography created for *Paper* in winter 2014. The imagery sits in a strange place between self-exploitation on the part of Kardashian and the questionable traditions of the male gaze on women in general – and in Goude's case in particular, women of colour.

The images from this shoot propelled Kardashian to a new level of fame, largely by dint of her deployment of her own naked form. The photo spread is effectively a striptease ending with an image of her standing on a simple plywood box against a caramel-coloured backdrop, her black dress held around her thighs, a Mikimoto pearl necklace looped around her neck. Her naked, oiled body catches highlights. In the final image she is devoid of pubic hair. Her facial expression is hard to describe: it's a smile, but equally she

Kim Kardashian at the 2021 Met Gala. Kardashian's control of her omnipresent public image
has reached the stage where she can replace her visible recognizable presence with a negative space;
a void into which any and every meaning can be projected by her continuously beguiled public.

might be in the middle of a complicit exclamation: 'Hey!' The champagne glass, gloves and bottle lie artfully arranged on the floor; the bottle is reflected in what is presumably a puddle of champagne.

I say 'reflected', but since the advent of Adobe's Photoshop as a stand-alone application in 1990, every image released in print or digitally has been subject to some form of post-production. The art of the retouch has gone from the deft use of airbrushes, shading and dodging and re-photography to the manipulation of the pixel, so that we can no longer be sure of what we are seeing as photographic reality. Even allowing for that, however, Kim Kardashian is something else. Amanda Fortini, who interviewed her for *Paper*, claims that her skin, nails, teeth, eyes and hair are so flawless in the flesh that it's as if 'she comes with a built-in filter of her own'.5 The lengthy roll call of skilful image makers and manipulators behind the images tells its own story.

The 'Break the Internet®' shoot serves as a good illustration of the relationship we have collectively built between channels and content. In 2018, Entech Media, the publisher of *Paper*, filed to make 'Break the Internet®' a registered trademark. So ubiquitous and easy has the spread of memes, tropes, images and animation become that the half-life of cultural events is impossible to predict. The images from this shoot appeared as print but took flight via the internet. Even now, visiting the relevant pages on *Paper*'s website, each image is adorned with clickable icons to enable sharing on various social media platforms.

I am an individual; we are a community

The spread of these images and many others has been facilitated by the empowerment of the individual as both consumer and distributor. It's possible to see this evolution as a natural consequence of a process that was instigated in the 20th century: namely, the fostering of the agency of the individual. Arguably, this rolling phenomenon has had a major impact on the culture of visual communication in the 21st century. What do I mean by this and how so?

Well, there is perhaps a gulf of difference between someone like me, who lived through the 'birth' of the internet as a usable tool and yet was unable to get his head around just how the technology functioned, and someone born after, say, the year 2000. It's a question of the culture in which we find ourselves. I am a 'boomer' – part of the generation born between 1946 and 1964 – while my daughter and her friends are digital natives. The former is astounded while the latter seems to take the wonder of the internet very much for granted.

To be part of the boomer generation is, I would suggest, in a developed Western nation, to be at least aware of the tenets and benefits of the post-war collective contract. This is hard to express concisely but if, as I mentioned earlier, you have had your education at the hands of the state; if your university and postgrad career was fully funded; if your children were born under the National Health Service or its equivalent; if your parents drew their state pension and, when elderly or infirm, were looked after with no money changing hands; if you grew up at a time when you could pop into a local library, swimming pool or gym; if you could rent a house for a reasonable sum from the local council; if you enjoyed parks; if the fire service and the police were present; if the graveyards and crematoria were efficiently run albeit a little municipal in atmosphere; if the buses and trains were managed, liveried and staffed by a central, publicly owned agency; if the flower beds on the roundabout were filled with daffodils each spring – then you would have had a sense of the collective spirit that infused much of the Western world during the years of rebuilding and reconstruction after the Second World War.

Forces were at work on promoting our sense of individuality, however – bent on disrupting that collective sense of responsibility and ownership. So where are the roots of that change, the great shift to the 'me' that has in turn fuelled the boom in visual communication between individuals?

Perhaps, in part, it goes back to Sigmund Freud as part of that great upheaval in intellectual thought that changed the philosophical landscape of fin-de-siècle Europe. Freud's ideas foreground the ego as the mediator of the unconscious mind, the id. The ego is 'the Ich' in German, which, of course, translates as 'the I'; 'Everybody's got one', as the Mike Sammes Singers, directed by John Lennon, remind us on the fade-out of 'I Am the Walrus'. Of course, the recognition and use of individuality and individual agency did not emerge from that one Viennese source, or from a Beatle. But I'm suggesting that some of the groundwork was laid for our current state of siloed, socially mediated solipsism in many subtle ways.

One of these is the construction of the means by which we can indulge in our individual searches for meaning in existence. In part, our obsession with individuality grew out of the discipline of psychoanalysis. Once codified and out there, the plausibility of the idea, the meaning of the individual, changed – even if not all of us can afford the luxury of a one-to-one exploration of the self on a leather couch with a kindly analyst.

There are other pieces of evidence of the change from 'we' to 'me'. Alfred Leete's design for the 'Your Country Needs You' image, featuring Lord Kitchener's foreshortened pointing finger, stern look and handlebar moustache, rightly became iconic. It's essentially a modern piece of advertising and first appeared on the cover of a magazine, the *London Opinion*. It was only

Leete's design broke the 'fourth wall' in an innovative way in order to appeal to the individual to act in the interests of the many.

deployed as a poster in late September 1914, after the first frenzy of enlistment, so its impact on the numbers of volunteers is difficult to determine. What's interesting about it in this context, though, is the way it places the demands of the collective onto the individual. The country (collective) demands that you (the individual) subsume yourself for the greater good. At that point in time, at the beginning of the 20th century, this seemed a reasonable request. It's hard to imagine the call-up to the army to fight in an ongoing war working in the same way today, with a similar campaign. But why? The answer cannot be pinned down easily. I'm happy, instead, to try tying together a few disparate strands of a changing culture that may help characterize the rise of the individual and, ultimately, its effect on visual culture.

The advent of psychoanalysis is only one element in the mixture of influences that altered our relationship to ourselves. Politics, too, played its part. Much has happened in the political sphere but a few things remain salient. The legacy of Margaret Hilda Thatcher has spread beyond its original domain of the United Kingdom. When she came to power as prime minister in 1979, the nation was not in the best shape economically or societally. The then Labour government was beset with troubles. The union with Scotland was an issue, and the collective bargaining power of the unions with their old

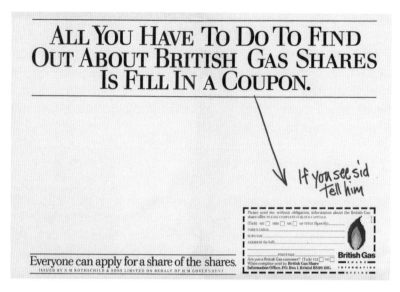

The childish 'humour' behind this advertising campaign to sell off national assets to the private sector was deemed necessary by Thatcher's Conservatives in order to soften the public attitude to their newly minted, often rabid adherence to free-market ideology.

alliance and connection to the Labour Party was a target for the newly elected female PM. The cult of the individual was fostered by a Conservative ethos that saw advertising as being in league with politics, not only helping to fight elections but to promote the selling off of publicly owned assets such as the railways, the national air carrier, water companies, bus companies and council housing – all with the view to creating a 'property-owning democracy' fed by the 'trickle-down' system unleashed by free-market economics and the deregulation of the financial markets – the so-called 'big bang'.

By the mid-1980s, childish but successful advertising campaigns ('Tell Sid' for the sell-off of the national gas industry, for example) created a sense that the individual could gain a foothold in the workings of the country in a way that had previously been the preserve of only the wealthy, or those with access to stockbrokers. My own family fell for it, owning some £133.00 worth of British Gas shares that were never traded or cashed in. Later, my wife and I bought a Smeg range cooker for our first house with the unasked-for windfall from the sell-off of the Abbey National building society: a mutual turned into a bank. In the meantime, the bulk of the shares from any sell-off were snapped up by the usual financial institutions.

In 1981, on the other side of the Atlantic, Ronald Reagan had become president of the USA and ushered in a new era of conservative economic policy-making. Reaganomics, as it became known, is essentially a free-market approach, shrinking the state and its take of taxes and so state expenditure, and thrusting the onus for survival onto the individual. Reaganomics was hard on some (mostly the poor), but its apologists point to it as ushering in an entrepreneurial decade wherein small companies could flourish and grow. Companies such as Apple, for example. The mythology of driven entrepreneurs working hard to create wealth is pervasive and, to some, persuasive. Such an idea has a tangential but powerful effect on the culture as a whole, and on visual communication. Cultural change can be bolstered by political thought.

Britannia Unchained is a pamphlet written in 2012 by Dominic Raab (who, between 2019 and 2021, was Foreign Secretary), Kwasi Kwarteng (Business Secretary), Priti Patel (Home Secretary), Liz Truss (once Trade Secretary and then Foreign Secretary) and Chris Skidmore, who until 2020 was Minister of State (Department for Business, Energy and Industrial Strategy) (Universities and Science). It's unclear what Skidmore subsequently did to put himself outside the inner circle, but he and his former co-authors celebrated individuality in a curious way. Their 'book' contains the following passage: 'Once they enter the workplace, the British are among the worst idlers in the world. We work among the lowest hours, we retire early and our productivity is poor. Whereas Indian children aspire to be doctors or businessmen, the British are more interested in football and pop music.'[6]

This is of course not true, of the British nor of Indians, and it never was. But it's a convenient (for the authors) characterization of the qualities of individuals in order to advance a spurious argument. To be clear, this execrable generalization is the work of people later appointed by Boris Johnson, ex-Bullingdon Club member, part-time journalist and prime minister, to run the country. *Britannia Unchained* is a sloppily argued bulletin containing the usual slew of economic percentile analysis bolstered by highly selective anecdotal 'evidence'. The whole thing is a paean to a particularly socially corrosive form of individualism. It posits the idea that government's role should not be to support the individual and to glue individuals together into society, but rather to create conditions in which people feel their only option is to 'work harder' as siloed beings in a brutal, sink-or-swim world.

Fast-forward to the COVID-19 pandemic and we can see how ten years of this ideology of state shrinkage, defunding of public services, so-called and unnecessary 'austerity' in the wake of the banking crisis and a squeeze on education, NHS capacity and social security has affected the country. Britain has seen the worst death rate in the world, and the worst economic fallout. It turns out that over 165,000 now deceased individuals really did need the government to step up and step in. Who but the state could glue

These images sum up the history of personal photography. The principal differences in the experience of camera use are the ubiquity of the camera (we no longer need to be reminded to take it with us) and the speed with which images are seen and shared.

everything together – and, to stretch the metaphor, make sure that there was enough glue, and that it was strong enough to do the job?

Individualism is not all bad, though; for one thing, the rise of the techno-logically enabled individual has had a tremendous impact in terms of creating visual communication. Everyone, it seems, is making images and showing them to each other. It's not by coincidence that the 21st century became the era of the selfie. 'Selfie' was the *Oxford English Dictionary*'s Word of the Year for 2013. Apocryphally, the term is Australian in origin, with a photo of a cut lip on a night out by an anonymous Aussie having kicked off the whole phenomenon.[7]

The ability to turn the camera on oneself is, of course, not new. Kodak Box Brownies, in 1900, allowed for a cable release, so enabling self-portraits. Then Edwin Land's Polaroid camera made possible a relatively instantaneous photographic view of the self. The game-changer was the arrival of the inter-net-enabled phone with camera, along with the network allowing peer-to-peer communication. The ability to share images of yourself over networks and garner 'likes' from 'friends' you may never have met is evidence of an epoch in the making. Issues of quantity and quality, though, are to the fore.

The confluence of politics and societal change laid the groundwork for the adoption of the ubiquitous smartphone by many the world over. How that powerful pocket computer has come to be used relies on visual communication. The two-way street it once represented has become a battleground for corporations. At the time of writing, Apple is introducing a feature on its phone operating system that will require users to opt in to being tracked by other apps. Facebook, which depends on scraping data from all sorts of interactions, is up in arms at this devolution of privacy to the individual. In America, the iPhone too will scan users' photo libraries looking for illegal images of child exploitation and porn as well as sending data on mental health to centralized servers. We shall see how these initiatives pan out.

Finding and making the tools for individual expression

The roots of individualism and its effects on visual culture exist both in mainstream capitalist culture and in the counterculture. The twin ideas of individuality and community were present at the beginning of the computer age, when networks and connections and the distribution of information were at the centre of the most engaged discourses. The year 1971 (when, incidentally, Steve Jobs and Steve Wozniak, the future co-founders of Apple, first met) saw the final edition of a publication called *The Whole Earth Catalog* (*WEC*) – and there is perhaps no better illustration of the nexus of hippiedom, individualism and consumerism than this weird, partly visual guide to the culture. The *WEC* originated as a kind of *samizdat* handbook for the individualist American spirit. When Stewart Brand started it in 1966/67, it was a catalogue masquerading as a manifesto and working as a tool.

In the age before the internet, information on how to do things like keep bees, husband a goat, dig a well, mix mortar or build a shelter was out there, but it was not aggregated. The *WEC* brought the possibility of access to tools closer, so that it was only a phone call away. During its relatively short existence the *WEC* is said to have moved from an early concentration on individualism to an emphasis on community. Steve Jobs once described it as 'Google before Google',[8] and it's true that the relationship it represented between individuality and community prefigured the way in which many of today's online communities work.

Jobs was reputedly fascinated by the *Whole Earth Catalog* and Stewart Brand's ethos. Brand, for his part, has disavowed the historical shorthand that blames him for everything from Google to Apple and all points in between. He's probably right to do so. But he undeniably had an impact on the culture – particularly the visual culture – of that time. This came about not only through the design and organization of the catalogue, but also the choice of imagery and the thinkers, books, writers and tools it featured.

There were astounding moments of visual invention in the *WEC*. Like others in the counterculture, Brand had heard the rumour that NASA, via the ATS-1 satellite in its geostationary orbit, had taken the first full pictures of Earth. Brand led a campaign for these images to be released. The image of Earth was made from several individual shots; once they were tiled together to create a composite image of the whole planet, this previously unseen view adorned the first edition of the *Whole Earth Catalog*. The so-called *Last Whole Earth Catalog* (1971) would also carry an image of the whole planet on its cover: a version of the famous 'Earthrise' image taken by Apollo 8 astronaut Bill Anders during his lunar orbit on Christmas Eve 1968.[9]

The making of the *WEC* was a collective effort of craft and skill. There's a photo by Richard Drew (an AP snapper) of Stewart Brand and the team working on the last issue in their studio at Menlo Park, CA. They are wielding scissors, creating paste-up under Anglepoise lamps, unknowingly prefiguring the access to information that the internet would bring. This team-oriented approach echoes the work of USCO (the US Company), the art and technology collective of which Brand was a part, whose output covered everything from happenings to psychedelic posters to sound installations. 'Be-ins', where people could inhabit installations for as long as they liked, underlined USCO's use of technology to effect and reflect social transformation.

The last physical *Whole Earth Catalog* looks like a self-published 500-page underground manifesto for self-sufficiency and individuated resilience. But it was ultimately distributed by Random House and won a National Book Award. Across its run of editions from 1967/68 to 1971 and sporadically thereafter, it sold millions of copies and was read by millions more. It was a bridge between the counterculture and commerce; its inky, hands-at-home, cut-and-paste vibe was coupled with an irreverent tone when discussing access to tools and skills with which to keep colonizing the world with ecological responsibility. To wit: 'surveying is the human way of pissing on all the corners of your property, so you know what's yours and what is theirs. it is also a way of leveling, finding corners, mapping. if you are going to use land, chances are you'll run into a survey. this book seems to cover the discipline and use of the surveyor's tools.'[10] This comes from the section on surveying and blasting, which goes on to recommend Charles Breed's book *Surveying* and the *Blaster's Handbook*.

ATS-I DTG(U) 356-6-/8/805 SEQ 6

ABOVE The Application Technology Satellite was launched in 1966. It was a geostationary satellite and carried the Spin Scan Cloud Camera that captured the first image of the full disc of the Earth on 11 December 1966, and in so doing arguably changing forever the way humanity sees itself and its home.

RIGHT The so-called 'Earthrise' images taken by Apollo 8's Bill Anders have been cited as among the most influential environmental images ever disseminated.

A photo by Richard Drew of Stewart Brand and the team working on the last issue of the *WEC*. They are wielding scissors, creating paste-up under Anglepoise lamps – using analogue techniques but unknowingly prefiguring the access to information that the internet would bring.

Page 14 of the *Last Whole Earth Catalog*, in the section on understanding purposive systems, contains this paragraph: 'There is no basic reason why one cannot design a control memory with a different technology, a technology which would allow the computer itself to alter the information stored in the control memory. Thus, we would have a computer that could alter its own character as required. To my knowledge very little conceptual work has been done in thinking through the implications of this extremely powerful possibility. The possibilities are so staggering and deep. The poor harried souls responsible for trying to understand the classical computer as we now know it wish this idea would go away.'[11]

Along with all the practical information about how to build a log cabin or store your seed potatoes, the last *WEC* manages to mention computers some 132 times. This at a point in history where IBM was shipping only 1,000 computers per week. Now remember that Steve Jobs was a fan of the *Whole Earth Catalog* and that Stewart Brand reputedly coined the term 'personal computer'. I don't want to labour the point – and, as we've said, Brand dismisses this connection as a lazy, join-the-dots approach to something quite complex. Of course, conjecture and connection do not amount to causality;

but there was a confluence of ideas at this point in time that resulted in the invention of the personal computer. Then, in the fullness of time, came the personal internet-enabled device in the shape of the smartphone. Fast-forward to 2020, and it's estimated that somewhere in the region of 3.8 billion smartphones were in use around the world.[12] Add to this perhaps a couple of billion usable computers (estimates vary), and we have a situation where there is a two-way street into the pocket and living space of every individual with access to the network. Who uses that street, and for what purpose? The answer varies. Friends and family? Sure. Advertisers and merchants? Of course. Politicians and those with nefarious intent to gain power? Naturally.

Meme, me me, MAGA, gaga

It's still possible, in parts of rural China, for people to wake up in the morning and find their village has been plastered in propaganda posters overnight. These may be exhorting support of the Party or hailing the productivity of the workers or even, more recently, trumpeting an environmental message. Such tactics of visual saturation hark back to the birth of revolutionary communism and the development of the kind of imagery designed to communicate with an illiterate population. From the mythical Stakhanovite heroism of the workers in 1930s Russia, depicted as muscled, questing, socialist over-producers, to the hagiographic depictions of Mao Zedong standing on the Gate of Heavenly Peace on the first day of October 1949 and announcing the birth of the People's Republic, the propaganda image has been a powerful political tool.[13] Now, although such posters appear only occasionally in the West (cf. Nigel Farage and 'Breaking Point', as discussed in Part Two, or the Conservatives' 1997 'Demon Eyes' poster featuring Tony Blair), propaganda and advertising have nevertheless successfully elided.

In the case of the Chinese village, arguably the point is not solely in what the posters exhort the populace to do, believe or simply see, but also in the power of the state to roll in, put the posters up and then roll out again.[14] This is blanket communication, akin to a carpet-bombing of imagery. Image saturation can create a kind of blindness to the content, but the fact of its existence on the walls and lamposts cannot be denied. And, as the People's Republic and other actors now know, the propaganda poster is only one somewhat outdated weapon in the armoury of communication that keeps the population politicized.

Our phones and computers – that two-way street in the pockets and parlours of internet users – have become the favoured channel through which,

in democracies, political parties seeking power can reach the crucial undecided voter. I say 'voter', singular, because the way that this industry has
evolved over the last decade has allowed for the targeting of ever smaller
cohorts of people, eventually leading to specific individuals.

The UK Parliament's *Inquiry into Disinformation and 'Fake News'*, undertaken in the wake of Donald Trump's election victory and the narrow win
for Vote Leave in the advisory and non-binding 2016 Brexit referendum,
took place in 2019. In the course of the proceedings, the frightening extent
to which mass communication can be nuanced to individual taste became
apparent. Inevitably, machine learning and artificial intelligence were
involved. The report says that 'three machine learning pipelines were used
to process both text and images. The software could be used to read photographs of people on websites, match them to their Facebook profiles, and
then target advertising at these individual profiles.'[15] There are further tools
out there, mostly unknown to users, that also help the machines to 'scrape'
data from other unrelated sites and build profiles of individuals. Companies
such as Cambridge Analytica, Facebook and Google can then use that data
in whichever way they see fit.

Gustav Klutsis, *Long Live Stalin's Breed of Stakhanovite Heroes* (1934, Tate). An amazing lithographed
photomontage: note the detail in the organization of the adoring crowd, and the freedom with
which scale and perspective have been used.

Further on in the report, the committee comments on Facebook Pixels: 'The Facebook Pixel is a piece of code placed on websites. The Pixel can be used to register when Facebook users visit the site. Facebook can use the information gathered by the Pixel to allow advertisers to target Facebook users who had visited that given site. AIQ definitely utilized Pixels and other tools to help in data collection and targeting efforts.'[16]

So much for the toolkit used to build the profiles. What did this individually targeted visual communication look like? After all, here we are at the new frontier of the interface between ideas and consumers; so, presumably, the anonymous designers of these ads must be pushing the envelope of graphics and typography, the better to connect with their audience of undecided voters?

Sadly, even a cursory glance at the ads deployed during the Brexit campaign or the Trump election campaign reveals a sorry lack of inspiration. As with the 'Breaking Point' poster, these propagandists aren't interested in the niceties of design or design innovation. What they are interested in is impact: both visual and emotional, as well as the connection between the two.

Perhaps the amateurish composition and typography functions as a non-threatening way of catching the viewer's eye. Perhaps it was felt too much design would get in the way of the message. Certainly, it became ridiculously easy to measure the effectiveness of these seemingly thrown-together ads. On the occasion of the third US presidential debate in 2016, the Trump campaign tested 175,000 different ads in a single day.[17] The Vote Leave campaign used a billion ads in its final week of campaigning. This unparalleled outpouring of potential connection with voters on an emotional and individual level is perhaps an inevitable consequence of the collision of machine learning and rapid iteration of ideas with the industry built around information and persuasion – advertising.

The full history of advertising can't be discussed here for obvious reasons, but the salient principles of mass communication to consumers were set fairly early on. The famous Victorian ad for Pears' Soap has been analysed *ad nauseum*, but there's a reason for that: it had all the ingredients of a powerful static Out of Home (OOH) nailed at the very birth of the advertising industry.

Advertising has always stolen or borrowed from high culture and the precedent for this was set in 1887, when Thomas Barrett bought the rights to Sir John Everett Millais's sentimental oil painting *A Child's World* (also known as 'Bubbles'). The significant thing here is not the simple fact of a work of art having been appropriated for commerce, but the ingredients that were brought together in so doing. Arguably the most important element is not the addition of a bar of soap to the foreground of the image (added after the acquisition of rights); nor is it the headline of the ad, with its lovely

The bar of Pears' Soap in the foreground was added after the rights to Millais's painting had been acquired. What are now common techniques of image manipulation and aspirational branding arguably originated here, in the mid-19th century.

rendering of the capital P and the strong compositional sense that almost gives it a contemporary feel. No; for me, it's the gentle expression of wonder on the face of the child. Without wishing to be too sentimental, there's something emotionally resonant about the subject matter and situation. Millais is working here in a symbolic tradition, rendering the image of his grandson spellbound by transient beauty that will soon disappear. It's a metaphor, of course, for life and for the brief innocence of childhood.

The power of the painting as advertising lies in the harnessing of this emotional tug. Nowhere in there is there an exhortation or injunction to buy. Instead – in 1888/89 – the ad is playing not only with our emotions and empathy, but also with ideas of aspiration. Appreciate Millais, and you will appreciate Pears' Soap.

Arguably, Barrett (who was the managing director of the soap company) was on safe ground deploying this image in this way. Millais was a famous and well-regarded artist, his work often reproduced in popular magazines. The Pre-Raphaelite attention to detail, skill and subject matter resonated well with the prevailing norms of Victorian middle-class sensibilities. Barrett got it right, without focus groups or testing of any kind. He knew the image was popular, he knew his product was good – his genius was in connecting the two.

Today, in terms of design and the construction of visual communication, increasingly little is left to chance. There are countless techniques available to map and understand consumers' responses to brands and products. A potential campaign can go to any number of agencies who will test the effectiveness of the idea using an armoury of techniques.

For example, eye-tracking technology is used to eliminate guesswork from the design process. So-called neuromarketing doesn't rely on the talent of, say, an Abram Games or a Tom Eckersley (see page 178) to occupy the advertising space with measured interpretive skill or illustrative inspiration. Instead, design, typography, colour and composition can be tweaked 'on the fly' by testing how the target audience reacts to closely tailored communication.

Traditional market research techniques are still used: gathering a group of people, showing them the work and asking their opinion. But at the more extreme end, marketeers are deploying fMRI technology to measure brain activity based on changes to blood flow to the areas of the cortex wired for seeing. By combining this technique with eye tracking, datasets can be produced that allow for the 'tweaking' of communication in order to make it penetrate the psyche of the viewer more effectively. This is potentially scary stuff for consumers, but moreover for designers it represents a potential demotion from inventor to a factotum of machines. We need to be careful. It's important to preserve the inventive autonomy of designers of visual culture, and not to allow everything in the service of commerce to emerge from a combination of focus groups and AI-derived datasets. But how?

There is a counter-stream to this ill-conceived race to develop visual communication driven by what we subconsciously wish to see, or are drawn to. The internet meme is a phenomenon that is a cross between a shared joke and a genetic mutation. It's not surprising. The term 'meme' was invented by the geneticist Richard Dawkins in his 1976 book *The Selfish Gene*. He wanted a word to convey the idea of a unit of cultural transmission. It's rather brilliant. As he points out, the word evokes memory, echoes the French word for 'same' (*même*) and is a contraction of the Greek *mimeme*, that which is imitated.

For a meme to succeed, it has to be distributed, changed and copied and yet retain something of its origins in all its expressions. It's a little like having children. It would be remiss of any overview of visual communication, when touching on the idea of the meme, to ignore the effect of 'I Can Has Cheezburger?' on the culture.

The impact of cats on the internet is perhaps a subject for another book, but the genesis of the pictorial meme lies in an image of a grey cat, apparently smiling. Emblazoned across it in upper-case, drop-shadowed Impact is

The designer Tom Eckersley, surrounded by the analogue tools of his trade and some of the results.

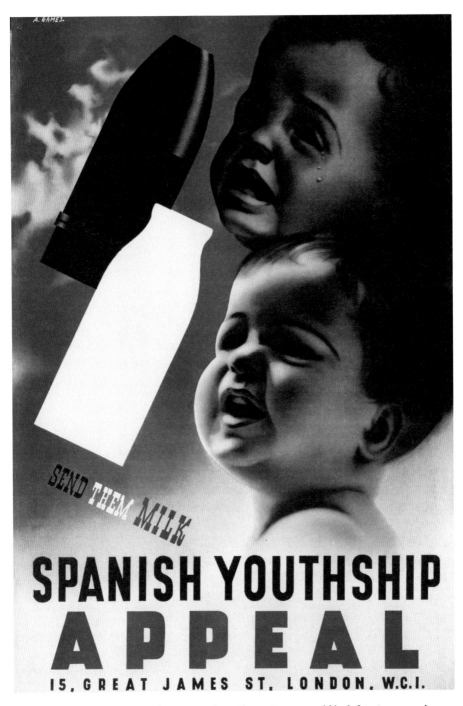

In the mid-twentieth century, designers such as Abram Games would be left to interpret the message and devise images that would deliver the 'shock' that Tom Purvis identified as one of the keys to powerful communication (see page 182).

the question 'I Can Has Cheezburger?' The reasons why this thing came into being are unclear. It inhabited a blog going by the same name, which has now expanded into an internet empire. The blog was originally linked to by an entrepreneur, Ben Huh, who then witnessed a spike in traffic to his own site. Sensing the attractive power of a funny cat picture with a ridiculous caption using badly set type, Huh then paid $10,000 to acquire the blog on which the original 'I Can Has...' appeared.[18]

By 2010, Huh was experiencing some 16 million unique visitors to the fifty-three or more interlinked websites that have become the Cheezburger Network. The Cheezburger Network displays content uploaded by users. It's still featuring cats and captions, Lolcats in the parlance, but has expanded to incorporate other genres of meme. Ten years ago, tens of thousands of users were submitting their self-generated content for consideration every day. Something like 1 per cent of the submissions to the site were used. Today, just one of the sites in the network is still attracting half a million users each month – a figure replicated or bettered by the other websites linked together in the group.[19] The point of this detour into the seemingly harmless world of Lolcats and their aid to time-wasting is simple: the approach to the generation of web-friendly content typified by Lolcats, Cheezburger, Fails and the rest of the internet's filler prefigured what came next.

In choosing a random image and adorning it with the most basic typographic style, but with a humorous edge, I contend that Lolcats paved the way for the similarly simple-seeming but poisonous propaganda of targeted political Facebook ads. The stuff pumped out to sway elections and referendums looks as though it might be home-made. Indeed, the look and feel of it harks back to the way images appeared on message boards such as 4chan back at the birth of the internet. It's a familiar, non-threatening aesthetic that doesn't look like it's had a ton of money spent on it or been 'designed' by experts. In this way, the meme garners a certain sense of authenticity. Replace the humour, though, with a pithily turned phrase warning about a (non-existent) 'threat', such as Turkey or Syria joining the European Union – or raise a question in the mind of the viewer about 'fairness' with the use of alternative or manipulated 'facts' – and you have the ingredients of a deceptively powerful piece of visual communication, ideal for the purposes of propaganda. Lolcat memes softened up the world to a plausible, propagandized political occupation of the digital space.[20]

Memes, then, can be powerful things. It's worth knowing that somewhere in the Carnegie Mellon University School of Computer Science, researchers are working on the maths (or as they would have it, math) to see if they can, by comparing text, image and meaning, invent a system that can 'generate meme descriptions using a simple pipeline'. As they point out: 'Meme is not only about the funny picture, the Internet culture, or the emotion that passes along, but also about the richness and uniqueness of its language: it is often highly structured with special written style, and forms interesting and subtle connotations that resonate among the readers.'[21] The project appears to be about creating a machine-learning pipeline to generate better memes. So even the shonky world of Lolcats is to be honed by machine logic, the better to make memes work.

Education, education, education

For those of us not involved in Natural Language Processing, the point of such an exercise may seem obscure. Do we really need to automate any further the process of filling up the internet? Where to find the answer? We keep coming back to the Bible, and in this case it's for a corruption of Matthew 5:5 in the Authorized Version: *Blessed are the geeks: for they shall inherit the earth.*

Today, the geek has been associated with the digital for some time. The development of arcane knowledge, the maths, the calculations and the logic required to understand and use computer programs, has created the geek-as-archetype. But geekdom was once inhabited by those pre-digital designers driven to understand the available technologies in order to produce the work.

In 1929, in London, Tom Purvis gave a paper to the Royal Society of Arts. Purvis was a designer whose solid block colour lithographs of British seaside scenes, parks, architecture, dining, products and leisure became a staple of advertising languages between the wars (see page 184). In this paper, he tries to square the circle of the relationship between art and commerce. He bemoans the lack of art education dedicated to the burgeoning field of advertising. He acknowledges that the London County Council is doing some good work through its schools at Central and Chelsea; and that further afield, in Bradford, there is an art school where students have decorated the 'motor-van' of a local business.

In a telling passage of the paper, he recalls his former boss: 'He was the hardest worker of the lot of us and an advertising genius. And when I felt I knew more than him – I left. I got a shock. I found that in my special desire to be a poster designer I knew nothing of the practical side of lithographic printing. Back I went into a printers, this time for roughly two years. I believe I could design, lithograph, mix the inks, do the printing and plaster the hoardings with a poster if someone should be willing to pay the enormous fee I should ask for this unique effort.'[22]

This strikes me as worth quoting because it illustrates the usefulness of the journeyman nature of training in creating visual communication for the purposes of commerce. Purvis is very clear on the function of the commercial or applied artist: it's to provide what he calls 'shock value', which in turn creates the 'kick', 'strength', 'visibility and immediate readability' in a piece of communication. To create this shock value, he says, 'this is where your artist, if he knows his job, should be left alone'.[23]

This is a somewhat different approach to the neuromarketers' testing and tweaking discussed above. Arguably, Purvis, who trained at Camberwell School of Art in London, was a product of the traditions in arts and manufactures education instigated by Henry Cole after the Great Exhibition of 1851. Art education, as it developed through the 20th century, became largely a feeder to and an adjunct of industry: the potteries, cutlery makers, lighting designers, furniture makers, knick-knack providers and advertisers. All of them came to rely on the output of courses in illustration, wood, metal, ceramics, fine art and graphics, as well as the specialist colleges for printing that bloomed in parallel with the technology that drove the industry. This was not a phenomenon limited to Great Britain, either. There was the *arts et manufactures* of France, the Bauhaus in Germany; the USA had the Rhode Island School, which had been in existence since 1877, or California College of the Arts, which came into being in 1907; then there was the School of the Art Institute of Chicago, another 19th-century addition. Clearly, when it came to fuelling the demand for expertise in originating and giving form, art and design schools were recognized by the state and industry around the world as essential components in the establishment of a commercial economy. They are arguably just as vital now; training in the techniques of generating quality visual communication is still important.

But commercial economies are seductive things, particularly when they are successful. The logic that the state should fund the education of the creators who fed industry disappeared when, counterintuitively, the UK Labour government introduced tuition fees for universities in 1998, albeit with a cap of £1,000. Perhaps the politicians of the left misunderstood the rapacious nature of markets when there is money to be made. But within a decade the cap had been moved up, first to £3,000, and then to above £9,000 per year by the coalition UK government that came to power in 2010.[24]

This created the conditions for the wholesale marketization of education. In the 'creative' sector, this means that universities such as University of the Arts London (UAL) are able to post an operating surplus of £8.4 million in one year. This is on top of a cash and short-term deposit balance that decreased to £234.6 million in 2020, down from £262.2 million in 2019.[25] The Royal College of Art, on the other hand, holds reserves of approximately

£158 million, having generated a surplus of over £12 million.[26] The RCA and UAL are the two top-ranked art schools in the world. Their impressive financial performance is a result of an influx of international students, who on average pay twice what a student from the UK or, until recently, the EU would pay. At the time of writing, UAL receives 46 per cent of its income from international fees. Similarly, the RCA has some 60 per cent of its students coming from outside the EU.

It's interesting to speculate on how this phenomenon will play out in the future. Students from all over the world are being educated in London and, by and large, being granted degrees. (No one pays tens of thousands of pounds to be told they have failed.) Let's presume that ways of thinking and making are honed within the hothouses of the studio, a melting pot of influences focused on the needs of industry. As this student diaspora returns to its home countries and cultures, over time there's the possibility of a 'flattening' of the culture. The peculiarities of geographic specificity, national styles and the needs of particular markets could experience a reduction in the diversity of ideas and execution in the work these students make once they are out there in the world. It's almost as if the system of education around visual communication is executing a globalist agenda.

Even if that's the case, it doesn't matter. The generation of students currently going through art school or learning to design visual communication in London are digital natives. They are not (yet) hung up on increasingly outdated ideas of national styles and boundaries between disciplines, or else they wouldn't be studying, absorbing, collaborating in the alchemical mix of London's elite finishing-schools-cum-art-colleges.

As a result, already, an advertisement seen on television or YouTube might look as though it has borrowed filters from Snapchat; filters from Snapchat appear on global teleconferencing platforms; YouTube content can look as if it's peopled by CGI-rendered beings; games running on consoles feature dramatic scripted sequences that look like movies; movies in turn can look like games. The intersectionality of different outputs in different channels turns on the mastery of the pixel. Even those die-hard analogue makers – and there are many – represent, distribute and show what they have made via digital channels. Digital is an ineluctable medium joining everything and everyone together in the developed and developing world.

Times have changed. Arriving at Brighton School of Art (then part of Brighton Polytechnic) in 1984, I did not know anyone or indeed much about my subject. I was keen, though. Meeting people on different courses, going to inductions in various bits of the studios, being able to use facilities that were not strictly part of the course I was on: all of this was part of the experience.

Purvis's solid block colour lithographs of British seaside scenes became a staple of advertising languages between the world wars.

Today, and with large sums of money changing hands, students tend to know their cohort before they arrive, finding them through social networks. Before enrolment, new students will have conversations with past students, the course tutors about the course content, aims, mark schemes, teaching and learning.

Putting students in the role of customers changes the dynamic of the educational experience. When I was teaching, I was always clear with potential students I interviewed that the course would unfold; that it was exploratory and collaborative and designed to grow some criticality, invention, fun, magic. Some potential students, thinking of themselves as customers, would demand to see the entire course content, briefs and all before making their decision. From their point of view, they were buying that content – but of course, they weren't. So I said 'no'. What they were buying was the chance, the time, to work out how to work, make and think. How to tell their stories better, make better results, engage with new techniques and ideas; how to fail in the process, and learn from it.

I would always say to a new cohort: 'There is no magic key to becoming the designer you wish to be. It's about thinking, making, working, failing, doing it again and getting better.' That's the process of making visual communication – and whether it's in an educational or a commercial setting, it should not be interrupted by the overweening growth of our dependence on machines, machine learning and the march of the digital.

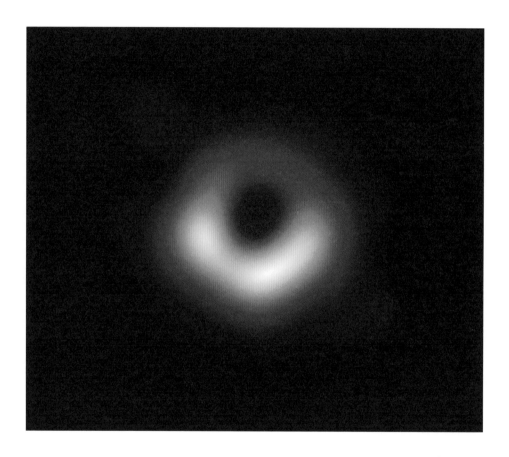

The most amazing image ever to be published in a newspaper, a supermassive black hole churning away in deep space, is on closer analysis perhaps not a true 'picture' of a black hole. Both the origins and the interpretation of the image are complex.

Part Five

Nothing is Real

Nothing is real – or is it?

One morning in April 2019, I was flicking through the newspaper on the iPad. Simple swipes, gestures involving me in a confluence of immense technological achievements: object-oriented computer languages, touchscreens, computing power, servers and graphic design, all coming together to deliver my experience of a newspaper on a screen. I flicked through some stories, some analysis, some editorial – and then on to the science section, where I found an amazing piece of visual communication.

Two things struck me about it. First, it was one of the most extraordinary things I had ever seen; and second, it was a picture in my newspaper's digital edition, with a caption and a column beneath it, just like an ordinary story. It could have been about a journalist making up quotes and being fired for it; or an elected official squandering public money on a vanity project like a garden bridge; but it wasn't. This was the least ordinary thing.

The story was that NASA had released an image of a black hole. This momentous piece of image-making and visual communication had been achieved using VLBI (Very-Long-Baseline Interferometry) and the Event Horizon Telescope (EHT). The EHT is a series of connected arrays around the world, and VLBI is a method of time-stamping their coordination through connection to an atomically powered clock source so that the array – spread around the Earth – continues to 'look' at the black hole as the Earth turns. The black hole is 6.5 billion times the size of our sun in the centre of the M87 galaxy, some 55 million light years away. The EHT builds the picture of the black hole's presence as the Earth spins, hurtling through space at 67,000 miles per hour.

It's an incredible technical achievement, but as I looked at the image on the iPad, I had to ask – what were we actually seeing here? It wasn't a black hole. At least, there is a black 'hole' at the centre of the image, but that's not a black hole *per se*, as a black hole cannot technically be 'seen'. According to Einstein, no light can escape from the dense gravity field. What we are actually seeing is an interferometrically derived rendition of the gases that are silhouetting the presence of a black hole. It is, by definition, not 'real'.

The dissemination of this image by NASA, via the internet and news agencies, represents a continuing faith by state actors in the value of the idea of scientific progress and in the power of the image. Furthermore, the notion of 'seeing' a black hole for the first time resonates with the quasi-religious idea that we are witnessing elements of nature that are far bigger, far more complex and far more terrible than anything humanity can think up for itself.

Perhaps for this reason, the image had to appear as if it were a normal photograph in news feeds, on Instagram, in newspapers and on TV. We had to be able to read it in the way that we read any other news image. The picture of the black hole, therefore, is indistinguishable in some ways from the special effects we're all used to seeing in cinematic renditions of space travel. Looked at in that way, it's disappointing in its ordinariness. It's familiar, but similar results can be achieved with the effects of refraction by shining a torch into a 50-mm prime lens.

The framed, colourized, composite 'photograph' made by NASA nevertheless has a clear function: to depict the un-depictable, to make the invisible visible and to unite humanity in wonder once again. It would seem that if the science is too complicated for the average person to comprehend, then the image has to do the heavy lifting – hence the beauty of the image. In order to communicate, NASA's astronomers have become aestheticians.

In some ways, looking at a spectacular representation of a black hole rather than a picture of the Earth signals an important shift in perspective for humans. The image of the black hole is the obverse of the image of the Earth rising that adorned the *Whole Earth Catalog*. Now, instead of looking back at ourselves on our fragile little blue oblate orb, we are looking out at an event horizon, beyond which is the unknowable, the bending of time and an infinite and certain destruction.

There are other connotations. In *The Society of the Spectacle* (1967), the writer, filmmaker and all-round disruptor Guy Debord wrote: 'All that once was directly lived has become mere representation. All real activity has been channeled into the global construction of the spectacle,' and further, 'The spectacle is capital accumulated to the point where it becomes image.'[1] There is no more spectacular image, I could argue, than that of a supermassive black hole churning away out in deep space. And of course the amount of capital behind the generation of that image is, as Debord suggests, astronomical.

Event Horizon Telescope arrays don't come cheap. It's difficult to put a hard figure on the cost of the EHT – the EU contributed some €13,975,744 to the BlackHoleCam partner organization. Furthermore, the team subsequently received another $12.7 million to fund a *movie* of a black hole. Capital is indeed important, and it translates into spectacle.

Visual communication and capital are the lifeblood of Debord's conception of spectacle. Technology has enabled the spectacle in ways that, a mere five years ago, would have been unimaginable to the ordinary person.

Technology depends upon capital. Now even more ordinary people are contributing to the existence and maintenance of the spectacle – the circus of visual communication and consumption that orientates, compels and shapes us as a society. Social media isn't called that for nothing.

The key to the shifts we are currently experiencing in the ways visual communication is being made to work rest in part on the development of AI or machine learning. The algorithm is the unseen driver of the culture. The latinized leap from the name of the 9th-century Persian mathematician al-Khwarizmi to 'Algoritmi' gave a name to the process that helps shape the spectacle. An algorithm sees a mathematical equation go through a set of predefined steps, incorporating various inputs to come up with an output. Such complex and mind-boggling automated computation results in suggestions for you to follow on your socials; image searches; smart electricity metering; trending notifications on Netflix and Twitter; contacts on LinkedIn; logistics in shipping and air travel; surge pricing; computer chess; computer games in general; bots; automated chats; and many more applications. The spectacle demands our participation and our attention, and there is an ever-growing stream of content designed to secure that attention and make us click through.

The Internet of Fake Things is, paradoxically, a real phenomenon wherein researchers work at developing systems that can scan the continuous outpourings of the web to identify what is real and what is fake. They do this using machine learning, a technology that is extremely good at pattern recognition and comparison. So what kind of things could the new fake-seeking algorithms be detailed to search for? Fake news, certainly; bot-generated internet chat and trolling, for sure; deepfakes and cheap fakes, talking heads and fake sex tapes, images and stories, points of origination, memes and tropes. We have reached a point in the history of viscomm where we need to invent machines to tell us what is real.

Earlier on, when we were looking at Chuck Close and photographic realism, or Nick Ut's photography, this was not a problem. The real was perceived to be, well, real. Photo-manipulation could airbrush history, of course; Leon Trotsky and Lev Kamenev were famously excised from an image of Lenin making a speech to the Red Army. Equally, in the hands of someone like Man Ray or Moholy-Nagy, images that would disturb and delight could come into being: crystalline tears on a woman's cheek (see page 190), or an oddly shaved head, or Herbert Bayer's self-portrait depicting himself as a man with a slice of arm missing. These were accepted 'sur-realities', born at the beginning of a certain kind of photographic image manipulation, the so-called Neues Sehen, which meant that photography was the only place where this kind of *true-made* image could be experienced. Perhaps because of

Man Ray's crystal tears played with the idea of the real at a time when image manipulation was not yet the norm.

the lack of a multiplicity of channels and clear signals that what we were seeing was *not* real, the real was never really in dispute.

Fast-forward to 2021, and we find Raffaela Spone of Bucks County, Pennsylvania, charged with doctoring images, using publicly available deep/cheap-fake technology, to misrepresent her teenage daughter's fellow cheerleaders with the alleged aim of having them kicked off their team. Investigators said that images of a trio of girls on the Victory Vipers squad had been altered so that they appeared to be nude, drinking and smoking. Ms Spone denied all the charges, but the issue as far as we are concerned is not whether or not she did it (she didn't) – nor who is or is not in the ascendancy in the hierarchy of the Victory Vipers. No. The concern here is in the veracity of the seen, and the context in which images are experienced.

Apps such as Zao, Reface, Jiggy and Morphin are designed to help users fill their feeds with amusing visuals. These are for fun. Jiggy, for example, allows the user to plant anyone's face on a professional dancer and thus 'make anyone dance'. But the deepfakes we should be concerned about are not necessarily fun apps like these, clogging up the internet with amusing ephemera – even if they are using power, creating emissions, demanding battery life be extended and more mobile devices be manufactured, and thus changing the geopolitics and economics of the world.[2]

Generative Adversarial Nets came into being in 2014 when a team of researchers at Cornell University published a paper called, unsurprisingly, 'Generative Adversarial Nets'.[3] They determined that by pitting one learning algorithm against another, the outcomes are randomized in such a way that they are able to ape, to a degree, the imperfections and complexity of nature. Their machine learning program was trained using a combination of the MNIST Handwritten Digit Database and the Toronto Faces Dataset.

There are databases in centres of learning all over the world upon which researchers working on machine learning can draw to train their programs in making images that are indistinguishable from real photographs of real people. The parameters of these databases are wide. For example, the AR Face Database includes seventy males and fifty-six females with 'All frontal views of: neutral expression, smile, anger, scream, left light on, right light on, all sides lights on, wearing sunglasses, wearing sunglasses and left light on, wearing sunglasses and right light on, wearing scarf, wearing scarf and left light on, wearing scarf and right light on...'[4] Another, Labeled Faces in the Wild, contains more than 13,000 unique people. The algorithms are able to map and 'understand' recurrent patterns or configurations and reassemble them into new patterns. If these patterns are the basic elements of a face, then the maths can put together the elements of 'a face' in such a way that we humans will read it as real, whether or not it actually is.

This kind of manipulation has profound potential to disrupt through disinformation. In April 2018, for example, a video was published on the news site Buzzfeed ostensibly featuring former US president Barack Obama calling US president Donald Trump 'a dipshit'.[5] This video quickly went viral – even more so when it was revealed that 'Obama' was voiced by Jordan Peele, the performer, writer and director famous for work including the Oscar-winning *Get Out* (2017). Seeing Obama deliver the injunction to 'stay woke, bitches' is a moment of cognitive dissonance employed as a shock tactic to warn of the dangers of deepfake technology deployed in the service of politics (see page 192).

But the deepfake phenomenon does not stop at clever satire of the kind Peele has made. The natural path along which we are going with the capacity to generate believable humans on screen ends with the real being indistinguishable from the fake. This means that actors may be replaced by avatars as a matter of course; and in the case of some actors, that may not be a bad thing. The evening news could be delivered on television by a talking head

Obama's injunction to 'stay woke, bitches' was a moment of cognitive dissonance enabled by deepfake technology – a phenomenon to which, I predict, we will have to become accustomed.

that is indistinguishable from a trusted source (i.e., an actual human). Indeed, in the world of increasingly high-definition broadcast technology, some newsreaders might prefer an unaged version of themselves that will never need make-up or surgical intervention to prepare for a hi-def close up.

In short: the real used not to be up for grabs, but now it most certainly is. Notwithstanding the judicious crop, the power of a real photojournalistic image such as Nick Ut's is indisputable. It served, in its time, to shift opinion on the validity of America's war in Vietnam. Equally, the unknown man carrying the shopping bags, standing in front of the tanks in Tiananmen Square, became an image that – momentarily, at least – signified a shift in the Chinese population slightly further towards a desire for so-called 'Western democracy'. Similarly, no one disputed the images that came from Srebrenica in the mid-1990s, alerting the world to an attempted geno-cide – but today it is possible to dispute the veracity of almost any image, simply because the ability to manufacture believable fakes is in the blood-stream of the culture.

The now infamous 5″ x 7″ colour photograph of Prince Andrew with his arm around the waist of the then seventeen-year-old Virginia Giuffre was found by Michael Thomas, a freelance photographer, in a bundle of images handed to him by Giuffre. And yet, when questioned about the image in interview, the prince has raised doubts as to whether the image is real, claim-ing that while he recognized himself in the picture with Ms Giuffre, it was impossible to know whether it had been faked. Enough uncertainty is now

The portrait of Mao Zedong in Tiananmen Square is a 15' × 20' oil painting that was only taken down once and replaced by a black and white photograph on Mao's death in 1976. The painting has evolved to an idealized image over time. There is a surreal quality to treating a building as a living room wall at this scale.

embedded in the general notion of believing what we see that a prince under questioning can (in his mind, at least) plausibly float the idea that persons unknown have manufactured an image designed to incriminate or embarrass him.

If we reach a point where our ability to trust our own eyes and ears is completely compromised, the consequence will be that trust is placed not in mainstream channels delivering information to us about the world, but instead in individuated and siloed 'trusted actors' who feed information, true or not, to those who believe in them. Truth becomes belief. Fact becomes fiction. Cults rise.

That might sound Orwellian, but in fact it's already happening. The behaviour of Kellyanne Conway, counsellor to the US president, during a *Meet the Press* interview on 22 January 2017 was a symptom of the creeping disease eating away at the culture of truth and the veracity of what we see. During the 'presser', she defended White House Press Secretary Sean Spicer's false statement about the attendance numbers of Donald Trump's inauguration, and floated the idea that Spicer was offering 'alternative facts'.[6] Comparative images of the crowds at Trump's and Obama's respective

Comparative images of the Obama and Trump inaugurations signally failed to counter the misinformation in the minds of those who chose to believe what they were told rather than what they saw.

inaugurations signally failed to counter the misinformation in the minds of those who chose to believe what they were told rather than what they could see. Visual communication of the truth made no difference to the views of Trump's faithful followers.

The phenomenon of alternative truth can be found everywhere. In March 2021, in the wake of yet another revelation about UK prime minister Boris Johnson's extramarital affair with tech entrepreneur Jennifer Arcuri, government press secretary Allegra Stratton described Johnson as someone who 'acts with integrity and is honest'.[7] For a time, there was a plan for proclamations such as this to be delivered from a new £2.6 million flag-bedecked press briefing room inside Number 9 Downing Street. The optics – the visual communication of government authority, of the importance of the flag, of patriotism – were to be used to add plausibility and authenticity, the ring of truth if you like, to anything the government might choose to tell us. Now, however, they won't. It seems the idea of holding a daily Q&A at which the UK press could interrogate the plausibility and veracity of government statements has palled in the wake of ongoing fallout from the pandemic, from the Grenfell Tower fire, from Windrush, from Brexit, etc., etc.

The new press room will still be put to use. It was designed for television: the predominance of the colour blue plays to the brand of the current incumbents of number 10, but blue always reproduces well on domestic TV screens. In terms of staging, the prime minister (or whoever) stands behind what looks like an oaken lectern, flanked by two artfully draped Union flags. The COVID-era hazard warning graphics (*Save Lives!*) on the front of the lectern have been ditched in favour of the Lion and Unicorn seal, dating from the Act of Union in 1603. These heraldic supporters are symbolic: the Lion is England and the Unicorn, Scotland. On the other oaken lecterns in the room are written the words 'Downing Street' in a roman typeface. Behind the central lectern, on the blue backdrop, is a ghostly blow-up of the Lion and Unicorn seal with its legend in middle French, 'Honi soit qui mal y pense' ('shame on those who think ill of it'). The hodge-podge of language, symbolism, colour and meaning in this arrangement, the threads of shadow-gap LED light, the look of matt veneer on the lecterns, the ordinariness of the concept, all lend it a turgid, workaday quality that suggests (mis) understanding of the potential of beaming this visual into the living rooms of the nation.

How much better could the visual communication of governmental competence and authority have been? The corporate blandness of the Pyongyang-lite room decor they've gone for, during the Johnson administration at least, is continuously upstaged by the unkempt and unruly, thinning blond thatch of the prime minister's hair. The press room at Number 9 Downing Street is designed to make us feel a certain way; depending on your sympathies, it may or may not work. Deliverers of today's messages increasingly rely on visual communication to trigger certain feelings in our breasts.

Feelings, nothing more than feelings

In the minds of those creating messages for us, how we feel about what is being said to us is as important as what is actually being said. Our emotional response is conditioned in part by how we receive the messaging. If there is a disconnect between what we are being told and how it's being delivered, we may not believe or invest in the message: it may seem more like fiction than fact. Or a lie rather than truth. But the space between fact and fiction, lie and truth, can be bridged by emotion.

Whether it's for politics or profit, the way we humans communicate visually is an adjunct and a driver of a moral or monetary economy; be it graphic, sculptural, dimensional, documentary or decorative, visual communication rarely, if ever, exists in a vacuum. There is exchange, economic, moral and emotional, implicit in every act of communication. By harnessing

The optics of the flag and of patriotism in the briefing room at 9 Downing Street were intended to lend plausibility and authenticity to the pronouncements of a prime minister and a government with a proven tenuous relationship to the truth.

technology to the act of communication, we are opening up new possibilities of experience and outcome, and at the same time edging ever closer to trying to predict and control what happens as a result.

In 2018, the *New York Times* launched 'Project Feels' – an attempt at getting mood-based targeting of ads to work at a variety of scales. If this somewhat creepy idea can be made to work, then we enter a new realm of communication in which our sense of authenticity is bolstered by how we feel about what we are seeing. Importantly, how we feel is being tracked and the advertising targeted to that feeling in real time. The removal of happenstance, of the chance encounter with emotional resonance by those who wish to communicate with us, has been happening for some time.

The digital, algorithmic tracking of our preferences resulting in the 'if you like this then you might like this' online experience means that increasingly, when it comes to communication, little is being left to chance. We opt in. We accept cookies. We are tracked. All this the better to find the emotional triggers that will inform us and get us to buy, vote, belong, act.

Project Feels and the like have the capacity to be truly innovative in reaching target audiences. For example, by analysing a crowd's social media use in a geographically specific space and by mapping the general feeling expressed via social channels in, say, a stadium, ads on the big screens could be targeted to reflect and enhance the mood of the crowd. The theory is that this kind of empathetic communication would hit people in their most open, reflective and vulnerable state. The language is interesting here. Though the marketeers seem to be tapping into ideas of empathy and feeling, the underpinnings of the language are those of war. Targets, hits, campaigns, launch, collateral, penetration, uplift, wins, shock...the troops in the agencies, the designers and art directors, account managers, the film directors, the animators and typographers, packaging designers and experience inventors, brand managers and social media innovators and marketeers: all of them are in a battle for our attention and our coin. Their battleground is the digital multiplex, the numerous channels we all inhabit on a daily basis.

We've gone from a few hundred thousand users exchanging files, back at the birth of internet connectivity, to around 5 billion users of the interconnected digital multiplex today. It's of course impossible to say how much of this communication continuously criss-crossing the globe is visual, or written, or the pure code, the zeros and ones supporting and sustaining the ecosystem. Then there is the invisible web, the dark web accessed through software known as Tor (The Onion Router). Most web users use the so-called surface web, which relies on the WYSIWYG principle: what you see is what you get. It's a medium that has become more visually, pictorially and semiotically oriented over the course of its development.

The XR identity encodes two simple ideas: Earth and time. The circle is Earth, and the two triangles touching points evoke an hourglass.

The so-called 'dark web' is a network that is largely invisible. Estimates of its size vary wildly, ranging from a few thousand pages to many times that number. It has a reputation as a site of nefarious activity, owing to the anonymity afforded by virtual private networks and the way traffic is bounced around different servers and nodes. Thus, a reputation for gun running and drug dealing has permeated people's understanding of the dark web and what it's for. Such sites dealing in bad things have existed and been seized by the authorities, but in truth, apart from hosting real criminal activity in the shape of drug and arms dealing and child abuse, the dark web is also a refuge for refuseniks and weirdos, scammers and frontiersmen and women; for message boards where racists can say things they're 'not allowed to say anymore' with impunity. In some ways, the dark web is very like the web as it was at the beginning – at the time of Geocities and 'web communities'.

Of course, one man's revolutionary is another man's freedom fighter: a refusenik and a weirdo can take many forms. Take, for example, the Extinction Rebellion movement. Since 2012, this movement has been trumpeting the effects of the Anthropocene on the gathering climate crisis and the potential this phenomenon has to severely disrupt, change or even end the way we live on the Earth (and by 'we', I mean all living things). In 2017,

I was teaching at the London College of Communication, where I ran a masters programme in Art Direction. One day, walking up the London Road towards where the college was located at Elephant and Castle, I along with many others was stopped in my tracks by polite, apologetic protesters who had stretched a banner across the road. This was the second barrier I had encountered: earlier, I had walked across Waterloo Bridge marvelling at its transformation into a garden of sorts. Trees had been installed in planters, and a huge pink flag with a strikingly angular logo on it had been unfurled and was being waved. I was struck by the design of the logo. At the time it was an anonymous but strong symbol. It has since been attributed to ESP, an artist who protects their anonymity. The symbol is powerful because it encodes two simple ideas: Earth and time. The circle is Earth and the two triangles, touching points, evoke an hourglass. It is simple, can be reproduced at any scale large and small, in black and white, can be drawn by a child, is extremely memorable and sits well on a T-shirt – the basic rules of good logo design.

In terms of symbolism, the XR logo also evokes the Lakota symbol, a First Nation symbol of the Americas representing the union of earth and sky: 'as above, so below'. The XR logo has about it a certain conceptual tightness that makes it look as though it has been in existence forever, which, if the Lakota is indeed the inspiration, is possibly quite close to the truth.

Extinction Rebellion's presence and 'cut-through' is attributable in no small part to their clever use of the guerrilla *affichage* of their printed materials. The posters and fliers have a curiously 'hands at home' feel about them. Purloined images, display headlines and the ubiquitous logo give their communication the feel of a *samizdat* campaign.[8] The XR logo is free to download from Extinction Rebellion's website and it can be used and reproduced by anyone for any reason, other than to make a profit from its use.[9] I cannot therefore include a reproduction of the XR logo in this book, unless it is part of a documentary photograph, as much as I would like to celebrate and strengthen the cause or draw people's attention to the power of visual communication rendered in this way. I'll have to dissect something else, I guess.

The CND symbol, designed in 1958 by Gerald Holtom, uses a combination of a bounding circle and the flag semaphore positions for the letters N and D – standing for Nuclear Disarmament. Holtom in interview also referenced a form of human gesture encoded in the symbol communicating despair, his own despair – the hands pointing downward at 'twenty to four', palms outfacing.[10] It's an oddly effective combination, the mechanistic referencing of semaphore, with its military background, and the gestural honesty of the despairing supplicant. Feeling is thus encoded in the CND symbol, alongside an alphabetic code (see page 200).

The CND symbol uses a combination of a bounding circle and the flag semaphore positions for the letters N and D, an oddly effective combination.

Invented by Sir Home Riggs Popham as a means of communication for the Royal Navy, the land-based signal code dates from 1803 and accounts for the numerous 'Telegraph Hills' that are dotted around the south of England. Using this innovative system, a signal could be sent from the admiralty in London all the way to Portsmouth in around fifteen minutes. Charles Pasley's improvements to the system with handheld flags resulted in the flag semaphore system used in the navy and by other military actors. That a militarily derived form of communication should be partly co-opted by Holtom, a conscientious objector, in his fight against mutually assured destruction is an ironic but powerful act of appropriation in pursuit of peace.

The semiology of semaphore has been appropriated many times. My favourite is Robert Freeman's photograph for the cover of the Beatles' 1965 LP, *Help!* The idea was originally to spell out the word 'help' with the Fabs holding the flags. Once the scene was shot, however, it was felt that the result was not graphically strong enough. The UK release spells out something that looks a bit like 'NUJV' (see page 202). '*NUJV! I need somebody/ NUJV! Not just anybody*' – as a lyric, it doesn't work quite as well; NUJV doesn't make you feel the same way as John Lennon's hoarsely heartfelt 'Help!'

Living with Brautigan's prediction

As a teenager, like many others, I went through a phase of reading whatever I could find. I would go into a bookshop and pick up anything. In a prefiguring of my behaviour in the stacks of the NAL, I would duck into Foyles on the Charing Cross Road, having made my way there by browsing the myriad guitar shops on Shaftesbury Avenue. Once inside I would walk the shelves, trailing a finger along the spines, and then just choose one book at random.

At the time I did not really understand the principles and processes of serendipity, and I still don't. The idea that the 'Three Princes of Serendip' – or Horace Walpole, who drew upon that fairy tale to coin the term – had any genuine sense of how to harness its power must be nonsense. Naturally enough, the serendipitous only reveals itself in hindsight, and this was the case with me and Richard Brautigan. I plucked the Picador edition of *The Revenge of the Lawn* off the shelf in 1978. It cost me a pound and featured sixty-two short stories that hooked me into his particularly Californian way of seeing the world. Of course, then, I had no idea about his poem 'All Watched Over by Machines of Loving Grace'; I could have picked up the poetry collection of the same title, which no doubt was next to *The Revenge of the Lawn* on the shelf. Instead, having devoured *Revenge*, I went back and got *A Confederate General from Big Sur*, Brautigan's first novel. I came across 'All Watched Over by Machines of Loving Grace' sometime in the 1990s, I forget quite when.

We can't reproduce the poem here, as it is copyrighted in such a way that the medium in which it appears has to be given away free – a restriction similar to the XR logo. However, it is a thing of beauty. It evokes an imaginary future epoch in which human beings are guarded, tended, supported and watched over by 'machines of loving grace'. This poem is one I turn to when I am feeling overwhelmed or overly fearful about where technology may be taking us. Perhaps it won't work out so badly after all? I'm not so sure, though.

Having moved house at the beginning of 2021, I had to update some basic documents including my driver's licence. This used to be a laborious affair involving trips to photo booths and lengthy form-filling at the post office. Now, though, a UK government database holds a photograph of me – the same one that's in my passport. That photograph is optimized and used by facial recognition software (see page 204). Puzzlingly, the government pressed ahead with the deployment of this kind of software despite knowing it had problems identifying people with darker skin tones.[11] Now, the UK Home Office guidelines on photo quality for the purposes of automated

The semiology of the semaphore has been appropriated many times. On the cover of the US release of the Beatles' 1965 LP *Help*, N-V-U-J is spelt out here by the Fab Four (see page 200).

recognition using systems run by its various partners runs to twenty-eight pages and precludes the use of photographs in which people are frowning or smiling, have their mouths open, or have temporary injuries like black eyes. We're also not allowed to flip the photo to its mirror image. All well and good and reasonable, you might think. But there are ethical and societal implications to the storing, retrieval and recognition of imagery by machines, and these implications are being played out in real time in real places.

In China, for example, the surveillance state is on a mission to determine who is and who is not trustworthy via a system of social credit. It seems that Shanghai is ahead of the game: as long ago as 2016, in the run-up to China's national social credit scheme going live on its planned date in 2020, the city rolled out the Honest Shanghai app. Developed with the Zhengxin Fangsheng software company, the app landed in November's 'honesty week', a seven-day festival of probity that had been running every November for over a decade. It invited the user to enter their national ID number and take a selfie – it then trawled various databases to build a profile of the user and offer a public rating, ranging from bad to good to very good, depending on the subject's behaviour. The full rollout of the social credit system administered by the People's Bank of China, the National Development and Reform Commission and the court system has been hampered by COVID-19; but it's coming soon and no doubt it will function, however complex it is. The Chinese are not alone in getting the infrastructure ready. In Moscow in October 2021, the Metro rolled out its FacePay system: a cashless, phoneless, cardless arrangement that simply requires travellers to link their bank, ID and Metro card via an app. Then a look into the camera opens the gates. Moscow has a further 175,000 plus surveillance cameras in operation.

The success of the social credit system as a mechanism for nudging a population into socially cohesive behaviours rests upon a panoply of variables: bill payments, sitting in the right seat for the fare you have paid, putting the bins out on time, not littering, not sticking your chewing gum under train seats – that kind of thing. But the whole idea hinges on facial recognition, and this is where the link to visual communication comes in. For the first time, the processing of facial photographs is visual communication at work in a context where humans are the subject, but machines are the viewers. We are indeed watched over by machines, or are about to be. It's where Brautigan's idea of 'loving grace' comes in that we have still to determine.

We keep coming back to this idea of what it is to feel, and how communication is designed to make us feel. This situation between humans and machines could also be something to do with empathy and emotion. Machines can learn to recognize the emotions we are expressing through our micro- and macro-facial expressions. By mapping these expressions, software can determine and learn the patterns that represent particular moods and emotions.

That may sound innocuous enough, but consider the possible lot of the post-COVID home-working call-centre employee. The employer/corporation installs an AI-enabled camera on the employee's computer. The camera scans the employee's face while they are working, while they are answering calls to the employer's customer base. This kind of surveillance opens the door to questions. Is the employee genuinely positively engaged with the customer? Did that eye-roll represent exasperation and an unwillingness to help? Does the employee look angry or sad most of the time? How does this connect to and influence productivity? How does the knowledge generated by this surveillance feed into Human Resources' need for annual assessments, employee rating on a bell curve, promotion or wage increases?

This is just one use of the technology. Emotion recognition is already being deployed in airport security, headhunting and hiring, in workplaces and in learning environments. In a darker turn of events, in 2021 a whistle-blowing software engineer claimed that the Chinese government was using emotion recognition software to convict Uyghurs in detention, where no other evidence was available.[12]

There are problems, of course, with simplifying human emotion and its transmission to a set of patterns. A trip to the website emojify.com reveals an experimental 'game' developed by scientists at the Leverhulme Centre for the Future of Intelligence and the Centre for the Study of Existential Risk at Cambridge University. The point of the game is to explore the underlying idea that changing the shape of your face does not necessarily mean that your mood has changed. Perhaps the engineers at the 'vocational skills education centres' in Xinjiang and elsewhere are ahead of the game.

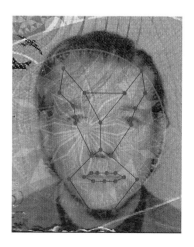

Facial recognition software uses between 20 and 70 recognition points. Now government agencies worldwide can identify and share subjects' and citizens' identities. In this tranche of visual communication, for the first time autonomous machines, not humans, are the viewers.

For profiling that uses pattern recognition to be effective, it needs to work from a very large and very nuanced dataset. Datasets like this are underpinned by the development of more sophisticated maths with which to automatically mine and frame the results. Then, terrifyingly, we can trust machines to truly read our innate visual communication signals in the same way our fellow humans can. You know when a smile does not reach the eyes, right? Machines – currently – do not. And yet the market for emotion recognition systems is growing.

Technologies designed to read the visual communication that humans use all the time are being marketed as tools of control. But they also link into the market research industry – the same organizations deploying eye-tracking technologies to map and record real-time emotional responses to all sorts of stimuli. The emotion recognition industry is now worth upwards of $20 billion and climbing. Companies such as Affectiva, through their iMotion brand, claimed in 2019 to have a database of 7.5 million faces from eighty-seven different countries – a number that will not decrease.

There are, of course, positive uses of this kind of technology. I like the idea that by means of mapping facial expression, a camera trained upon someone flying a commercial airliner with 300 souls aboard might pick up on undue stress, tiredness or a sudden compulsion to put the plane into a dive. I like the idea that remote monitoring can focus on wellness and wellbeing. But – and this is a big but – the systemic simplification of the unknowable complexity of human emotion should not be used to drive, shape and inspire the means by which we create visual communication.

To go too far down that route could eventually remove humans from the act of creation. Once machine learning has determined the patterns that work on us and can map our responses and tweak communication in real time for maximum effect (software used by the gambling industry already does this), what options do we have left? We either accept and become consumers of automated visual communication, or we rebel. I'm for the latter. But what would such a rebellion involve?

Keeping it real

At times, visual communication stimulates the culture, prefigures progress and in some cases can take the sting out of potentially alarming innovation. Look at Elon Musk's images of his Starship SN11 SpaceX rocket and compare them to those used by pulp comics of the 1940s–50s such as *Amazing Tales* and *Dan Dare*. This is rocket design as visual communication at scale, on a sculptural level and on a cultural level: there is a retro-futurological cast to

ABOVE SpaceX launched Starship SN11 on a test flight in March 2021. It performed well until it came to landing when, due to what Elon Musk called 'a plumbing problem', it exploded in a massive fireball. Subsequent Starships have proved to be spectacularly successful.

LEFT Dan Dare's spaceships featured in the *Eagle* comic in stories set in the late 1990s. This imagined spacecraft and Musk's Starship seem to share an aesthetic shaped by a boyish enthusiasm for space travel.

the representation of the ship on SpaceX's website.[13] The nose fins and the apparently seamless one-piece fuselage are redolent of Klaatu's silver space saucer. It is not rocket science, but it is science fiction. However, the form of these things in real life must be determined by aeronautics, ballistics and engineering in a way that the sci-fi versions were not. Sending four 'amateur' astronauts into orbit, as SpaceX did in 2021, in a ship controlled from the ground means there is some serious engineering at work. It's this combination of hard engineering and 'soft power' that has helped to create acceptance of the brand mythology Musk has built over the years.

Various other cultural artefacts and ideas have been appropriated by Musk in his amazing attempts to advance humankind. Leaving aside the name he and his partner, the musician Grimes, gave to their first child (a robotic X Æ A-12), he's adopted or invented a range of cultural triggers with which to strengthen his presence on the world stage. For example, Tesla, Inc. – Musk's car company – took its name from Nikola Tesla, the outsider competitor to Thomas Edison and a revolutionary genius in his harnessing of electricity. For space, Musk has looked to rock 'n' roll: 'Starship' is a neologism coined by Grace Slick and her collaborators in the wake of the demise of their band Jefferson Airplane. (The next vehicle up in the heirarchy, I presume.) It's this casual evocation of pop culture that gives Musk ventures a certain legitimacy, bridging reality and fiction as they do. That gap between the real and the fictional is in continuous flux, to such a degree that it's becoming difficult for the average person to know what's what. In 2021 William Shatner – Captain James T. Kirk out of *Star Trek* – transitioned from actor to spaceman at the whim of Jeff Bezos and his Blue Origin rocket ship.

Another example of how strangely fictional the real world is becoming can be found in the realms of academe. In April 2019, scientists at Cornell University used what they call DASH (DNA-based Assembly and Synthesis of Hierarchical) materials to create a DNA-based material that can rearrange itself to form new shapes and structures. With the characteristics of life in self-organization, metabolization and locomotion, these 'machines' were described by Dan Luo, one of their scientist progenitors, thus: 'We are not making something that's alive, but we are creating materials that are much more lifelike than have ever been seen before.'[14] They look amazingly sci-fi and, as ever, how these things look and how they are transmitted visually to the general populace is as important as what they actually do. I read about this development with incredulity. Not alive, but lifelike? The very existence of such things, let alone their depiction, sends the mind down strange avenues of possibility. This may not be the place to speculate on what will happen when a DASH-based material is conjoined with an AI program that has learned to recognize, encode and express emotion. Therefore,

I will stop. I think we can all imagine, and either embrace or reject, that future as and when it comes.

The foundations for visual communication enacted by automatons, on the fly, in real time, are already being laid – sometimes in unexpected places. The UK and Japan have already seen trials of the CARESSES (Culture-Aware Robots and Environmental Sensor Systems for Elderly Support) programme, in which 'culturally competent' wheeled robots called 'Pepper' interact with the residents of care homes. The interaction is rudimentary, but apparently effective in reducing feelings of loneliness and improving mental health. The robots can gesture with their almost humanoid articulated arms; they can ask questions (once programmed with their interlocutor's interests); they can play the person's favourite music.

It's a strange mental image: a white plastic robot with glowing eyes and the height and stance of a toddler, playing Duke Ellington's 'Mood Indigo' while gesticulating at an elderly person in an institutional reclining chair. This work, by the University of Bedfordshire and the Advinia Group, which runs the care homes, is designed to enhance people's experience of the care home, to fill the gaps in their day, and that has to be a good thing.

Pepper the robot, created in 2014 by SoftBank Robotics, seemingly in the middle of an eye roll while entertaining and informing an older person. Subtle facial expression is still some way off in robotics.

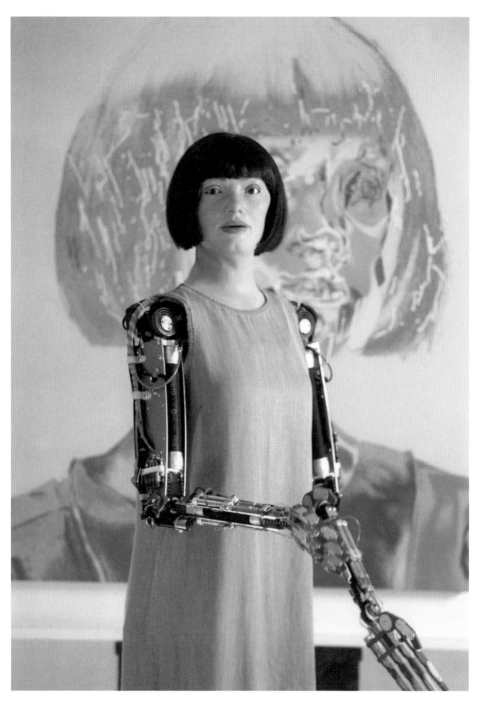

Invented by Aidan Meller and completed in 2019, robot Ai-Da's punning name reflects her (its?) AI-enabled ability to produce what her inventors are calling 'art'. In spite of the remarkable technology on display, her spoken delivery owes a good deal to Gerry Anderson's Supermarionation techniques.

But sentient, culturally competent robotics are to my mind the thin end of a wedge that includes emotionally targeted, automated, digitally enhanced visual communication.

Let's go back to the idea of rebellion. Before we get to the point where emotionally literate cyborgs are designing the communication we see, replete with emotional triggers known to work on us, we have the means to build a bulwark against the potential flood of the aforementioned emotionally targeted, automated, digitally enhanced visual communication. We know what's coming across the drawbridge, so what do we do to defend ourselves?

Clues to the shape the revolution must take, or perhaps more accurately the resistance, are easy to find. Richard Sennett's book *The Craftsman* (2008) is a paean to quality. In it he evokes many examples of how, in essence, the combination of skill plus time in the making of things results in good work. Sennett is acutely aware of the impact of machines on the things we create. Citing P. N. Furbank's critical biography of Denis Diderot, the 18th-century writer, art critic and encyclopaedist, Sennett reproduces this prescient fragment: 'There are machines so hard to describe and skills so elusive', wrote Diderot, '...it has often been necessary to get hold of such machines, set them in operation and lend one's hand to the work.'[15] That might have worked for our Denis, but maybe not so much for us in the here and now. Everything in Diderot's time was naturally analogue. Machines at the birth of the industrial revolution were simply designed to transfer and amplify the capacity for work. They were mosty analogous to human processes.

So, the steam-driven beam engine could drive a pump or belt that previously would have been driven by the muscles of man or animal, or by a water wheel. A threshing machine could winnow wheat in greater quantities than a woman in a field with a mesh and a breeze. A metal stamping machine, driven by a belt, driven by steam, would make 'toys' – badges, buckles and buttons – in the workshops of Birmingham. And, of course, the carding machines, spinning jennies and weaving looms helped to drive the industrial revolution into its self-sustained take-off in the damp towns of the north of England, where cotton and wool behaved well in the rainy atmosphere. Machines increased horsepower and speed, making industrial design possible and ultimately necessary.

Diderot wanted to understand machines, and in his time it was possible to do so by becoming involved in the work. In Diderot's case, perhaps he was fascinated by the processes of bringing his *Encyclopédie* into being – printing and typesetting, paper-making and inks. With a bit of training, anyone can set type. Over time, and with practice, we become skilful. The hand, guided by the eye, expresses the idea formed by the mind. That's how we make things. Or how we used to.

Today I think it's safe to say that there is no one person who could, for example, understand and work with all the processes involved in making a semi- or superconductor, or any kind of microchip. As individuals, we cannot therefore understand today's machines simply by becoming involved in the work they do. My use of the MacBook on which I am writing these words will never lead me to a working practical understanding of the components within.

It's the same for other iterative processes. Users of compositing software like Adobe's InDesign are happy to set paragraphs of type without having to get too involved in the tricky processes of kerning and justification, unless they wish to. InDesign is such a clever program that kerning occurs automatically where the pairs are tabled in character sets. The laborious process of typesetting, of graphic organization, is no longer necessarily laborious in and of itself. But this convenience in the iterative processes of creating visual communication is a double-edged sword.

I had the privilege once of sitting on a panel at the School of Architecture at UCLA. There were presentations by various historians and architects. They were all fascinating in terms of content, research and ideas. All of them were delivered to the audience using PowerPoint, the Microsoft presentation tool.

Without fail, all of these people, practised in critical thinking around the issues of architecture and its aesthetics, had taken full advantage of the presentational features in the PowerPoint program. It was a visual car crash. Lime green headlines in Arial, stretched to fit the frame, peeled away from the virtual background to reveal the next slide. Pages sliding left and right. Animated random bars and shapes deployed for no reason, flashes flashing and hexagons morphing to create page transitions. Pictures dropping and bouncing with faux gravity. I recall two thoughts going through my mind as I watched this cavalcade of ill-conceived and bizarrely executed visuals. One, why would Bill Gates sign off on a toolkit packed with features designed to create such ugly amateur aesthetics; and two, what would Max Miedinger think?

Miedinger was a typographer from Switzerland working for the Haas type foundry in Münchenstein, just to the south of Basel. Commissioned to develop an open and legible typeface to rival others on the market at the time (like the Berthold foundry's Akzidenz-Grotesk or the Stempel foundry's DIN), Miedinger, in cahoots with company owner Edouard Hoffman, developed Neue Haas Grotesk over a couple of years starting in 1955/56 and using Akzidenz as a starting point. There was a misguided impetus to develop a character set devoid of any extraneous meaning – an impossibility, as Helvetica (as it came to be called in 1960) rapidly became the go-to, along with Akzidenz, for the midcentury modernist designer. Its supposed neutrality is loaded with meaning. Taking something like Helvetica – a set of glyphs so perfectly wrought, over time, with the eye and hand of the craftsman Miedinger – and then putting its digital derivatives into PowerPoint, where they can be stretched, coloured, twisted, badly spaced, wiped, peeled and squashed, seems to me to be an act of visual barbarism. In part, it's the casual use of these tools that we should revolt against.

Quality

The nature of work, and the striving for quality in that work, is something that has been argued for since *Homo faber* first discovered how to grip, hold, turn and manipulate materials and tools. There was direct contact between the maker and the object made. Making things engendered craft and the accumulation of skill through experience. Then machines arrived, and interpolated themselves between an idea and its execution. Inevitably, the machines that so incensed Ruskin, William Morris and the Luddites evolved – and as a result, some interesting parallels emerged between then and now, and between different fields of manufacture.

The beginnings of the first industrial revolution were seeded in so-called cottage industries. Elements of any manufacturing process – for lock-making, pin-making, the making of clothing, buttons, elements of guns and other goods – could be 'put out' to be made in people's homes or small workshops. This decentralized piecework system was loaded in favour of the employer, with workers often sewing, stamping, filing, cutting and making in the squalor of their tenements and slums. The point here is not about working conditions in the 19th century, but rather that the toolset for iterative processes has now found its way back into the home via the personal computer. The second industrial revolution was and is fuelled by the process of 'putting out'; WFH is now the acronym for working from home.

It is of course the revolution in DTP, desktop publishing, to which I refer. When I worked on my postgrad qualification, we were privileged to be provided with writing and research rooms in the warren of the Victoria and Albert Museum's backstage area. In those rooms was a bunch of Apple Macintosh 128ks (or possibly Macintosh Plusses). The beige-coloured personal computer was an amazing thing back in 1988. Its one-piece body with integrated floppy drive and 9″ monochrome screen had a carry handle at the back, implying portability. In truth it weighed a fair bit, and although you could buy a padded carry case for it with a shoulder strap, the idea of lugging it around on the tube was frankly mad.

It's hard to emphasize the degree to which the Mac communicated to its user the joys of computing in the new era. Leaving aside Ridley Scott's prophetic *1984*-themed TV ad (Orwell again), the user interface was full of promise and, compared to other computer interfaces, humanity. The machine booted up with a little Susan Kare-designed 'Happy Mac' smiley face and the Jim Reekes-designed C-major chord you are greeted with today.[16] Importantly, the options for making publishable materials on those machines were extremely limited compared to what we can now do. Also importantly, the choice of typefaces was limited to a few – Times was in there and so was Helvetica, along with Geneva and Palatino, Monaco and Courier, the monospaced 'typewriter' one.

Choosing Helvetica gave a text a coolly modern feel on the tiny black-and-white screen. There were inkjet printers now, too, so our printouts had a nice solid black and actually looked like what we had put together. It was a step on from the typewriter. But DTP was in its infancy. Within a few years, colour screens had arrived and simple templates could be populated with text flowed into columns and decorated with clip art. The devolution of design had started: arguably, everyone now had the potential to become a designer.

Except they didn't. Joseph Beuys's maxim 'everyone an artist' doesn't apply here. There are no absolutes in what constitutes art, let alone good art; but design is a process developed by humans to answer a set of questions or problems in a systematic way. And the design of visual communication is, or should be, subject to the same rigour and judgment. How do we develop that rigour and judgment? Learn the tools and the rules. In short – get educated about the rules before you start to break them.

Access to the manipulation of the iterative processes of design has been democratized. Ridley Scott's vision of the 'freedom' that personal computing could engender has turned out a bit differently, with the simple interface of the Apple computer turning into the front end of a closed-loop system where no modifications by the user are allowed. Unlike PCs, where different components and programming languages can be used, Apple's products are almost hermetically sealed. Unless you are an adept who is part of the 'hackintosh' community, the means to make your own visual communication is simplified, locked down with an intuitive graphic user interface and at your fingertips.

The hand is still in play when it comes to making things via the computer. The capacitive screen that we are all familiar with, which allows us to swipe, pinch, zoom, 'pick up', drag and drop, is the gestural interface that will soon be the default way of controlling software, either with the fingers or with a stylus or pen. So the story of the tools we use to design comes full circle. The monk from the scriptorium in York a thousand years ago, transported here by some means, would be as unable as I am to understand the mechanics of the computational power that allows us to write and draw and move things on a screen. But he would understand the stylus, the Apple pen, the Wacom… the hand grips the stylus and gesture creates a mark. Today that mark might be a letterform, or a CAD drawing, or a NURBS.

The role of letterforms has remained significant over the centuries. Computer programs are written in languages and so the alphabet, the Roman/Greek-derived alphabet, is at the root of what makes computers work. Just how the letterforms that first appeared on ancient tablets, columns, plinths and friezes have come to be the codified organizing character set that makes scripted computer languages work is a mysterious journey with its roots in science that stretches from Charles Babbage and Ada Lovelace through to Turing, Gates, Jobs, Wozniak and countless unknown coders.

In terms of this journey, I find a pleasing symmetry in where we started with the human hand and its efficacy, and in the difference between one and zero – and how, through the embrace of zero, the development of civilization was effectively accelerated. That acceleration continues, aided by the computer. But what drives computation? The one and the zero, of course, form the basis of the most basic binary machine code, which the higher-level languages, the assembly code, directly relates to. Assembly code is a set of English-like standard instructions – you can read them, up to a point – that needs an 'assembler', a kind of translator to convert it into machine code that is directly executable by the computer's processor or microchip.

So it's 0 and 1, A, B and C…et cetera. Written words that translate to two simple numbers, one and zero, represented by numerals that in turn translate directly to the on and off states that codify all computerized instructions. The 19th-century mathematician and logician George Boole created an algebraic way of thinking that identified two states as 'true' and 'false'. A true statement might have a value of X and a false statement a value of Y. Computer logic lends itself to Boolean terms, so 'true' could be 1 and 'false' 0. Not many complex ideas can be expressed in such simple terms, but Boolean expressions can be built as a series of logic gates. In this way, everything we do in our digital, digitized world can be accomplished.

All of this flows from the most fundamental visual communication: the invention of type forms, glyphs derived from the skills of scribes who were compelled to codify their communication, resulting in the new form of scripts. Once they were written by hand and now they appear at a keystroke. Nevertheless, it's those same letterforms, originally created by hand, that now make the modern world work. The signifiers of open vowels and plosives; the signs for incremental integers; whole numbers and letters rendered as glyphs combining to drive the machines that churn through the algorithms and calculations in distant server farms and mainframes, in our phones, laptops, tablets and desktops, in satellites far above us.

The result is the automation of affect.

The delivery of emotional triggers and tugs via devices generated and delivered by machines leads us ever onwards in our continuous and continuing (for how long?) interchange of visual communication. The presence of machines and machine code in our daily lives should not, however, militate against the investment of ourselves in the making of communication. It is quite possible and desirable to make affecting and effective communication or sculptural, interactive works of wonder. I use the word 'interactive' guardedly, for our relationship with the world is interactive regardless of whether we use a pencil or an iPad. But in terms of work that is suffused with humanity but delivered with the help of machines, I think immediately of the work of Hudson-Powell, for example, or Troika, Norbert Schoerner, Refik Anadol, Anicka Yi, Audrey Large, Daniel Rozin and naturally (for me) Tomato. There are many others, too, all of whom, at their best, seem to rub the analogue up against the digital, thus creating a friction that produces human warmth.

Perhaps this is where we can live with Brautigan's prediction: in a space between the digital and the analogue, where humanity does not fully devolve its work in terms of creating aesthetics, meaning and emotion to machines. Instead, in this in-between space, we humans maintain the machines' mechanical status as our tools rather than our teachers. This does not mean we shouldn't learn from their capacity to improve our lives, or deploy those capabilities. We should be wary, though, lest our reliance on machines comes to allow the signifiers of humanity in visual communication to be aped, copied, codified and used to the extent where, now the pixel has been mastered, we can't tell the difference between something made by automatons for the masses and something made by us, for each other.

Epilogue

I am not sure where I stand at this point in our journey. It's the end of the narrative, but I will carry on after the endpapers, as will you. The path I've chosen through the landscape of visual communication has been necessarily partial, personal and partisan. We've spent a little more time on some topics than others, but in the course of the journey, we've experienced the landscape much as a tourist might – glimpsing some things in passing, and in other cases making a studied effort to stop and understand their qualities.

The common factor in the experience of this wide range of sights and stimuli, it seems to me, is emotion. How we connect emotionally with our fellow human beings is central to how we experience visual communication. The ends to which that emotional connection is put – whether commercial, political, or purely aesthetic – determines, to some degree, the value we place on visual communication. It ends up being ephemera or preserved material culture. Or in some cases, both.

The trajectory of civilization has seen us continually invent and reinvent not only the channels of communication, but the technologies we need to use them. How we fill these channels has changed in terms of technique. The difference between learning the analogue skills of lithography or letter-press, and learning how to use Photoshop or InDesign or create content for YouTube, is pretty marked. It comes down, I think, to automation. Whether it's kerning letters or creating a halftone screen, for many designers the push of a virtual button has replaced the action of the hand on materials.

But this is OK. I am not arguing here for a return to some prelapsarian state where machines and machine learning did not exist. What I think I *am* arguing for is a return to, or an embracing of, criticality. Along with a well-developed critical stance comes some adherence to quality and, as a result, a better relationship with the truth of what people do as designers, communicators and consumers.

What I mean by criticality is an analytical way of looking at the world, wedded to the pursuit of truth (or veracity, authenticity, reality – whatever you want to call it). In some settings, of course, criticality can feed the development of cynical uses of communicators' skills (cf. the propagandists and some advertisers), and this is also something we should guard against.

The way to build criticality is to invest in research. We talked earlier about libraries, both as signifiers and repositories of knowledge. Anyone involved in making their way in creating or even consuming communication (and that's all of us, really) should be building a library. That library might take the form of books on shelves, but it's more vital, expandable, accessible, dynamic, portable, useful and above all personal if it resides in the head. A library that lives in the head is not about display – it's a set of references, a set of coordinates against which we can measure our position creatively, morally and culturally as we move through life.

Back in the mid-1990s I was writing for a number of magazines, including *Blueprint*, as well as working as part of the Tomato studio. The magazine sent me to Paris to interview Philippe Starck. At some point in the interview he said, 'The more you respect people, the more people love you. And they love you by buying your products. What one needs is not all these objects but just love.'[17] At the time, I didn't pick up on the obvious contradiction – Starck has filled the world with more objects than anyone can count, so there probably should have been a 'but' at the beginning of his last sentence – and I

```
1001001 00100000 01101000 01100001 01110110 01100101 00100000 01100001 00100000 01110100 0110010
1110010 01101001 01100010 01101100 01100001 00100000 01100110 01100101 01100101 01101100 0110100
1110111 00100000 01110100 01101000 01100101 00100000 01101100 01100001 01111001 00100000 0010000
1100011 01101111 01110101 01101110 01110100 01110010 01111001 00100000 01110111 01100101 0010000
1100001 01110110 01100101 01100101 00100000 01101111 01101111 01101110 01110100 01101111 0111010
0100000 01110111 01100001 01111001 00101110 00100000 01010100 01100001 01101111 01101100 0110111
0010110 00100000 01110100 01100101 01100101 00100000 01100110 01101111 01110010 01100101 0101000
0100000 01110111 01101111 01110010 01100000 01101001 01101110 01100111 01100111 01101100 0110111
1110100 01100000 01101001 01101111 01110101 01110010 00100000 01100011 01100111 00100000 0110100
0100000 01110100 01101000 01100101 01101110 00100000 01100001 01110010 01100101 01100101 0110001
1100101 00100000 00100000 01110011 01110100 01100101 01110000 01110000 01100101 01110010 0010000
1101000 01110101 00100000 01100100 01110000 01110100 01100000 01101000 01110010 01100101 0010100
1110000 00100000 01110111 01101000 01100001 01110100 00100000 01100101 01110110 01100001 0010010
1101111 01100000 01101001 01100101 01110100 01110000 00100000 01100011 01110111 01100101 0111010
1000000 01101100 01101000 01100011 00101111 00100000 01101101 01110011 00100000 01100100 0111001
1100010 01110011 01110011 00100000 01100101 00100000 01100101 01101000 01100001 01101110 0110011
1101100 00100000 01001010 01101111 01101110 00100000 01100111 01110011 01101111 01101101 0111001
1101110 01101011 00100000 01110100 01101111 01100000 01100111 01110011 01101111 00100000 0110010
1110000 01110100 01100000 01101101 01110111 00100000 01100100 01110010 01101000 01101111 0110100
1100111 00100000 01110100 01100001 01100111 00100000 01101111 01110011 01110000 01101101 0110100
1110001 01101110 01100000 01111101 01110100 00100000 01100001 01110100 01100110 01100100 0010000
1000000 01101100 01100001 01100100 01101001 00100000 01110010 01110101 01110110 01100100 0111001
0100000 01100111 01101001 01110010 01101100 01100110 01110010 01110101 01100101 01101110 0110010
0100000 01100001 01101110 01100100 01110011 00100000 01100011 01101111 01101110 01110000 0110110
0100000 01100101 01101110 01110011 00100000 01101100 00100000 01101110 01100100 01101111 0111100
1110101 01110111 01101001 00100000 01101000 00100000 01101110 01110011 01101001 00100000 0111001
0100000 01110100 01100001 01100111 00100000 01100011 01101101 01100101 01101110 01100100 0110010
0101100 01100111 01101001 01100111 01110010 01101111 01110010 01110101 01110000 01101101 0111001
0100000 01100111 01101111 01110010 01100000 01100100 01100001 01101110 01101001 00100000 0010000
0100000 01100001 01101110 01100100 01110011 00100000 01100111 01110010 01110101 01100101 0110010
0100000 01100101 00100000 01110011 01101000 01101111 01110101 01101100 01100100 00100000 0110100
1110001 01110101 01101001 01110100 01100101 00100000 01110011 01100101 01100101 01101101 0010000
1101001 01110011 01101100 01101001 01101011 01100101 00100000 01100001 00100000 01100111 0110110
1100000 01100001 01101110 01100100 00100000 01110010 01101111 01101101 01100001 01101110 0110001
1101001 01110011 01101101 00100000 01100001 01101100 01100100 00100000 01100101 01101110 0110010
1100000 01110011 00100000 01110100 01101000 01100101 00100000 01100100 01101001 01110110 0110010
1101110 01101001 01110100 01111001 00100000 01101111 01101110 00100000 01101000 01101001 0111001
1110011 01100000 01100101 01101001 01100111 01101000 01110100 00100000 01100001 01101110 0110100
1000000 01110110 01101001 01110011 01101001 01101111 01101110 01110011 00100000 01101111 0110011
1101100 00100000 01101001 01101110 01101110 01101111 01100011 01100101 01101110 01100011 0110101
1100001 01101110 01100100 00100000 01101001 01101110 01101110 01101111 01100011 01100101 0110010
1100001 01101110 01100100 00100000 01101001 01101110 01110000 01100101 01110010 01101001 0110010
1110000 01100001 01100111 01100001 01101110 00100000 01100010 01101100 01101111 01101111 0110100
1100100 00100000 01100110 01101100 01101111 01110111 01101001 01101110 01100111 00100000 0111001
0100000 01110100 01101000 01100101 00100000 01110011 01101111 01101001 01101100 00100000 0110011
0101100 01100111 01101001 01110011 01110100 01100101 01101110 01101001 01101110 01100111 0111001
0100000 01110100 01101111 00100000 01110100 01101000 01100101 00100000 01110000 01100001 0111100
1110011 01110011 01101001 01101111 01101110 00100000 01101111 01100110 00100000 01110100 0110100
1100000 01100101 00100000 01110011 01100101 01100001 01110011 01101111 01101110 01110011 0110110
1100000 01100001 01101110 01100100 00100000 01110100 01101000 01100101 00100000 01110011 0111100
1110100 01100001 01100111 01100101 01110011 00100000 01101111 01100110 00100000 01101100 0110100
0100000 01101001 01100110 01100101 00100000 01101001 01101110 00100000 01110100 01101000 0110101
0100000 01101001 01101110 01110100 01100101 01110010 01110110 01100001 01101100 01110011 0010000
1101111 01100110 00100000 01100100 01101001 01110011 01100001 01110000 01110000 01101111 0110100
1101001 01101110 01110100 01101101 01100101 01101110 01110100 00100000 01100001 01101110 0110100
1100100 00100000 01100100 01100101 01101100 01101001 01100111 01101000 01110100 00101100 0010000
0101100 00100000 01101111 01100110 00100000 01101000 01101111 01110000 01100101 00100000 0110000
0100000 01100001 01101110 01100100 00100000 01100100 01100101 01110011 01110000 01100001 0110100
1101001 01110010 00101100 00100000 01101111 01100110 00100000 01110011 01110101 01100011 0110011
1100011 01100101 01110011 01110011 00100000 01100001 01101110 01100100 00100000 01100110 0110100
1100001 01101001 01101100 01110101 01110010 01100101 00101110 00100000 01010100 01101000 0110010
1100101 00100000 01110011 01100101 01100001 01110011 01101111 01101110 01110011 00100000 0110110
1101111 01100110 00100000 01101100 01101001 01100110 01100101 00100000 01100001 01101110 0110010
0100000 01100100 01100101 01100001 01110100 01101000 00101100 00100000 01101111 01100110 0010000
1101100 01101111 01110110 01100101 00100000 01100001 01101110 01100100 00100000 01101100 0110111
1110011 01110011 00100000 01100001 01101110 01100100 00100000 01100111 01100001 01101001 0110111
1101110 00100000 01100001 01101110 01100100 00100000 01101100 01101111 01110011 01110011 0010000
0100000 01100001 01101110 01100100 00100000 01100100 01100101 01100001 01110100 01101000 0110011
0100000 01110111 01100101 01110010 01100101 00100000 01100001 01101100 01101100 00100000 0110100
1100000 01100001 01110010 01110100 00100000 01101111 01100110 00100000 01101110 01100001 0111010
1110100 01110101 01110010 01100001 01101100 00100000 01100011 01111001 01100011 01101100 0110101
0101100 00100000 01100001 01101110 01100100 00100000 01101110 01101111 01110100 01101000 0110100
1101001 01101110 01100111 00100000 01100011 01101111 01110101 01101100 01100100 00100000 0110110
1100000 01100101 01101110 01100100 00100000 01101001 01110100 00101110 00100000 01000001 0110110
1101100 01101100 00100000 01100011 01101000 01100001 01101110 01100111 01100101 01110011 0010000
1100001 01101110 01100100 00100000 01100001 01101100 01101100 00100000 01110100 01101000 0110010
1100000 01101001 01101110 01100111 01110011 00100000 01110000 01100001 01110011 01110011 0010000
1100000 01100001 01110111 01100001 01111001 00101100 00100000 01100001 01101110 01100100 0010000
1101110 01101111 01110100 01101000 01101001 01101110 01100111 00100000 01110010 01100101 0110110
1100001 01101100 01101100 01111001 00100000 01100100 01101001 01100101 01110011 00101110 0010000
0100000 01001001 01101110 00100000 01110100 01101000 01100101 00100000 01110111 01101111 0111001
1101100 01100100 00100000 01101111 01100110 00100000 01101110 01100001 01110100 01110101 0111001
1110010 01100101 00101100 00100000 01100101 01110110 01100101 01110010 01111001 01110100 0110100
1101000 01101001 01101110 01100111 00100000 01101001 01110011 00100000 01101001 01101110 0010000
1100000 01100011 01101111 01101110 01110011 01110100 01100001 01101110 01110100 00100000 0110110
1101100 01110101 01111000 00101100 00100000 01100001 01101110 01100100 00100000 01101110 0110111
1101111 01110100 01101000 01101001 01101110 01100111 00100000 01101001 01110011 00100000 0111001
1100101 01110110 01100101 01110010 00100000 01110100 01101000 01100101 00100000 01110011 0110100
1100001 01101101 01100101 00101110 00100000 01001010 01110101 01110011 01110100 00100000 0110001
1110011 00100000 01100110 01101100 01101111 01110111 01100101 01110010 01110011 00100000 0110010
1101111 01110000 01100101 01101110 00100000 01100001 01101110 01100100 00100000 01100011 0110110
1101100 01101111 01110011 01100101 00100000 01101001 01101110 00100000 01110100 01101000 0110010
0100000 01101101 01101111 01110010 01101110 01101001 01101110 01100111 00101100 01100001 0010000
1100110 01110100 01100101 01110010 00100000 01110100 01101000 01100101 01111001 00100000 0110110
1100001 01110110 01100101 00100000 01100100 01101001 01100101 01100100 00101100 00100000 0110100
1101001 01110011 01101111 00100000 01110100 01101000 01100101 00100000 01110011 01100001 0110110
1101101 01100101 00100000 01101001 01110011 00100000 01110100 01110010 01110101 01100101 0010000
1101111 01100110 00100000 01110101 01110011 00101110 00100000 01010111 01100101 00100000 0110011
1101111 01101101 01100101 00100000 01100001 01101110 01100100 00100000 01100111 01101111 0010000
1100001 01101110 01100100 00100000 01110111 01100101 00100000 01100111 01101111 00101110 0010000
0100000 01001110 01101111 01110100 01101000 01101001 01101110 01100111 00100000 01101001 0111011
0100000 01110010 01100101 01100001 01101100 00101110 11100010 10000000 1001100
0100000 01101110 01101111 01110100 01101000 01101001 01101110 01100111 00100000 01101100 0110000
```

A set of binary instructions offers a pleasing symmetry with where we started: with the human hand and its efficacy in creating letterforms. The difference between 1 and 0 accelerated the processes of civilization and now underpins computer languages.

came back from the interview in a kind of trance. The editor who had commissioned it said at the time that he feared I had been hypnotized.

The idea that Starck floated into the conversation, that love is all we need, was of course not new. But I think it was the fact that it was delivered by this very famous designer in a shiny office in La Défense that caught me persuasively off guard. Similarly, in terms of the sentiment, in Stephen Hillenburg's remarkable animated series *SpongeBob SquarePants*, SpongeBob's archenemy Plankton finally gets his hands on the secret recipe for Krabby Patties. Plankton's victory is Pyrrhic, however, as customers at the Krusty Krab find his short-order cookery repulsive. The patties don't taste the same because Plankton, being evil, does not make them with love.

Adrian Shaughnessy, in his useful and truthful book *How to Be a Graphic Designer, Without Losing Your Soul*, proselytizes for something similar, namely 'dedication and a love of your craft'.[18] Richard Sennett, too, expands the idea into the realm of pride – it is difficult, after all, to be proud of something you do not love. As he puts it: 'Pride in one's work lies at the heart of craftsmanship.'[19]

So, to elide Starck, Sennett and Shaughnessy, love, pride and craft could be the triumvirate of qualities we critically seek to apply to what we choose to make, and to what we choose to consume. I find it hard to disagree with embracing ideas whose dimensions are so human.

Hello, human – what are you going to do?

Notes

Introduction

1   Tate, gallery label, 2015.

Part One

1   I saw this drawing at the National Gallery, between lockdowns during the pandemic of 2020/21. I have always found it interesting that part of any research process requires the researcher to be open to happenstance, to remain in an open-minded state of 'flow'. Flow is a slippery concept outlined by Mihaly Csikszentmihalyi and Jeanne Nakamura: 'There's this focus that, once it becomes intense, leads to a sense of ecstasy, a sense of clarity: you know exactly what you want to do from one moment to the other; you get immediate feedback' (https://www.ted.com/talks/ mihaly_csikszentmihalyi_flow_the_secret_to_happiness). I have tried to cultivate a permanent state of openness to this feedback, and so this narrative is constructed as a kind of switched-on *dérive*. Whether it is successful, I leave to the reader.

2   See 'Out of Hand', *Eye* (Summer 2011), http://www.eyemagazine.com/feature/article/ out-of-hand. Heidegger also wrote 'Man does not "have" hands, but the hand holds the essence of man, because the word as the essential realm of the hand is the ground of the essence of man. The word as what is inscribed and what appears to the regard is the written word, i.e., script. And the word as script is handwriting.' *Parmenides*, trans. Andre Schuwer and Richard Rojcewicz (Indiana University Press, [1942–3] 1992), pp. 80–81.

3   There are handprints in the caves of Quesang in Tibet that have been dated to between 169,000 and 226,000 years old. The prints were pushed, possibly by Denisovan children, into travertine, the fluid form of limestone before it hardens over time. Some scientists are of the opinion that this qualifies as art, as the hands deliberately changed the form of the medium. This may be the case, but who can say? For our purposes, it's the use of technique and colour that represents the starting point of a journey largely concerned with the graphic.

4   In a project instigated by Sally Shaw, director of the First Sight Gallery in Colchester, England.

5   A. Gilman, 'Explaining the Upper Palaeolithic revolution', in M. Spriggs (ed.), *Marxist Perspectives in Archaeology* (Cambridge University Press, 1984), pp. 115–26.

6   Literally from the Greek *tele* ('distance') and *graphia* ('description of'), down through Old French and into English, conveying the idea of distance writing.

7   'Stan' features the sound of a pen scratching on paper as a syncopated part of the rhythm track.

8   'Germany's thicket of rules and standards shields roughly 150 professions from competition, from ski instructors to well-diggers. Stiff fines await uncertified practitioners. German authorities conduct thousands of enforcement raids each year' (https://www.forbes.com/sites/timworstall/2016/10/19/think-how-much-richer- germany-could-be-if-it-didnt-have-the-medieval-guilds/?sh=e4d00121fbee).

9   The marble carvers of ancient Greece and Rome should of course be acknowledged: friezes, metopes, Ionic and Corinthian capitals. The exquisite carving of Roman

letterforms and numerals on countless plinths and panels are the wellspring of much of Western typographic history. But in this journey we cannot embrace and contextualize all human attempts at communication. I chose to look at the rose window in Lincoln through familiarity and interest, and because cathedrals and cathedral cities represent once again, for our purposes, the locus of the inception of modern visual communication.

10 Prefiguring Wycliffe, John Ball picked up on this symbology with his aphorism 'When Adam delved and Eve span, Who was then the gentleman?' – raising the question of just how far a peasant could be thought of as a position ordained by God, a key proposition in the peasant's revolt of the 14th century.

11 Jim Cheshire, 'Stained Glass', *Victorian Review*, 43:1 (Spring 2008), pp. 71–75.

12 See ibid. for more detail on this process.

13 H. J. Dow, 'The Rose-Window', *Journal of the Warburg and Courtauld Institutes*, 20:3/4 (July–December 1957), pp. 248–97.

14 Robert Lawlor, *Sacred Geometry* (Thames & Hudson, 1982), p. 16.

15 Almost inevitably, there is a precedent for this system in China. The ancient philosophical idea of yin and yang, represented in the *I-Ching*, also uses an extrapolation of binary, the origin of which is lost in legend and could date to between 300 and 1000 BCE.

16 See https://www.theguardian.com/environment/2021/jun/09/raccoon-dogs-britain-non-native-pest-invasive-species. The use of the tanuki pelt as a source of bristles for calligraphic brushes represents a deep connection to Japanese folklore. The tanuki appears in any number of stories as a shape-shifting, mischievous actor who may take the form of a beautiful woman, or imitate Shinto ceremonies by appearing as a Buddhist monk. Crucially, tanuki in folklore are also able to write and at times have taken pride in developing calligraphic styles that combine Chinese flourishes with machine-produced Japanese characters. Legendarily the tanuki can also deploy its scrotum as a cloak or, in extremis, a sail.

17 See David Pye, *The Nature and Art of Workmanship* (Cambridge University Press, 1978).

18 Poem 19 (Polara), as preserved on folio 4 of the 16th-century Codex Augustaneus 9 Guelferbytanus.

19 Michael Squire, *Papers of the British School at Rome*, 84 (October 2016), pp. 179–240, https://doi.org/10.1017/S0068246216000064.

20 See R. H. Bloch's *One Toss of the Dice* (Liveright, 2017) for an exhaustive and inspiring explanation of the poem, its origins and context.

21 Richard Polt, 'A Brief History of Typewriters', http://site.xavier.edu/polt/typewriters/tw-history.html.

22 See Peter Mayer, 'Concrete Poems Just Are', *Eye* (Spring 1996), http://www.eyemagazine.com/feature/article/concrete-poems-just-are.

23 Gretchen McCulloch, *Because Internet* (Harvill Secker, 2019).

24 Ibid.

25 Ibid. p. 179.

26 See 'Emojineering Part 1: Machine Learning for Emoji Trends', *Medium*, https://instagram-engineering.com/emojineering-part-1-machine-learning-for-emoji-trendsmachine-learning-for-emoji-trends-7f5f9cb979ad.

27 'It is really true what philosophy tells us, that life must be understood backwards. But with this, one forgets the second proposition, that it must be lived forwards.' Søren Kierkegaard, *Journalen JJ*: 167, Søren Kierkegaards Skrifter, vol. 18, p. 306 (Søren Kierkegaard Research Center, [1843] 1997).

28 See 'Most popular social networks worldwide as of July 2021', *Statista*, https://www.statista.com/statistics/272014/global-social-networks-ranked-by-number-of-users/.

29 In Iran, Afghanistan, Nigeria and various other places, the thumbs-up is an obscene insult meaning roughly 'sit on it', equivalent to holding up a middle finger. *The Social Dilemma*, a 2020 Netflix docudrama, contains interesting discourses on social media from many of its progenitors, including those who worked on the thumbs-up 'like' gesture. It's fair to say that they are not impressed with the Facebook thumb's effect on people.

Part Two

1 The year 1611 is also when John Tradescant introduced the blackcurrant to England. The world of chemical dyes was some way away, so strongly coloured fruits such as blackcurrants were among the resources used to create colour in the domestic sphere. Others include beetroot, onion skins, spinach, orange peel, kale stalks and damsons.

2 England lagged behind in the adoption of print, and the King James Bible, though significant for England, was published in the wake of the transmission of the Lutheran Bible in the German-speaking lands of Europe. Luther's Protestantism was bolstered by the alacrity with which the printing press was adopted in mainland Europe, a point well made in Niall Ferguson's excellent history of networks and hierarchies *The Square and the Tower* (Penguin, 2018), pp. 82–84.

3 Peter Bain and Peter Shaw (eds), *Blackletter: Type and National Identity* (Princeton Architectural Press, 1999).

4 Melvyn Bragg, *The Book of Books: The Radical Impact of the King James Bible 1611–2011* (Hodder, 2011).

5 See Aaron Bastani, *Fully Automated Luxury Consumerism* (Verso, 2019), p. 240. This does seem like an extraordinary number.

6 See Jeremiah E. Dittmar, 'Information Technology and Economic Change: The Impact of the Printing Press', *The Quarterly Journal of Economics*, 126:3 (August 2011), pp. 1133–72 (p. 1144).

7 In a strangely circular aside, antimony had been known to the ancient world – a 5,000-year-old vase made of the material is in the Louvre in Paris – for millennia. The mineral stibnite is the naturally occurring form of antimony sulphide and is the pigment used in kohl, the cosmetic used by Jezebel, who of course features in the Gutenberg Bible. Medieval typesetters' and the general populace's reliance on antimony's medicinal and laxative properties is less relevant here but does represent the ferment of scientific discovery, metallurgy and trade that at least in part drove the printing revolution in Europe.

8 See https://mises.org/library/i-pencil.

9 Hellmut Lehmann-Haupt, 'Book Illustration in Augsburg in the Fifteenth Century', *Metropolitan Museum Studies*, 4:1 (February 1932), pp. 3–17.

10 Suzanne Beisel, 'The Story of Lithograph City', *The Annals of Iowa*, 36:6 (Fall 1962), pp. 466–68.

11 See e.g. *Hornblower* (1951), *The Cruel Sea* (1953) or *Jason and the Argonauts* (1963).

12 The year 2021 saw the launch of a new blue called YInMn Blue, the result of a scientific experiment at Oregon State University where yttrium, indium and manganese oxides were combined at high temperatures, resulting in an intense new blue.

13   The comedy writer Eddie Braben penned a sketch for comedy duo Morecambe and Wise in which a news vendor calls out the name of the publication he is selling. Street cries of London were typically mangled by the accent: '*Morny Stannit, Morny Stannit*' was an approximation of *Evening Standard*, a popular London evening paper. Ernie Wise buys a copy from Eric Morecambe's newsseller and unfolds it as he walks away; the masthead reads *Morny Stannit*.

14   Will Slauter, 'The Rise of the Newspaper', in Richard R. John and Jonathan Silberstein-Loeb, *Making News: The Political Economy of Journalism in Britain and America from the Glorious Revolution to the Internet* (Oxford University Press, 2015), pp. 19–46.

15   Coldset web offset rotary presses were usually used for newsprint or other publications that required continuously fed reels of paper (webs). The ink dries by means of natural evaporation. Heatset presses are generally sheet fed using four-colour processes and use heat to dry the finished print, evaporating the oils and leaving the pigment. Sheets are run through cold rollers immediately after.

16   Sara Blair points out that Horgan's artistic sensibilities were in tune with the time and even he, as one of the progenitors of the press, felt that any image needed the hand of the artist to elevate it from the ordinary. See 'Object Lesson' in Blair, *How the Other Half Looks: The Lower East Side and the Afterlives of Images* (Princeton University Press, 2018), pp. 16–28.

17   Nigel Farage, LBC Radio interview, 28 April 2019.

18   See https://www.heraldscotland.com/news/15369469.edinburgh-firm-behind-ukips-notorious-breaking-point-advert-brexit-referendum/.

19   See https://www.independent.co.uk/environment/global-warming-data-centres-to-consume-three-times-as-much-energy-in-next-decade-experts-warn-a6830086.html.

20   See https://variety.com/2019/digital/news/netflix-loses-title-top-downstream-bandwidth-application-1203330313/.

Part Three

1   P. K. Aravind, 'The Hypercubical Dance – A Solution to Abbott's Problem in "Flatland"?' *The Mathematical Gazette*, 91: 521, pp. 193–97.

2   See https://www.laphamsquarterly.org/data-infographic/: a stereogram from Luigi Perozzo, 'Della rappresentazione grafica di una collettività di individui nella successione del tempo, e in particolore dei diagrammi a trei coordinate', *Annali di Statistica*, 2:12 (1880). Several ways of representing 3-D data were developed from around 1870 as more statistical data became available. Expanding from the 2-D plane to the 3-D allowed for greater illustrative possibilities and therefore greater ease of interpretation and understanding.

3   Scott Blake, 'My Chuck Close Problem', 9 July 2012, https://hyperallergic.com/54104/my-chuck-close-problem/.

4   As he later put it: 'for when the eye was removed from the prism – in which all looked beautiful – I found that the faithless pencil had only left traces on the paper melancholy to behold.' See https://www.metmuseum.org/toah/hd/tlbt/hd_tlbt.htm.

5   Catherine Flynn, 'From Dowel to Tesseract: Joyce and De Stijl from "Cyclops" to "Finnegans Wake"', *European Joyce Studies*, 24 (2016), pp. 20–45.

6   The opening title cards of Hitchcock's *To Catch a Thief* (1955) also have a nod to perspective, following the line of the window of the locked-off shot of the travel agent's shop on which the film opens. The device appears to make Cary Grant's credit slightly bigger than Grace Kelly's. There is no credit for title design.

7   Rowan Moore, 'Eileen Gray's E1027 – review', *Guardian*, 30 June 2013, https://www.theguardian.com/artanddesign/2013/jun/30/eileen-gray-e1027-corbusier-review.

8   The designer, planner and architect Charlotte Perriand collaborated with Le Corbusier on the Unité along with other architects. Perhaps tellingly, Perriand's brief was to design the kitchen spaces for the apartments.

9   Ralph Renwick, Jr, 'Dadaism: Semantic Anarchy', *ETC: A Review of General Semantics*, 15:3 (Spring 1958), pp. 201–9.

10   Hugo Ball, *Flight Out of Time: A Dada Diary* (University of California Press, [1974] 1996), p. xxiii.

11   'Dada', *Studio International* (January 1972), p. 27.

12   See 'Schlemmer's *The Triadic Ballet*', https://www.getty.edu/research/exhibitions_events/exhibitions/bauhaus/new_artist/body_spirit/interactive/.

13   We might also spare a thought for Elsa von Freytag-Loringhoven, who was part of the inner circle of Dada and modernist thought and practice and may well have been the source of the original urinal. See Siri Hustvedt, *Memories of the Future* (Hodder and Stoughton, 2019).

14   See 'Multi D&AD award winner Alan Waldie dies aged 76', *Campaign*, https://www.campaignlive.co.uk/article/multi-d-ad-award-winner-alan-waldie-dies-aged-76/1418421.

15   See Jared Diamond, *Guns, Germs and Steel* (Vintage, 1997).

16   See 'Chris Parks – "Rendering Gravity on One Computer Would Have Taken 7000 Years"', *Creative Chair*, https://creativechair.org/chris-parks/.

Part Four

1   In June 2021, Sir Tim Berners-Lee created a non-fungible token to auction an image he had made of the source code for the world wide web. See Alex Hern, 'Tim Berners-Lee defends auction of NFT representing web's source code', *Guardian*, 23 June 2021, https://www.theguardian.com/technology/2021/jun/23/tim-berners-lee-defends-auction-nft-web-source-code.

2   This whole episode was made possible by the development of a precursor to the internet, called the NSFNET, which was developed to link science and educational establishments. The National Science Foundation Network built on the work of Arpanet, the military networking project on which the first Transmission Control and Internet Protocols (TCP/IP) were developed. Tim Berners-Lee stood on the shoulders of these innovations when he coined the Universal Resource Locators that linked the Hypertext Transfer Protocols (http) with which web pages were named.

3   This is caveated by the impossibility of determining what the research methods and comparators are. It's almost irrelevant. We know that we are in an exponential spiral of data processing and creation. See https://techjury.net/blog/how-much-data-is-created-every-day/#gref and https://iorgforum.org/case-study/some-amazing-statistics-about-online-data-creation-and-growth-rates/.

4   This terminology may be a runner for an update on *The Shock of the New*.

5   See A. Fortini, 'No Filter: An Afternoon with Kim Kardashian', *Paper* (Winter 2014), https://www.papermag.com/break-the-internet-kim-kardashian-cover-1427450475.html?rebelltitem=14#rebelltitem14.

6   Kwasi Kwarteng et al., *Britannia Unchained: Global Lessons for Growth and Prosperity* (Palgrave Macmillan, 2012), p. 61.

7   See https://theculturetrip.com/north-america/usa/new-york/articles/history-of-the-selfie-a-photo-phenomenon/.

8   In his 2005 Stanford University commencement speech; see https://www.youtube.com/watch?v=Hd_ptbiPoXM.

9   I say so-called here because the Whole Earth approach to things didn't just end with the last edition of the catalogue. There were addenda and revisions published, and ultimately the group gathered around Brand founded *Wired* magazine.

10 *The Last Whole Earth Catalog* (1971), p. 78. See https://archive.org/details/B-001-013-719/mode/2up.

11 Ibid. p. 14.

12 See https://www.bankmycell.com/blog/how-many-phones-are-in-the-world.

13 In 1935, Aleksei Grigorievich Stakhanov reputedly mined 102 tons of coal in six hours, exceeding his quota by a factor of 14. As a consequence he literally became the poster boy for the Russian Communist Party's efforts at creating a socialist state.

14 See Kai Strittmatter, *We Have Been Harmonised: Life in China's Surveillance State* (Old Street Publishing, 2019).

15 See https://www.parliament.uk/globalassets/documents/commons-committees/culture-media-and-sport/Fake_news_evidence/Vote-Leave-50-Million-Ads.pdf.

16 See *Disinformation and 'fake news': Final Report*, www.parliament.uk, https://publications.parliament.uk/pa/cm201719/cmselect/cmcumeds/1791/179102.htm. AggregateIQ (AIQ) is a Canadian political consultancy and technology company. The company was part of the network of interests involved in information campaigns around various elections and referendums including Brexit and the 2016 Trump election campaign.

17 Issie Lapowsky, 'Here's How Facebook Actually Won Trump the Presidency', *Wired*, 15 November 2016, https://www.wired.com/2016/11/facebook-won-trump-election-not-just-fake-news/.

18 Jenna Wortham, 'Once Just a Site With Funny Cat Pictures, and Now a Web Empire', *New York Times*, 14 June 2010, https://www.nytimes.com/2010/06/14/technology/internet/14burger.html.

19 See https://www.similarweb.com/website/icanhas.cheezburger.com/#overview.

20 Deborah N. Dike, 'Countering Political Narratives through Nairaland Meme Pictures', *Cahiers d'Etudes Africaines*, 58:230 (2018), pp. 493–512.

21 William Yang Wang and Miaomiao Wen (School of Computer Science, Carnegie Mellon University), 'I Can Has Cheezburger? A Nonparanormal Approach to Combining Textual and Visual Information for Predicting and Generating Popular Meme Descriptions', NAACL (2015), p. 1.

22 Tom Purvis, 'Commercial Art', *Journal of the Royal Society of Arts*, 77:3990 (1929), pp. 649–64; p. 652.

23 Ibid.

24 Nick Clegg – the man who vowed to the electorate and particularly to the National Union of Students not to raise tuition fees, and then, having been given a sniff of power in the UK coalition government, immediately reneged on his promise – is at the time of writing vice president of global affairs and communications at Facebook.

25 UAL Financial Statement 2020.

26 RCA Annual Report 2020.

Part Five

1   See *Situationist International Online*, https://www.cddc.vt.edu/sionline/si/tsots01.html.

2   Afghanistan has, for example, an estimated \$1 trillion 'motherlode' of iron and copper, plus increasingly desirable deposits of rare earth metals and lithium, the essential ingredient in the manufacture of the lithium-ion batteries that now power everything from your headphones to your mobile and, once the petrol engine has been sidelined, will power your electric car.

3   Ian J. Goodfellow, Jean Pouget-Abadie, Mehdi Mirza, Bing Xu, David Warde-Farley, Sherjil Ozair, Aaron Courville and Yoshua Bengio, 'Generative Adversarial Networks' (Universite de Montréal, 2014).

4   See http://www2.ece.ohio-state.edu/~aleix/ARdatabase.html.

5   See https://www.youtube.com/watch?v=cQ54GDm1eL0.

6   *Meet the Press*, 22 January 2017, https://m.youtube.com/watch?v=VSrEEDQgFc8.

7   'PM's Spokesperson says of affair row: "He acts with integrity"', *Guardian*, 30 March 2021.

8   See https://www.extinctionsymbol.info/.

9   See https://rebellion.global/.

10   See https://cnduk.org/the-symbol/.

11   These were early problems with this type of software that have now been largely resolved. For example, back in 2015, Google was forced to apologize after its facial recognition software labelled a Black couple as 'gorillas'; see https://www.bbc.co.uk/news/technology-33347866.

12   See https://www.bbc.co.uk/news/technology-57101248.

13   See https://www.spacex.com/vehicles/starship/.

14   See https://news.cornell.edu/stories/2019/04/engineers-create-lifelike-material-artificial-metabolism.

15   Richard Sennett, *The Craftsman* (Penguin, 2008), p. 97.

16   See https://reekes.net/sosumi-story-mac-startup-sound/.

17   Michael Horsham, 'Love and the Argos catalogue', *Blueprint*, June 1996, pp. 1–5.

18   Adrian Shaughnessy, *How to Be a Graphic Designer, Without Losing Your Soul* (Princeton Architectural Press, 2005), p. 134.

19   Richard Sennett, *The Craftsman* (Penguin, 2008), p. 294.

Further Reading

Albers, Josef, *Interaction of Color*, 1963

Barthes, Roland, *Elements of Semiology*, 1967

Bastani, Aaron, *Fully Automated Luxury Communism*, 2019

Bendazzi, Giannalberto, *Cartoons*, 1994

Berardi, Franco 'Bifo', *Futurability*, 2017

Berger, John, *Ways of Seeing*, 1972

Berman, Marshall, *All That is Solid Melts into Air*, 1982

Bloch, R. Howard, *One Toss of the Dice*, 2016

Brautigan, Richard, *Revenge of the Lawn*, 1971

Bringhurst, Robert, *The Elements of Typographic Style*, 1992

Brockman, John, *What to Think About Machines That Think*, 2015

Chude-Sokei, Louis Onuorah, *The Sound of Culture*, 2016

Crawford, Matthew, *The Case For Working With Your Hands*, 2009

Daniels, Les, *Comix*, 1971

Debord, Guy, *The Society of the Spectacle*, 1994

Diamond, Jared, *Guns, Germs and Steel*, 1997

Dunne, Anthony, *Hertzian Tales*, 1999

Farrell, C., Knights, S., Green, A., and Skeaping, W., eds, *This Is Not a Drill*, 2019

Ferguson, Niall, *The Square and the Tower*, 2017

Foer, Franklin, *World Without Mind*, 2017

Foster, Hal, *The Anti-Aesthetic*, 1983

Foster, Hal, *The Return of the Real*, 1996

Fry, Roger, *Vision and Design*, 1920

Giedion, Sigfried, *Mechanization Takes Command*, 1948

Glickman, Michael, *Crop Circles*, 1992

Grunitzky, Claude, *Transculturalism*, 2004

Harari, Yuval Noah, *Homo Deus*, 2015

Harari, Yuval Noah, *Sapiens*, 2011

Harris, Alexandra, *Romantic Moderns*, 2010

Heidegger, M., *Basic Writings*, 1977

Ingold, Tim, *Making*, 2013

Jencks, Charles, *The Post-Modern Reader*, 1992

Jobling, Paul, and Crowley, David, *Graphic Design*, 1996

Knabb, Ken, ed., *Situationist International Anthology*, 1981

Koestler, Arthur, *The Act of Creation*, 1964

Kubler, George, *The Shape of Time*, 1962

Lavrentiev, Aleksandr Nikolaevich, and Nasarov, Yuri, *Russian Design*, 1995

Lawlor, Robert, *Sacred Geometry*, 1982

Lawrence, David, *British Rail Designed 1948–1997*, 2018

Leonard, Mark, *Britain TM*, 1997

Livingston, Alan and Isabella, *Graphic Design and Designers*, 1992

McCloud, Scott, *Understanding Comics*, 1993

McCulloch, Gretchen, *Because Internet*, 2019

McLuhan, Marshall, *The Gutenberg Galaxy*, 2011

Orwell, George, *Why I Write*, 1946

Papanek, Victor, *Design for the Real World*, 1974

Pater, Ruben, *The Politics of Design*, 2016

Rowland, Kurt F., *A History of the Modern Movement*, 1973

Sacks, David, *The Alphabet*, 2003

Sandbrook, Dominic, *The Great British Dream Factory*, 2015

Schick, Nina, *Deep Fakes*, 2020

Schumacher, E. F., *Small is Beautiful*, 1973

Sennett, Richard, *The Craftsman*, 2009

Shane, Janelle, *You Look Like a Thing and I Love You*, 2019

Sontag, Susan, *On Photography*, 1977

Spencer, Herbert, *The Liberated Page*, 1987

St Clair, Kassia, *The Secret Lives of Colour*, 2018

Storr, Will, *The Science of Storytelling*, 2019

Strittmatter, Kai, *We Have Been Harmonized*, 2019

Thompson, Philip, and Davenport, Peter, eds, *Dictionary of Visual Language*, 1980

Thunberg, Greta, *No One Is Too Small to Make a Difference*, 2019

Virilio, Paul, Rose, Julia, *The Vision Machine*, 1994

Watts, Alan, *Nature, Man and Woman*, 1958

Weinersmith, Kelly and Zach, *Soonish*, 2017

Wildman, Eugene, ed., *Experiments in Prose*, 1969

Williams, Heathcote, *Boris Johnson*, 2016

Wu, Tim, *The Attention Merchants*, 2016

Zuboff, Shoshana, *The Age of Surveillance Capitalism*, 2019

Acknowledgements

I am grateful to the various friends and colleagues who, when they have asked me what I have been up to, have had to suffer an elongated lecture, extemporization, or set of questions around the idea of visual communication its role in our lives and its history. In particular, early adopters like Frank Chambers with advice on contracts and source material and then once some words existed, Susannah Walker, Martin Green, Matthew Smith, David Crowley, Claire Catterall read, and then asked me useful questions. Simon Taylor and Norbert Schoerner, too, have either offered invaluable advice, conversation and/or encouragement, usually all three. Richard Asquith and Nick Fuller asked some pertinent questions and David Redhead too, helping me to focus on the shortcomings of the manuscript. I hope I have done enough to address their thinking. James Lance deserves mention for his constant creative support. David McCarthy, too. Going back in time, I would like to thank in no particular order Graham, Dirk, John, Simon, Steve, Jeremy, Juanita, Karl, Rick, Dylan, Jason, Joel, Tom, Tota and Anthony and everyone involved in Tomato over the years. I don't think I would have had the chutzpah, or the knowledge and experience to attempt something like this book were it not for the support, collaboration and occasional, or rather perpetual, challenge that working in that studio provided. Further back in time still Jonathan Woodham, Gillian Naylor, Judy Attfield, Paul Greenhalgh and Charles Saumarez Smith and every tutor I had were both instructional and inspirational. I would also like to thank Lucas Dietrich for pushing me to create enough of a framework for Thames & Hudson to commission the book and Evie Tarr and Sally Nicholls, who have been invaluable collaborators, the latter doing great work on the images. Camilla Rockwell deserves a special mention for wading through, trimming and correcting the prose. Lastly, I have to thank my wider family, my brother Anthony and my beautiful sister Theresa, and Mum and Dad of course. Lastly, my life partner, love and wife Oona and my darling daughter Natalie for putting up with me in the process of working on this project. My dog Keith was always there for me too, the cat Blossom, present also, but clearly less interested.

Illustration Credits

Index